The Li... ... ...
...an (

THE LIFE OF
EMERSON

VAN WYCK BROOKS

HAS WRITTEN:

THE ORDEAL OF MARK TWAIN
THE PILGRIMAGE OF HENRY JAMES
EMERSON AND OTHERS

Published by
E. P. DUTTON & CO., INC.

THE LIFE OF
EMERSON

BY

VAN WYCK BROOKS

Author of "The Pilgrimage of Henry James,"
"The Ordeal of Mark Twain," etc.

NEW YORK

THE LITERARY GUILD

1932

THE LIFE OF
EMERSON

CHAPTER I

MISS MARY MOODY EMERSON lived in
her shroud. She had stitched it all herself,
and when death refused to come she had put it on
as a nightgown, then as a day-gown. She was even
seen on horseback once, in Concord, cantering
through the village street, attired for the grave,
with a scarlet shawl thrown about her shoulders.

Miss Emerson was the daughter of the former
minister of Concord, who had died in the Revolution. She was a dwarf, four feet three inches tall,
with a bold, pinkish face, a blue flash in her eyes,
and yellow hair cropped close under a mobcap.
She was short and erect as an adder about to strike.
As an infant she had beheld from a window of the
Manse the manœuvres of the minute-men in the
meadow by the bridge; but she had been left an
orphan early, and for half a century now she had
drifted about the back-country of Maine and Massachusetts, drifted from one rustic boarding-house
to another, shaking her finger, for she was an autocrat and a prophetess and as fiery as the pit. She
was poor, obscure, uncomely, but an Emerson still,
of the seed of the ruling caste, the child of six generations of a sovereign priesthood. Her fellow-
boarders observed that her thimble was bright and
unworn. She used it not for sewing but as a seal.

7

Night and day she wrote, wrote, wrote. Letters, an interminable diary, prayers, ejaculations, mystical dreams, asseverations, exalted and melancholy, of her submission to the Eternal. She could not sit, she could not sleep: a demon drove her pen. For she had survived, a witness of the lofty and terrible religion of John Calvin, to rebuke what she regarded as the poor, pale, unpoetical humanitarianism of the new day. Her voice was the voice of a sibyl, issuing from the caves of the past.

She was queerer than Dick's hatband. She was thought to have the power of uttering more disagreeable things in twenty minutes than any other person living. She kept pace with nobody; she had received, she said, the fatal gift of penetration, and her mission was to undermine the vanity of the shallow. Was some high matter broached in conversation? Did some rash suppliant invite Miss Emerson's opinion? "Mrs. Brown," the sibyl replied, "how's your cat?" Was some lady praised too warmly in her presence? She pricked the panegyric: "Is it a coloured woman of whom you were speaking?" ("Give us peace in our boarders," she wrote on one occasion, and, when shown the misspelling, said it would do as it was.) She tore into a chaise or out of it, one of her nephews observed, into the house or out of it, into the conversation, the character of a stranger, disdaining all the gradations by which others timed their steps; and if she found that anything was dear and sacred to you she instantly flung broken crockery at it. But her oddities were never designed: they sprang from her isola-

tion, from a certain twist in her destiny. Of Talley-
rand she said, "I fear he is not organized for a
future state," and of another fallen angel, "What a
poet would Byron have been if he had been bred
a Calvinist!" But the Byrons and the Talleyrands
were the darlings of her imagination. She loved
life, she loved manners, beauty, distinction, genius.
She was born to command, to dictate, to inspire.
"For the love of superior virtue," she said, "is
mine own gift from God." And who could have
numbered the waste places of her journey, "the
secret martyrdom of youth, heavier than the stake,
the narrow limits which know no outlet, the bitter
dregs of the cup"? Loving the world, the world that
had passed her by, she had fallen in love with
death: no "easeful death," but the flaming death of
the saints. She had her bed made in the form of
a coffin. She invoked the worms as the Beatrice
who would lead her to paradise.

But death was not to be wheedled. "O dear
worms!" she wrote. "Most valuable companions!"
They were deaf to Miss Emerson's entreaties: she
was doomed to live. "Tedious indisposition," she
noted in her diary. "Hoped, as it took a new form,
it would open the cool sweet grave." And again:
"If one could choose, and without crime be gib-
beted—were it not altogether better than the long
drooping away by age without mentality or devotion?" But mentality and devotion she had; and,
since she was obliged to give up the prospect of
dying, she continued to live with a vengeance. She
carried her shroud, like Saladin, into the battle.

A bread-and-water diet; an inheritance of one hundred dollars, with a small share in a farm. She had to "finger the very farthing candle-ends"—the duty assigned to her pride. But poverty was the least of her cares: she had never felt pinched as a girl with ten dollars a year "for clothes and charity." For the rest, "I could never have adorned the garden," Miss Emerson said. "I never expected connections and matrimony. My taste was formed in romance, and I knew I was not destined to please." So she baked and swept and carded, in her lonely retreats, and toiled away at Plato and at Cicero's Letters. Not for her were "the pales of the initiated by birth, wealth, talents and patronage. As a traveller enters some fine palace," she said, "and finds all the doors closed, and he only allowed the use of some avenues and passages, so have I wandered from the cradle over the apartments of social affections, or the cabinets of natural and moral philosophy, the recesses of ancient and modern lore." She knew Plotinus and Coleridge as well as she knew her Milton; and Wordsworth and Madame de Staël. And she never lost faith that, some day, she would, in spite of all failures, know true friendship. For hers was "that greatest of gifts, the capacity to love the All-perfect." (Regardless of personal happiness. "Happiness? 'Tis itself.")

What rapturous hours she experienced in these long-drawn years of seclusion! "For culture," she wrote, "can solitude be spared? Solitude, the safeguard of mediocrity, is to genius the stern friend, the cold obscure shelter where moult the eagle wings which will bear one farther than suns and stars." In her Thebaid in Maine—a farm called "The Vale" where she boarded with her sister— she consorted with angels and archangels; she swam in her native element, "the fiery depths of Calvinism, with its high and mysterious elections to eternal bliss, and all its attendant wonders." To be "alive with God" was enough, to be able to "wake up the soul amid the dreary scenes of monotonous Sabbaths, when Nature looked like a pulpit." And in her passionate prayers, in her visions of the dying bed that would some day reflect lustre on her darkest fate, she apostrophized Eternity. No deceitful promises there, no fantastic illusions! No riddles concealed by the shrouds of loitering Time! None of Time's Arachnean webs, which decoy and destroy! No memory of defeats in virtue! "We exist in Eternity," she wrote. "Dissolve the body and the night is gone, the stars are extinguished, and we measure duration by the number of our thoughts, by the activity of reason, the discovery of truths, the acquirement of virtue, the approach to God. . . . The grey-headed god (of Time) throws his shadows all around, and his slaves catch, now at this, now at that, one at the halo he throws around poetry, or pebbles, bugs or bubbles. Sometimes they climb, sometimes creep into the meanest holes—but they are all alike in vanishing, like the shadow of a cloud."

Hours of rapture indeed! "How many stars," she exclaimed, "have set and risen, suns perhaps expired, and angels lost their glory, since I have droned in this place!" Had she missed so much, "cowering in the nest of quiet"? "Life truly resembles a river, ever the same, never the same. And perhaps a greater variety of internal emotions would be felt by remaining with books in one place, than pursuing the waves which are ever the same. Is the melancholy bird of night, covered with the dark foliage of the willow and cypress, less gratified than the gay lark amid flowers and suns? . . . 'Tis not in the nature of existence, while there is a God, to be without the pale of excitement." But sometimes she had her doubts. She remembered her visits to Boston, in the early years of the century, her brilliant brother William—Waldo's father— her nephews in their childhood. (Heirs of the shining world that she admired from afar.) And then a longing like despair was to her farthest cavern sent. And her old desire for the worm was not so greedy as to find herself once more in those pleasurable haunts.

The curtain rose before her. It was 1810: a Sunday evening in William's cheerful parlour. A tray stood on the sideboard, with decanters of wine and spirits, tumblers and glasses. There was William himself, the minister of the First Church of Boston, tall and fair, with his large, expressive eyes, so graceful and bland in manner. The Anthology Club was assembling; one by one the members were dropping in. There was William Ellery Channing, already famous at thirty, the little man with the flying pulse whose sermons were like a mountain speaking. Judge Story was there; and the

shaggy Daniel Webster, the lawyer from New
Hampshire; and the smiling Buckminster, elegant
in face and figure, with a voice such as Boston had
never heard before, Buckminster of whom people
were saying that he "celebrated the marriage of
Unitarianism with literature." For these new Unitarian doctrines, cold and weak and thin, Miss
Emerson felt nothing but scorn; but literature, ah,
that was another matter! And literature was the
burning topic at her brother's house. They were
publishing a magazine, *The Monthly Anthology,*
to "apply caustic and lancet to the disorders of the
American press"; and they met to discuss the
manuscripts over their supper. On "the merits of
Gray as a poet." On "Mr. Goethe's new novel." On
"Dante Alighieri, an Italian bard." (What strange
names were beginning to be heard in Boston!)
They were ministers, for the most part, though
far from other-worldly; and the magazine was not
to be destitute of the manners of a gentleman, nor
a stranger to genteel amusements. It was going to
take note of Theatres, Museums, Balls, and whatever polite diversions the town might afford.

Miss Emerson thought of her forbears, the godly
lives and deaths of her sainted kindred. Her
brother was a new shoot on this old stem! How
would Peter Bulkeley have regarded him—the
founder of the line, the founder of the town of
Concord, whose only care had been to "excel in
holiness"? And Father Moody of York, and Joseph
Emerson of Malden, and her father, William of
Concord, the Revolutionary chaplain? "Painful

preachers" to a man, enthusiasts like herself, "wrestling scholars," they would never have known their blood in this genial worldling. To one, as he lay on his deathbed, the Angel of Death had appeared, tapping on the window, and he had bidden the frightened family open the door. Another, when some of his parishioners had risen to leave the church in the midst of the service, cried out, "Come back, you graceless sinners, come back!" And when they ventured into the tavern of a Saturday night, he had followed them, dragged them forth and driven them home. A third, when his house was burning, stood by and sang, "There is a house not made with hands." How sombre they were, how severe in their antique Hebraism! They were associated in Miss Emerson's mind with the Fates and the Eumenides, with Nemesis, with all that was grandest in the Greek mythology.

Times had certainly changed!—with these Boston ministers, sitting over their wine, discussing books from England. And yet Miss Emerson listened like a child. Not when they spoke of theology! (This counting and weighing of texts was beneath contempt. How cold it was, how formal! To think that the faith of Calvin had led to these pale negations!) But they talked about Byron and Wordsworth and *Paradise Lost,* and how destitute America was of science and curious research. They were starting an Athenæum, and Buckminster had just come home from London and Paris with a whole shipful of treasures (Chalmers's *British Essayists,* a set of the British poets, topographical works on ancient Greece and Rome, *The Botanical Magazine, The Naval Chronicle,* books in Italian and Spanish, dictionaries of all the modern tongues). William, whose orations warmed the hearts of the Federalists, had edited a collection of hymns, taking pains to exclude those in which the voice of poetry was silent. And Judge Story had published a poem of his own. A Handel and Haydn Society was in the air, and a gallery of painting and sculpture. A new spirit was coming over Boston. One might almost have thought the Periclean Age was about to be born again.

Miss Emerson had her doubts about all these innovations, this babel of arts and inventions. What sort of civilization was it going to produce? One thing only she knew: the world of her fiery forbears had vanished forever, and this new world lacked the grandeur that belonged to a Doric and unphilosophical age. But it thrilled her none the less. What vistas opened before her! A world of Madame de Staëls, a world such as the Greeks and Romans had known. And then she thought of her nephews, asleep in the nursery. With a race like theirs, and with all these opportunities, what a future lay before them! The majority, she said to herself, would ever be in swaddlings, but never the children of her own tragic line. They were to be Byrons and Talleyrands, too. No mere apes of men, no crawling sycophants, but spiritual monarchs after the ancestral pattern.

ers or the flight of birds." She, more than any one else, had taught him to write; she had put him on his mettle, she had supervised his studies, exhorted, rebuked, incited him. With what fervour she had reproved him in his college days because Cæsar and Cicero stirred him more than the memory of his own Revolutionary grandfather! His ancestors were the constant theme of her discourse. Not praise, not men's acceptance of their doing, had absorbed their thought, but the Spirit's errand through them. They were, these Emersons of old, or so they seemed to the boy as he listened, awestruck, like the noble rock-maple tree which all around their villages bled for the service of man.

He was always listening. An obscure little boy, chubby, awkward, affectionate as a puppy, with a sluggish mind, a mind heavy and overcast, like a summer sky that is charged with electricity. At a word, a gesture, at the trembling of a petal, the flutter of a bird's wing in some elm on the Common, a flash as of lightning traversed him. His eyes blazed; then all was cloudy once more. A shrinking, retreating little creature, but full of wonder, he was all suggestibility, and so easily pleased. Everything he saw and heard seemed to unite in a harmony that amused and elated him. His aunt's anecdotes, the calm voice of his mother, the spare, comely lines of the old Puritan furniture, the ring of the horses' hoofs in the quiet, brick-faced streets, the pears in the neighbouring garden, the gracious contours of the buildings, the schoolhouse with its plume-like cupola spoke of some happy congruity, firm and exhilarating, at the heart of things.

He was naturally, unreasonably cheerful, this quivering little boy who loved to roam over the Common spouting Scott and Campbell. The mere sight of a handful of carnelians and agates bouncing over the pavement give him a fairy pleasure. But he was happiest in Concord. In summer, when school was out, he and his brothers flew to the Manse like migrating birds in March. No Dilworth's Spelling-book there, no gruelling chores, but long days and long thoughts, timeless, tideless, golden. It was a valley of good omen for the Emerson boys, this dwelling-place of their fathers, with its ancient Indian cornfields and the meadows by the lazy river. Memories of the heroic past—of the learned Peter Bulkeley, the founder of their family, of the clearing of the wilderness, of righteous compacts with Indians friendly and unfriendly, of the visits of the great men of the province to this first inland settlement, Winthrop and Dudley, and John Eliot, and Whitefield, who had come from England, of the assembling of the Provincial Congress, with Hancock at its head, of the Revolution and the battle by the bridge, and the coming of Harvard College which, escaping from the beleaguered neighbourhood of Boston, took refuge under the elms on the green—these memories lay there in the minds of the inhabitants like a rich leaf-mould, covering, fertilizing the unknown roots that were to flower from the generous soil. The very houses had this air of an autumn that was full of promise. Dusky and weather-beaten, but strong and shapely, as they rose above their straggling gardens and orchards, they betokened a toil that was really the toil of preparation.

The Manse, perhaps, especially. A long avenue, bordered by ash-trees and waving grass, led up to this ample dwelling, with its lofty, rounded, over-hanging roof, with its silvery, vine-covered walls, its dim little windows and the lilacs that clustered between them. It was dark and dusty within; the timbers were blackened with smoke, and the cav-ernous chambers were crowded with queer old high-backed chairs and short-legged tables, with beds and chests of drawers that might have come over in the "Mayflower." Funereal prints of grim Puritan divines stared down from the walls. There were sheds at the rear and a barn and pigeon-houses, and an old stone pigsty, overgrown with weeds. But the garden was a riot of luxuriant ver-dure. Currant-bushes and peach-trees, pears and quinces crowded one another. Muskmelons grew there, watermelons, "crook-necks," and the rus-tling, swaying corn. Thousands of sheeny insects, with green body and crêpe wing, overhung the meadow that stretched down to the river, and all day long the bees sucked honey from the flowers.

The gate at the head of the avenue was always open, and few horses passed the Manse without stopping. For who enjoyed a friendly chat more than Doctor Ripley? The pastor of Concord, the father and counsellor of this population of two thousand souls, he had lived in the Manse for more than a generation. He had married, in fact, the widow of his predecessor, the first William Emerson, of the days of the Revolution; and there were no guests he relished as much as his five step-grandsons.

How grave he was, how droll, this courtly, valiant, best-beloved grandsire, with his rusty coat, his high boots and his iron spectacles! No mortal was hardier than he, or more credulous and opinionative. None quicker on his horse, when the fire-bell rang, with his buckets and bag beside him; none fitter (a visitor said), as a man of anecdote, for the company of kings and John Quincy Adams. No scholar, yet terse and often elegant in his speech. His prayers (against lightning, "that it may not lick up our spirits"), his public rejoicings (in the face of sickness and insanity, "that we have not been tossed to and fro until the dawning of the day, that we have not been a terror to ourselves and others") were a school of style. His table-talk no less. Pleasant it was to hear him observe, as he sat at supper, in his cloak and velvet cap, that his "last cup was not potent in any way, neither in sugar, nor cream, nor souchong; it was so equally and universally defective that he thought it easier to make another than to mend that." Large, open and simple in his nature, with the robust wisdom of some Indian sagamore, he was the heir of an ancestral charity, a lingering survivor, as he seemed to one of these boys, of the old proud camp and army of the Puritans.

A sample of the heroic mould. "Great, grim,

earnest men," wrote Ralph Emerson years later, when this oak had fallen at the age of ninety, "I belong by natural affinity to other thoughts and schools than yours, but my affection hovers respectfully about your retiring footprints, your unpainted churches, strict platforms, and sad offices; the iron-grey deacon and the wearisome prayer rich with the diction of ages." All these things were the history of his own race; and well he remembered as a boy driving about the village at the Doctor's side, hearing as they passed each house the story of the Bloods and the Barretts, the Hosmers and the Hoars and the Buttricks, of all the worthies of Concord, not to mention the nine parishioners who had made a schism in the Church and who had come, every one of them, to a bad end. Once they drove out to a funeral at Nine Acre Corner where the father of the house had died and the eldest son, about to come into his estate, had fallen into evil ways. "Sir," said Doctor Ripley, as he entered the house, addressing each mourner in turn, "Sir, I condole with you. Madam, I condole with you. Sir, I knew your great-grandfather. When I came to this town, your great-grandfather was a substantial farmer in this very place, a member of the Church, and an excellent citizen. Your grandfather followed him, and was a virtuous man. Now your father is to be carried to his grave, full of labours and virtues. There is none of that large family left but you, and it rests with you to bear up the good name and usefulness of your ancestors. Sir, if you fail—Ichabod—the glory is departed."

So spoke the patriarch, for whom every farm in Concord was a principality. Nor did the Doctor hold himself in low esteem, or his petitions, that the Lord could entertain them lightly. One August afternoon, when he and Ralph and the hired man were busy in the hay-field, the Doctor looked up reproachfully at the sky where a thunder-cloud was gathering to spoil his hay. Raking very fast, he called out to his man, "We are in the Lord's hand; mind your rake, George! We are in the Lord's hand"; looking up at the cloud the while, as if to say, "You know me; this field is mine—Doctor Ripley's—thine own servant!"

Everything in Concord sang to the boy's ear and eye. Thrilling it was when George came in at breakfast and asked if he was to "drive the cow into the battlefield." Gay was the sound of the whetting of the scythe, delicious the scent of strawberries on his hands, and the solid sunshine of the pumpkins. And the breath of the warm south wind that drew him to the top of the ridge along the turnpike, where the mountains shimmered in the distance through the summer haze. And the thistleballs floating upward, and the droning of the bees in the still spaces of the woods; the blue river in the grass at the foot of the meadow, the water, soft as milk, when he went for a swim. And the flags and the rushes that bordered the torpid stream, the yellow water-lily, the pickerel-weed, with its long stalk crowned with a blue spire. Best of all were the rambles about the fields, the measured marches to the beat of the resounding ballads this boy enjoyed so much—"Child Dyring" and the "Battle of Harlaw" or "Warsaw's Last Champion" (when he brandished a cut stick and plunged it into the swarm of airy enemies his fancy arrayed about him). For him Concord was more eloquent than all the oracles of Greece. He was going to return to it in time, after far wanderings. And through him this village was to become another Delphi.

CHAPTER III

H E was growing rapidly, this favourite grandson, this favourite nephew, who preferred to be called Waldo instead of Ralph. The plump little spouter of rhymes had been transformed into a tall, spindling hobbledehoy. All his life he was to be greeted by his friends with a "Seems to me you are looking thinner than when I last saw you." He had long arms and longer legs, a narrow chest, sloping shoulders, a wedge-shaped head, a big bony nose, large, soft eyes and a curved, full mouth. His voice was slow and musical, and occasionally when he spoke there was a flash in his expression that vaguely suggested some strange inner power.

He was aware of this power himself, a curious ebbing force that came at moments and filled him as the wind fills a sail. At moments, only at moments, and usually when he was alone: it seldom came to him in the presence of others. In company he was torpid, awkward, mute; he laughed, he blushed, he had no power of face. He felt as if any whipper-snapper could eat him whole. What boy, what gossiping girl, could not daunt and tether him, out-state and pull him down and leave him rolling in the dust? He retreated before every confident person; he seemed to be bereaved of his organs; he listened like a willow; he took the con-

tagion of every one's views and utterly lost his own.
He felt like a waif and a straw; and then, without
warning, as he sat in his room alone or strolled on
the Common, the ebbing flood would return. And
it seemed to him at these moments that he had the
keeping of a secret too great to be told, that a divine
man dwelt near him in a hollow tree.

What was the meaning of these gleams and premonitions, this dancing chorus of hopes and visions
that hovered before him? Intimations, suggestions
of what? Tantalizing, unpossessed! Yesterday he
felt like a doctor; to-day, a dunce. Of one thing
alone he was certain: he lived in a world of marvels. The forms of the shells on the beach, the sight
of a boat on a pond imparadised him. (Was it
prosy in the eyes of others, that piece of fairy
timber capering on the waves? How the light loved
it, and the wind!) He saw a boy pick up an old tin
milk-pan that was rusting by the roadside and poise
it on the top of a stick. A battered, mouldy old
pan, but what elegant curves it described, twirling
there in the sunshine! He would wade through
snow-puddles, under a clouded sky, enjoying the
inconvenience, delighted with the chemistry of the
slush, glad to the brink of fear.

Grace, beauty, power were all about him. And
what miracles of skill! He remembered struggling
with a calf, as a little boy in Concord; he was trying to drag the calf into the barn, and the Irish
girl put her finger in its mouth and led it in directly. He remembered struggling with a rowboat;
he was trying to drag the rowboat out of the river,

and the hired man put a round stick beneath it, and the boat was on wheels in a jiffy. And how clever the Indians were! (He had watched them in the summer when they camped by the Concord River.) For strings they helped themselves with the fibre of the milkweed, or with spruce-root or the withe-bush; they made their bows of hickory, or a fir-bough, at a pinch; they would sew together a roof out of the bark of the hemlock, and hats from the bark of the birch-trees. Miracles, every one!

The world was alive with these marvels. Rays of light shot through it in all directions. Wonderful was the fact that two bits of gypsum became luminous when he rubbed them together in the dark— that his penknife, magnetized, would hold a needle—that blue and gamboge made green when he painted a mountain. Great was the charm of drawing vases by scrawling, with ink, heavy, random lines and then doubling the paper, so that what had been chaotic suddenly became symmetrical. And hallooing to an echo at the pond and getting musical replies. He produced these harmonies himself, so he was a part of the force that he felt at the heart of Nature! He would have to think this out. It was very exciting!

At fourteen Emerson entered Harvard; at eighteen he took his degree. Four years of a rambling, browsing, fitfully laborious obscurity. Not for him were the wine-parties of the gilded few, the fast horses, the dancing, the swaggering ways of the Southerners with their elegant swallowtail coats and their famous calfskin boots. (But how gay, how imperious they were in their jaunty indolence! Dancing and riding were too much for his own unskillful joints, not to mention his pocketbook, but he loved to watch them. This nonchalance filled him with a kind of awe.) Not for him were the routs in Boston, the clandestine visits to the theatre, at the risk of a ten-dollar fine. Not for him did old Morse, the stage-driver, draw up in the college yard and blow his horn, the signal for the flight. Nor did the juiceless learning of the curriculum greatly attract him, the logic, tough as hickory, the unpalatable doses of Paley and Locke, dear to the hard head of Andrews Norton. They were slightly repellent, these venerable Harvard professors, these harsh Unitarian monks. "Doctor Pop" touched one's fancy with his dry humour, and President Kirkland's face, all smiles and dimples, was somewhat reassuring. But for Emerson the conventionally grave had as little charm as the conventionally gay. As a poor boy, the son of a minister's widow, he served as a faculty messenger, he waited on table at commons, he had to depend on scholarships. For the rest, he followed his own whims, grave and gay alike.

They were often grave enough. Not to scribble nonsense does one rise at four-thirty on a winter morning, and in such a room, a carpetless, curtainless chamber in Hollis Hall. Or smash the ice in one's pitcher; or bruise one's numbed fingers, to light the candle, with flint and steel; or twist and turn at one's high desk, endeavouring to collect one's thoughts. One must have a real motive: some notable poem in mind, or an essay on the Character of Socrates. And the writing itself must be one's whole incentive. There is no great joy in winning a prize for declamation when one's thirty dollars must go to pay the baker's bill at home.

Writing was his greatest pleasure. No stripes of the day, no small humiliation, could vex him very long if, in his own room once more in the evening, he could accurately paint the fact in his journal. A thin skin like his had its compensations: he got his revenge by a sharpened observation. For years he had been keeping this journal; he had filled a dozen notebooks with little essays on history, religion, manners, passages from letters that seemed especially happy, lists of "poetical phrases" that enlarged his vocabulary, stylistic exercises in the manner of Bacon or Burton. He loved these old authors in whose books the English tongue had its teeth and bones and muscles largest and strongest, loved their vigorous phrases and peculiar words, their power of condensation, the richness of their cadence. Now he would copy out some song of Ben Jonson, or some lines from Beaumont and Fletcher, now attempt a poem of his own, on Marathon, for instance, after Byron, or a ballad, or a sally of sonorous couplets in the vein of Pope. Or jot down some sentence, his own or quoted, on the history or the character of the Greeks. (What wild wisdom the Greeks had, an elegance wild and handsome as the sunshine!) Especially he liked to collect the words and phrases that had stirred his blood as he read like blasts of triumph. From Shakespeare, Seneca, Moses, John or Paul.

The daydreams came and went. A splotch of colour on a wall charmed his eye, a fandango of shadows, the nonchalant pose of some labourer. He was going to be a painter, perhaps. Then he planned a romance: how Talbot came into town as poor as Béranger's Romeo, and built his plain cottage with such beauty that it eclipsed all the villas of the grandees—for he cut his garden-walks in curves of inimitable beauty and added a fountain-jet that tapped a mountain. (Was there something prophetic in this?) Then chemistry, physics, astronomy played the coquette with his fancy. There seemed to be a hundred Emersons, jostling one another down there in the depths, each listening to some call from without, struggling to rise to the surface ahead of the rest. How pantomorphic human nature was! He revelled in all these visions that seemed to suggest his wealth. He could scarcely wait to begin the journey of greatness. It glowed and towered in magnificence before his eyes.

But most of all the poets smote and aroused him. He sat there, torpid as a clod, and suddenly at a phrase the rigid fibres relaxed and his whole frame expanded to the welcome heats; life returned to a finger, a hand, a foot; he felt as it were wings unfolding at his side, and he saw his right to the heavens and the farthest fields of the earth. He had been but a moment before as a ship aground, and the waters returned beneath him, and he put forth his sails and turned his head to the sea. What power these poets had! That was the power he had vaguely discerned in himself! He too was going to invite men drenched in Time to come out of Time and taste their native immortal air. The high prize of eloquence was going to be his, the joy of uttering what no one else could utter, what all men must receive.

Nor was Harvard really dull. Was the gracious Ticknor dull, the new professor of belles-lettres, with his glowing descriptions of the great streams of French and Spanish literature? Was Edward Everett dull, Everett whose every word made a picture, whose every gesture was the movement of a sorcerer's wand? One had only to ask the students who were flocking to hear this Abelard, flocking from remote villages in Tennessee and Kentucky.

For the sun that was rising over Boston was rising over Harvard also. Who could resist the radiant beauty of Everett—that voice with its rich tones, its precise and perfect utterance, or the new learning he was pouring out with such grace, such happy abundance? In Emerson's eyes Everett was garlanded with legends: he had visited Greece as a friend of Byron, he had known Canova in Rome, and how fragrant were his discourses on the Orphic poets, on the ante-Homeric remains, how stirring his apostrophes to Liberty, his lectures on Greek freedom and the ancient republics! The words he spoke became classical at Harvard; and as he stood there on the platform, before the new panorama of Athens that had just been presented to the college, he seemed like a Grecian statue come to life.

There were other magicians in Cambridge, in Boston, whose bright images Emerson carried home to his bedroom. The air was alive with voices announcing the new age. Daniel Webster's, for one —the majestic Webster, his father's old friend, black as a thundercloud, with his terrible animal force, who brought the strength of a savage into the height of culture. (A man who could measure himself with a ton of coals, whose head turned on a pivot as deep as the orbit of the sphere, it moved so slowly and grandly!) His theme was the Revolution, the destiny of the dawning Republic; and to Emerson he seemed the symbol of the power and possibility of man. There was Dr. Channing too, that other friend of his father's, the spokesman of Young America. Buckminster had expressed the hope that the American genius would take a bolder flight, and Noah Webster was appealing to his countrymen to cast off the Old World models and develop a literature based on their own life and traits. And what did Channing say?—"To avail ourselves of the higher literature of other nations, we must place ourselves on a level with them. . . . A people into whose minds the thoughts of foreigners are poured perpetually needs an energy within itself to resist, to modify this mighty influence. . . . The true sovereigns of a country are those who determine its mind, and we cannot consent to lodge this superiority in the hands of strangers. . . . A foreign literature will always in a manner be foreign. It has sprung from the soul of another people, which, however like, is still not our own soul. . . . A country, like an individual, has dignity and power only in proportion as it is self-formed." What a challenge these words contained! Literature—this was the note of the hour—could express, could arouse, all that was lofty and profound in life. And through literature America was about to come into its own.

Emerson listened to these orators with a strange excitement. Time enough later to weigh and measure their doctrines. They were Pied Pipers—that was his main impression; and the stones danced when they spoke. A triumph of pure power, and how beautiful and surprising! They seemed to say that the world was beginning again, that America was going to realize the promise of the Revolution, that Boston had been appointed by destiny to lead the civilization of the continent. And they proved that man was a mover, that life as one knew it was simply a troubled sleep. What hidden forces lay below the threshold of the human consciousness, waiting to be kindled! A word, a picture evoked for his inward eye, and he felt as if he were a Plato, a Cæsar, a Dante. It was all there within him, the germ of every human thought and action; and, if in him, in every responsive soul.

CHAPTER IV

WILLIAM ELLERY CHANNING was the demiurge of Boston. A small, nervous man, with a rapid, elastic step, thin, pale, of an almost unearthly refinement, with hollow eyes and furrows about his mouth, he would mount his pulpit on Sunday and utter words that electrified New England. Then, as often as not, he collapsed and spent the rest of the week in his garden at Newport collecting his strength for another impassioned hour.

He had lived as a child in Newport. The son of a prosperous merchant, he was known in those days as "Little King Pepin." A delicate boy, but muscular and exuberant, overflowing with animal spirits: he was famous as a wrestler, and his favourite sport was climbing the mastheads of the vessels at the wharves. Then his father lost his fortune, and the boy went South as a tutor. At twenty he returned, completely changed. His friends were shocked when they saw him. His manner was anxious and careworn; he looked like an invalid; he took his meals in haste and never appeared in society, buried himself in his study and gave himself over to intense religious exercises. He slept on the bare floor, sprang up in the middle of the night, went out for long walks in the winter darkness. And all

34

for the sake of what? Some nebulous creed that
no one could quite make out. It was certainly not
the faith of the Pilgrim Fathers. He had squared
his accounts with that when he was a boy. His
father had taken him to hear a sermon on the theme
of Damnation. It appalled him at the moment;
then, to his own astonishment, as they were driving
home in the chaise, he found that he was whistling.
That was the end of Calvinism for him.

When Channing whistled—if his friends had
only known it—that was the end of Calvinism for
Boston. For he soon made himself heard in the
metropolis. He had read Rousseau and Godwin
and was full of the French Revolution; he had
read Wordsworth's *Excursion,* in the days when it
was ridiculed by *The Edinburgh Review,* and found
it a revelation. It contained, he said, a theology
far more spiritual than that of the Unitarians or
the Trinitarians. (For, although he was generally
regarded as a Unitarian divine, he looked upon all
sects as merely "vestibules.") The Revolution for
him had broken the shells of abstract creeds and revealed the kernel of religion as the moral sentiment: all dogmas beside this were mere transient
figments of the brain. "The divine attributes," he
wrote, "are first developed in ourselves and thence
transferred to our Creator. The idea of God, sublime and awful as it is, is the idea of our own spiritual nature, purified and enlarged to infinity. In ourselves are the elements of the Divinity." He was
really a mystical enthusiast, with a passionate faith
in man's intellectual being, in the powers and dig-

nity of the mind. The old faith, the doctrine of total depravity, filled him with abhorrence. It had banished, he felt, all reverence for the beauty of life.

He had just passed forty in 1821, the year of Emerson's graduation from Harvard; and already he was known as the "counsellor of the people." He was setting out for Europe to visit Wordsworth and Coleridge and to study the social life of the French and Italians. He returned brimming over with more ideas than ever. He threw himself into the Abolition movement, at the risk of all his influence. He subscribed to every movement of reform. Nothing was too wild for Channing: the only thing he feared was the apathy of the public. He hated the "selfish prudence" of New England. But he had little hope of the modification of society by outward revolution. The change must come from within, through the richest growth of human personality. Through manners, art, music, poetry, dancing. ("Why should not gracefulness be spread through the whole community?") He decried distinctions of property. "The principle of exclusiveness," he said, "keeps society uninteresting." He spoke of the frankness of the Southerners and their generous confidence, so different from the avarice and coldness of the North; of the animation produced in Scotch society when Burns, the Ayrshire peasant, broke in upon its tameness. He called for a "bold, free tone in conversation," for a greater breadth of reading. ("Our reading is confined too much to English books. We ought to know the different modes of viewing and discussing great subjects in different nations.") He begged the public to protect and foster the arts. ("The eye to see beauty is developed by nothing less than making beauty.") He even spoke of the kitchen. "Anyone," he said, "who would teach how to make bread and cook potatoes well would be a public benefactor."

Such were the themes that Channing discussed in the pulpit, or in private conversation; and all Boston hastened to do his bidding. "The idea of forming a superior race of men" was the burden of all his preaching. "Conformity," he insisted, "benumbs and cramps genius and creative power. What faculties slumber within, weighed down by the chains of custom!" He kept in touch with the new German philosophers, with the French psychologists and critics. He would say surprising things, as, for instance, that there seemed to be two souls in the human body, one that never suspended its action and had the care of the involuntary motions, that dealt in natural magic, premonitions, antipathies, instincts, and the other the vulgar, waking, practical soul. He had picked these theories up in the course of his reading or thought them out in his long, silent walks by the sea at Newport. For he loved the roar of the breakers on the beach. He had certain favourite seats among the rocks, the rocks where Berkeley had sat a century before and conceived his *Alciphron,* his theory that Nature was the language of God.

a struggle against the chaos that threatened to engulf him. He had entered the House of Pain.

For a dozen years Emerson was destined to live there, years of illness, frustration, false beginnings, of calamity and confusion. That plague of his family, consumption, so soon to destroy his two favourite brothers, had seized upon him also: a "stricture of the chest," accompanied by extreme depression. The school was abandoned. William sailed for Germany. Should his brother follow? Where was the money to come from? He tutored for a while, taught school for short sessions at Chelmsford, at Roxbury. Then he entered the Divinity School at Cambridge. Some years before, in college, wondering about his vocation, he had thought of consulting the *sortes Virgilianæ*. He had opened Dryden's translation at the line: "Go, let the gods and temples claim thy care." Prophetic it seemed; prophetic it really was, though not as it seemed. He had never doubted his destiny.

He had only mistaken the form. It was not to be the Church, or not for long; and as Mary Emerson watched him during these years her doubts grew graver and graver. He had scarcely entered the Divinity School when his eyes gave out; his uncle sent him to Florida. He returned, apparently better, and went on with his studies; and his Aunt Mary's hopes rose for a while when he first began to preach, then took the pulpit of the Second Church of Boston. But his constitution was "all clay, no iron"; and preaching made things worse. "My lungs," he had written once, "sing sexton and

sorrow whenever I ask them to shout a sermon for
me." Yet, strangely enough, as he noted in another
letter, after a merry or only a gossiping hour he
lost all sense of this mouse that was nibbling his
chest. The truth was very clear: his whole nature
revolted against the pulpit. He resigned, in the end,
over a technicality: he could not sincerely admin-
ister the Communion. What he really felt he wrote
in his journal: "Forms remain, but the soul is well-
nigh gone. Calvinism stands, fear I, by pride and
ignorance; and Unitarianism, as a sect, stands
by the opposition of Calvinism. It is cold and
cheerless."

He had made a mistake. He had adopted the ancestral vocation, as if by the mere force of inher-
ited habit. To the old Church, Aunt Mary's fiery
Calvinism, he looked back with respect and even a
kind of affection. It was narrow, blind, revengeful,
and Calvin, he felt, was a monstrous old prig. The
breath of a hot village of Teutonic peasants!—but
at least it had been, in its day, a school of feeling, a
school even of greatness, sublime, poetic. The Unitarian faith was a mere shell beside it, an intellectual form from which the heart had departed. It
could never command his allegiance. Besides, he
was not suited for the ministry. The sexton of the
Second Church said that he never made his "best
impression at a funeral"—he seemed to be ill-at-
ease, too shy and retiring; and an old Revolutionary veteran on his deathbed rose up in anger and
remarked that he didn't understand the business of
consolation. He revolted from "official goodness";

he could not bear to consider himself an "example," and preaching seemed a "pledge." What were these forms, these dogmas, that he was supposed to defend? "Flimsy sophistries," he called them in his journal, "that have covered nations, unclean cobwebs that have reached their long gangling threads over whole ages, issuing from the dark bowels of Athanasius and Calvin."

He had made a grave mistake, and one that left him at thirty sick and disheartened. (With a dubious reputation. For nobody understood him. Why had he entered the Church in this lackadaisical way? It was said and believed by many that his mind was deranged.) Nor was this his only misfortune. He had fallen in love, he had married Ellen Tucker, and his wife was dead in another eighteen months. He had met her in Concord, New Hampshire—the daughter of a Boston merchant. She was seventeen, merry and gay but already stricken with consumption. She seemed to be growing better, and they went South together in the hope of curing the disease, but all in vain. For two years after her death, till the day he sailed for Europe, Emerson walked to Roxbury every morning to visit Ellen's grave.

Everything, apparently, had gone amiss. Emerson had lost his profession, he had no plans; his wife was dead; his brothers, Charles and Edward, were burning themselves away. (They were both studying law, and both had made brilliant records. Charles had a chance of life, but Edward was failing rapidly. He had entered Webster's office as confidential agent, but, eaten up with ambition, he had broken down completely and become a violent maniac. He had soon recovered his reason but had had to give up his career and go to Porto Rico. He was working there as a clerk—waiting for death.) A doom seemed to hover over Emerson's family. Yet under the surface of his life, dark as it was at the moment, a purpose was taking form in his mind.

He knew he was born for victory.

CHAPTER V

FOR years his greatest pleasure had been strolling in the country. He would shut up his books on a summer afternoon, put on his old clothes and his oldest hat and slip out into some little cowpath where he knew he could defy observation. That point gained, he would amuse himself for hours picking blueberries and other trash of the woods. He remembered these walks in winter, he looked forward to them in the spring. He did not know another creature who had the same humour or would even have thought it respectable.

Strange thoughts came to him as he idled about the pastures. The trees, the flowers, the hills seemed somehow alive. Not merely as trees and flowers: they suggested some general life of which his own was a part. He would suddenly lose the sense of his personality, and then this general life rose up within him. It was stronger and better than his own; and when he relaxed and gave it the freest passage, he felt an infinite force traversing his soul.

It was something that filled all Nature, as Wordsworth said; and he was a part of Nature. But Nature was plainly an effect of the universal cause; and he felt that he shared in both the cause and the effect. He was able to detach himself from this floating world. He was able even to shape it! Had he not as a boy discovered that, chaotic as it seemed, he could play on the world as a kind of musical instrument and draw wonderful harmonies out of the chaos? It was not a chaos then! Harmony lay within it, a power that expressed itself by means of laws. And this power flowed through him—he became its agent—whenever he put himself in a position to receive it.

This train of ideas had become his ruling passion. It had drawn him to the reading of Plato and the Neo-Platonists and the Sacred Books of India, where he found his own thoughts expressed in a beautiful rhetoric. It had drawn him also to the Quakers at New Bedford, who were having a schism and revival in 1828. He visited them often, especially Mary Rotch. "What is this Inner Light?" he asked her. "It is not a thing to be talked about," she replied. But he drew her out, and she said she had been driven inward, in these years of the Quaker Schism, till she had learned to *have no choice,* to acquiesce without understanding the reason when she found that she felt an obstruction to any course of action. She felt it was a presumption to press through this reluctance and choose for herself. And she said the result was a kind of sublime tranquillity, an absolute assurance of higher direction.

This was the feeling that Emerson had shared so often. You listened, you obeyed, and then you acted with all the force of the unconscious. It was not your petty will that directed you then, your limited intelligence, your personal self with its prejudices, but a deep inward necessity. You surrendered to the spontaneous life within you, and your nature flowed with the river of the universe.

The old Greek thinkers constantly spoke of this force. "The soul," said Pythagoras, "is an emanation of the Divinity, a part of the soul of the world, a ray from the source of light." And Heraclitus: "That common light which enlightens all at once is only the divine reason spread through all thinking beings by an immediate effusion." This corresponded with Plato's idea of the Good, the unity that lies forever at the base of things, an undying fire, constantly in flux, but always obedient to the same divine laws. This One, this Over-Soul, as Emerson thought of it, was represented in every one of its particles; so the laws that governed Nature governed the mind, and man was not merely an effect but shared in the creative forces that produced him. In the outer world one saw the laws more clearly expressed than in man, for there they met with no conscious resistance. In the flowers, the birds, the stars, in the study of the natural sciences, one could see the divine scheme face to face. And man too had it in his power to live as harmoniously as they. But man was disunited from the stream of Nature. His customs, prejudices, habits, his ignorance and blindness cut him off from the source of his natural sublimity. If he looked within himself he would find the laws, and, by following their clue, achieve his rightful inheritance.

Emerson had found his faith. It was gathering

about it a metaphysical form, for here was the conclusion expressed by Plato; here was the conclusion of the Neo-Platonists too, for whom the soul and the cosmos were so closely related, for whom the cosmos indeed was a sort of external diagram of the soul. And here was Kant's doctrine of the moral law that lies at the heart of life. But the source of this faith was Emerson's unconscious nature, into which had been poured for so many years such a flood of heroic suggestions: a uniquely candid nature, strong and happily organized, that rang with "inner voices," the voices of his Aunt Mary, of Concord and Boston, of Plutarch, Virgil, Homer, that responded with a special intensity to the beauties of human behaviour, in history and the world about it, responded only to these—for Emerson had long practised a kind of auto-suggestion: he had kept his mind fixed, with a rigorous will, upon those things alone that contribute to the health of the soul. None was more passive than he before Shakespeare, Goethe, Plato: he became a mere organ of hearing before them and yielded himself to the laws of these mighty beings. He was a Proteus himself, with a faculty of enjoying the universe through the powers of different men. His imagination had lived in the great ages of history: in the grandest strokes of the poets he had always felt most at home. *He* would have acted so, so thought, so builded, in the situations they painted. The Platonic "ideas" of things were the sole realities: things actually were what humanity ought to make them. Emerson had come to live in this

Elysian air, and he couldn't but think that what
was true of him must also be true of others. What
was real to him had only to be pointed out for the
world to awake from its sleep and become an
earthly paradise.

"What faculties," Channing had said, "what
faculties slumber within, weighed down by the
chains of custom!" What undiscovered powers,
Emerson said to himself, lay in the soul! Poetry
made him a poet, painting a painter. The soldier's,
the sailor's life, the sculptor's life: he took delight
in each. Stupendous were the riches of human nature! And every man had all the capital in him, if
he only knew how to turn it, had the power to
exist not as a flint but a sun. The sages of India had
been tormented by this thought. The raising of
man to a higher level of consciousness, a continuous state of inspiration, by calling into play the
forces of the subconscious being—this had been the
object of all their philosophy. They had known,
these demiurges, that man, naked man, not man
overburdened with tradition, with the weight of
custom, had within him the power to build the
world anew; and something in his own circumstances, the fresh, frank emptiness of a young nation, had recreated this faith in Emerson's heart.
"When I consider," he wrote, "the capacities of
man and see how near alike they all are, and that
they always seem to be on the verge of all that is
great, and [are] yet invisibly retained in inactivity
and unacquaintance with [their] powers, it seems
as if men were like the neuters of the hive, every

one of which is capable of transformation into the queen bee." Let them shake off tradition first! For what was tradition but a series of hardened intuitions, translated into the terms of a past experience! Since every one was a part of the divine, he had only to plunge within to receive the inspiration of the source.

Emerson had found his faith. His own path, meanwhile, lay clear before him. "I read," he was very soon to write in his journal, "I read my commission in every cipher of nature, and know that I was made for another office, a professor of the Joyous Science, a detector and delineator of occult harmonies and unpublished beauties, a herald of civility, nobility, learning and wisdom; an affirmer of the One Law yet as one who should affirm it in music and dancing." Whence had he received this conception of his own rôle? From the dim forbears who, for two centuries, had represented for their people the idea of a life redeemed from the darkness of egoism? From Channing, who had referred so earnestly to the opportunity of the American man of letters? From Fichte, Carlyle, Milton, with his inspired descriptions of the office of the writer? No doubt all these voices had contributed to form his intention; and he certainly felt that the world's great age was about to begin anew, could begin, rather, would and should begin, if the scholar assumed, as he must, the leadership that was proper to him. "Who can doubt," he noted, "the potences of an individual mind who sees the shock given to torpid races, torpid for ages, by Mohammed, a vibration propagated over Asia and Africa, and not yet exhausted? What then of Manu? What of Buddha?" He had seen a teacher of physics lay a magnet among filings of steel, "and the force," he observed, "the force of that subtle fluid, entering into each fragment, arranged them all in mathematical lines, and each metallic atom became in its turn a magnet communicating all the force it received of the loadstone." Many a great writer had acted in just this way upon his people, till every soul tingled and trembled with life. The prophet, the scholar, was the great awakener, the "geometer of men's forces," and something told him that this office had been reserved for him.

The world, he said to himself, should be like the Dance of Plotinus in which "the bodies are moved in a beautiful manner, as parts of the whole," moved and moving in ecstasy; or, if one had to think of it in terms not of poetry but of prose, then the prose should be heightened prose, and each person should fulfil his part with intensity and faith. And who so much as the writer had it in his power to quicken the general rhythm? The Over-Soul was a reservoir of power, of which every great thought and noble action, the deeds of all the heroes, the dreams of all the poets, were emanations. Grace, beauty, skill, love, friendship—wherever these appeared, the laws of life were plainly in operation. He would look into himself and report his own perceptions, reveal as far as he could the possibilities that lay in the soul of man.

Such was to be his task. He was almost ready to

perform it, but first he needed a whip to make his top spin.

Travel, a year in Europe, the sight, the touch of three or four living writers. There was Landor, for instance, whose lightness and Greek grace had become his ideal of style. And Coleridge, that true citizen of the universe, the critical spirit whose opinions deserved to be written in steel; and Wordsworth with his feeling of the divinity immanent in the natural world. But among all these tonic streams of contemporary thought there was one that had mingled with his heart's blood, a strange, cloudy genius whose essays on German literature he had read with the utmost excitement in the British reviews. Carlyle: he had heard the name of the brooding berserker, had pictured this prophet emerging from the woods of the North, a Viking mourning over the decay of his race who had come to restore the heroic virtues of the past. What blasts of the trumpet these essays were, and how they confirmed his own profoundest convictions! Man was not a clothes-horse, to be encumbered forever with the useless trappings of tradition. Away with the cold rationalizings of modern philosophy! Away with mechanism and calculation, the shibboleths of the new industrial age! Not consciousness but the unconscious, not the will but the involuntary, not mechanics but dynamics, not argument but intuition was the way of health. And how superbly the prophet expressed this faith! He was digging down amid the débris of history for those half-forgotten men who had been the grand movers and initiators, the men who had given themselves whole-heartedly to a leading instinct, who had liberated and brought into action the deep forces and energies of life and whose presence, re-constituted in words more vibrant than flesh and blood, would arouse a world that was running to cerebration. That science the prophet spoke of, not the science of the logic-mongers, but a science that addressed the springs of love and wonder, Enthu-siasm, Poetry, Religion—that was the science Em-erson had been born to affirm. He must know this master, this elder brother, see him and hear him speak. For what was it Goethe said?—"My thought becomes infinitely more real to me as soon as another shares it."

He sailed from Boston on Christmas Day, 1832. A trading brig, bound for the Mediterranean, with a cargo of mahogany, tobacco and coffee, with pork and beans for breakfast, dinner, and supper, and the weather as the staple of conversation. There was no room here for the spectres of theology. He ate with a truckman's appetite, and, strangely, here on the sea he began to taste the earth. He watched the Yankee sailors with their clever hands: had he ever known before how many fingers he had, or the faculties of a knife or a needle? He had descended from the clouds indeed, for this was human power, even the power of which Carlyle had written. Praise to these men of action, who could strike a porpoise and make oil of his blubber, who could bleed a sick sailor and mend the box of

their pump, who could ride the roughest storm
and find their way from Boston across three thousand miles of water to a little gut of inland sea! No
mere logic there, no mere mechanism, but instinct
and the unconscious, the natural play of energy.

He had lost all sense of effort and strain; he was
ready for the visible and audible earth to pour its
blood into his veins. The second phase of his education had begun, the phase of facts that illumines
the phase of books—that endless alternation by
which power ascends to its climax: theory confirmed and corrected by experience, theory again,
deepened by deeper experience, wider theory,
wider experience, intenser at every stage. At
Malta, in the high battlements of the castle, in the
jabbering groups of Moors, Greeks, Sicilians,
friars, beggars, the sense of colour and form
dawned upon Emerson, the key of the pictures, the
sculpture that lay before him. There were the
churches: never again could his eye accept as final
the bare, cold interior of the American meeting-
house. Sicily came, and the fountain of Arethusa,
the "gloomy Dis," the flowers that Proserpine
gathered. Then the Villa d'Este, the eternal poem
of gardens. And all the traces of the great men who
had made the history of the world: Cicero's villa
and Tasso's grave, Byron's house in Florence and
Petrarch's at Arquà. And the mighty works of
Napoleon, the roads, the Simplon tunnel. They
were not pictures for Emerson: they were confirmations. He had come to Europe to see what
humankind had accomplished, and here on every

side were tokens of the force of which he had read. It was no illusion then that the corners of history had been turned by the concentrated power of individuals, that all this beauty and strength had been gradually built up by human initiative, the initiative of single men working on the responsive mass.

And then there was natural science. In Florence he visited Amici, marvelled over those telescopes, the most powerful in Europe, and witnessed the professor's experiments with polarized light. Feats of skill had always electrified him, but as he watched physicists and chemists at their work, as he read textbooks of the sciences, he was more and more struck by the analogies, the correspondences, the identities that existed between all the parts of the natural world. The experiments of the chemists illumined his own observations. There were men like iron, like salt, like air, like water, and you could study and predict their behaviour in the element they resembled almost as well as in their actual lives. But his great lesson came in the Jardin des Plantes in Paris. There were animals from every country, lions from Algiers, elephants from Siam, the venerable ibis, the vulture (who reminded him of an auctioneer), hazy fishes, insects, snakes. Mountain, morass, prairie and jungle, ocean and river, the mines and the atmosphere had been ransacked to furnish types of each class of beings, to render account of the three kingdoms of Nature. The universe was a wilder puzzle than ever as he glanced along this bewildering series of

animated forms, with the upheaving principle of
life incipient in the very rock, the transparent
lumps of amber, with gnats and flies within them,
the radiant spar and stalactites, the huge blocks of
quartz, the gold in threads, in plates, in crystals,
in dust, the silver taken from the earth molten by
fire; and strange thoughts stirred in him as he
stood there. He yielded to a singular conviction
that in all these rich groups of natural productions
there was not a form, grotesque, savage or beautiful, but expressed some property in man, the ob-
server. He felt an occult relation between the
crawling scorpion, the flowering zoöphyte and
himself. He felt the centipede in him, the cayman,
the eagle, the fox. He was moved by mysterious
sympathics. He was one with all these creatures.
Nature was a living whole.

But the greatest events of the year were the men
he met. He visited Thorwaldsen's studio in Rome;
in Paris he dined with the aged Lafayette—he
might have been living for an hour in the days of
the Revolution. And Horatio Greenough, in
Florence, the first of American sculptors, an ardent, eloquent man with the face of another Achilles, introduced him to Landor. (Greenough was
himself worth knowing. As a boy in Boston he had
carved flowers on the handles of his toys and made
bas-reliefs of his playmates and had often been late
to school because he had loitered to admire some
wooden eagle over a doorway. He was living in
Florence now, planning his colossal statue of
Washington, and he spoke of the advantage of the

Greeks in working in schools and fraternities and said that art would never prosper at home till Americans abandoned their shy, jealous ways and worked in society also.) Landor received his guest in a cloud of pictures at his Villa Gherardesca— an erect, muscular man, paradoxical, downright, with a passionate love of freedom and justice as elements in which alone genius could work. His conversation brought all history together and touched it with the freshest Grecian light. And Emerson felt, as never so clearly before, the value of the pure literary spirit.

In London, he called upon Coleridge—prematurely old, heavy, bent, shambling, with a soft white face and the bluest of eyes—who burst at once into a eulogy of Channing and an outcry against the folly of Unitarianism. (Another confirmation!—though not perhaps quite in Coleridge's sense, for the latter went on to talk of *trinism* and *tetrakism* and soon left Emerson far behind in the clouds.) Then he went to Rydal Mount to pay homage to Wordsworth. The poet spoke of America, of the dubious effect of superficial schooling, of the need of a civil war to knit society together, of the too much making of money, the necessity for all Americans to cultivate the conservative, the insanity of Thomas Carlyle, the obscenity of Goethe. He was tame and limited enough till suddenly, in his garden, standing on the gravel walk where thousands of his lines had been composed, he began to speak of his poetry. He had just returned from Fingal's Cave at Staffa and remarked, with perfect simplicity, "If you are interested in my verses, perhaps you will like to hear these lines." Then he drew himself up, like a schoolboy declaiming, and recited three new sonnets with the greatest animation.

Two days before, Emerson had visited Carlyle in the wild and desolate hills of Craigenputtock. He had borne with him a letter from the Baron d'Eichthal, a French Jew in Rome, a friend of the prophet's brother, but no one in England or Scotland seemed to know where the prophet himself was living. At last he had got the address from the secretary of the University of Edinburgh and found his way to Dumfries, then hired an old rusty gig and driven the sixteen miles to the lonely farm of Mohammed-in-the-desert. A dreary scene indeed: peat-bogs, stunted trees, black cattle, the grimmest of houses, so still one could hear the sheep munching the grass a quarter of a mile away. A weekly cart from Dumfries brought parcels and letters, and the prophet smoked his pipe and, like Montaigne, "put his ear close by himself, and held his breath and listened."

Emerson stayed over-night and besieged the oracle. "I will go with that man," he had said to himself, as Hazlitt had said of Coleridge, for no writer had made the world seem so alive. He took history up in his hand and shook it, this giant of the North, with his great gaunt skull and his mad Scotch wit, till the paper formulas blew away in the wind and what remained was the naked force of men. Those who had shown the plasticity of life, who had opened the gates of the unconscious and flooded the dry earth with its fertilizing currents, were the heroes he worshipped; and as Emerson listened to the riotous play of his humour he felt as if he had drunk the blood of all these heroes.

His torpor seemed to have vanished for good and all when, from the gig that returned on the following morning, he waved farewell to the prophet of Craigenputtock (his friend, as he knew, forever). And looking back, as he turned his face towards home, he saw that his apprentice years were over. He owed much to this journey. He had had to struggle to preserve his freedom of judgment, not to be overborne by the power of Europe, to be pleased only by that which was fit for him; and this had immensely strengthened his self-confidence. He could form in future a juster view of the great, he who had met the greatest. Moreover, he had witnessed on every side the effects of the action of representative men on the malleable earth; and Carlyle had made him feel, in that long night of talk, the practical relation his thought might bear to his own time and country. All he had seen and heard in these months of travel had confirmed him in his convictions; his health was re-established; he was ready for the work of his life. The future rose before him, an enchanted path.

CHAPTER VI

THE sun had emerged from the clouds. Strange that a few months could have wrought such a change in Emerson. He had come home charged with life, faith, vigour. He felt the master stirring in him.

Where was he to live? For a moment he thought of Maine, and again of the Berkshires. Perhaps the dry air of the hills would restore Edward and Charles, and together, in some quiet village, with a few friends about them, they might edit and write a magazine. But Edward's case was hopeless now, and Charles had settled in Concord: he was studying law in Samuel Hoar's office and had just become engaged to the Squire's daughter, Elizabeth. Was not Concord, after all, the predestined spot?

How many memories were associated with this little town! Personal memories, family memories, national memories. The happiest hours of his youth had been passed in these peaceful meadows, redolent of the lives of his forbears. There too the Revolution had begun, the struggle for an independence that had still to be confirmed in the spiritual sphere. In solitude, amid the black cattle of the Highlands, Carlyle had nursed his mighty prophet's heart; and Wordsworth had sat him down at the foot of Helvellyn, far from cities, to obey the heavenly vision. Concord was as wild as Windermere, and Concord was only eighteen miles from Boston. So be it then!—with every muse befriending. "Hail to the quiet fields of my fathers!" Emerson wrote in his journal. "Not wholly unattended by supernatural friendship and favour let me come hither."

So Emerson returned to the Manse. Dr. Ripley had asked him to come there with his mother and board, for the present at least. His first wife's estate had been settled in the meanwhile: twenty-two thousand dollars—twelve hundred a year. With this, and another eight hundred or so from lectures, they could live without a care. They would have to count out Edward, but Charles was near them. William had gone to New York. He had come home from Göttingen with too many doubts to be happy in the ministry, although Goethe, upon whom he had called in Germany, had advised him to put aside his scruples. He had taken up the law and was living on Staten Island, and he seemed to be marked out there for a sober success.

Then suddenly Emerson found himself engaged again to be married—to Lydia Jackson of Plymouth. He must look for a house of his own, large enough for his mother, and Charles and Elizabeth too, when they were married. A house on the Boston turnpike happened to be empty, built for his son by Coolidge, the Boston merchant. It was cheap at thirty-five hundred, and a small addition

—a parlour behind the study and a bedroom above
—would make it ample; and with two acres of
ground they could have a liberal garden.

The marriage took place on September 14, 1835,
in Lydia's house at Plymouth. A beautiful town,
Plymouth, with its two hundred ponds, with its
warm, sandy wood-roads and its great dome-like
lindens and the long sea-line always visible from
the tops of the hills. No humble cottage-village like
Concord, but a proud seaport, with stately man-
sions—Lydia's own house had been framed in
England. Emerson had preached there and had
always liked it. They had lordly ways in Plymouth,
ways of the world one seldom saw at home.
A siesta in the afternoon: the ladies drew their
blinds and took a nap (all lying on their backs, just
as if their fathers had never been Pilgrims). They
had gypsy suppers on the beach, and drove along
the shore, and yielded themselves to the *dolce far
niente:* it was quite Italian, like Newport. Lydia
would have liked to live there, with all her friends.
But Plymouth was no place for rambling. Too
many streets! (And would Lydia be willing to
change her name a little? *Lidian Emerson.* The
words ran together so much more pleasantly.)

So they drove back together in a chaise to Concord. The new house was awaiting them, with
Emerson's mother and Charles already installed.
A spacious house indeed, square, plain, white, with
a Doric portico—not a Plymouth mansion, no, nor
a Concord cottage either, but the sage's golden
mean. High ceilings, airy chambers; a garden by

the brook for Lidian's favourite flowers, the bulbs and seeds from Plymouth, the tulips and the roses; an orchard and a barn. And a study at the front, on the ground-floor, facing northward: a sanctum for the sage. A bright crimson carpet, a gay sprigged wall-paper, red velvet chairs, a round mahogany table, a rocking-chair in the centre, a fireplace with a stove. Books to the ceiling on one side, engravings on the walls, heads of Goethe, Dante, Pindar, Virgil, Newton. A little bronze figure of Goethe on the mantel, and Flaxman's statuette of Psyche with the butterfly wings; and over the fireplace a copy of Michael Angelo's "Three Fates," made by young Wall of New Bedford. When the fresh wind blew, Emerson placed in one of the western windows an Æolian harp made by Lidian's brother; and as he listened to it, fitfully singing in the breeze, the wild and gentle melodies of Wales and Provence rang through him again. Its notes mingled, on spring and summer days, with the trilling of the birds; for outside, between the windows, stood a balsam fir-tree, and in its branches, when the sun was out, robins and cedar-birds, orioles and goldfinches, warblers and cat-birds loved to foregather.

It was truly a Sabine farm. The land was low but not marshy, and he could trust the long ridge opposite to shut off the north winds. The barn had a carpenter's bench, two planes, a saw, a chisel, a vise and a square. (Great institutions, these planes, whose invention no man knew. One would have to watch a carpenter for a month to learn all the tricks that might be played with them. Great was Tubal Cain!) The nail-box stood in the snuggest corner, filled well with nails and gimlet, pincers and screwdriver. (An old joy of youth, this catlike love of garrets, barns and corn-chambers, and all the conveniences of long housekeeping.) There were all too many trees about the yard. For Emerson went scrambling in the woods with Peter Howe, collecting six fine hemlocks; and presently thirty more arrived from Waltham, a gift from Dr. Hobbs and Uncle Ripley—white pines and two or three chestnuts. He would have to buy those nine extra acres to find room for them all.

Pathetic, he felt, these graceful trees, rooted there, so patient and helpless, would-be men, creatures, by a feebler effort, of the soul that had made himself, with their long boughs and drooping leaves weeping their strait imprisonment. For the flowers, he would have liked to put dittany in his greenhouse, asphodel, nepenthe, moly, rue and poppy, plants that stirred his fancy—put even pansies there, the droll and elfish pansy. But roses, dahlias, tulips? A poet could be forgiven if he liked the wild flowers better than all of Lidian's bulbs. A poet with an orchard, an orchard fit for Plato! Early apples, sweet and sour, York and Roxbury russets, red cherries, purple plums, greengages, quinces, currants, and all the pears in New England: Gravenstein, Chelmsford, Seckel, Bartlett, Winter Nelis, Green Princess, Flemish Beauties and the Golden Beurré of Bilboa. He approved of Madden's rule for an orchard, as Dr. Johnson reported it—"Enough to eat, enough to lay up, enough to be stolen, and enough to rot on the ground." And nothing was as good as a pear, although there were only ten minutes in which it was really ripe. (A stirring sight, this pear-tree. It grew like the ash Yggdrasil; it had every property that ought to belong to a plant; it accepted all kinds of nourishment and could almost live on none. Grubs, worms, flies, bugs attacked it. It yielded them all a share of its generous juices; but when they left their eggs in its broad leaves it thickened its fibre and shook the vermin off. A good object-lesson for a man of letters. Watch a pear-tree and learn how to handle your critics!)

In the morning, after breakfast, Emerson spent an hour in the orchard, pruning and stirring the earth about his shrubs. Sometimes his mother joined him for a little talk, hardy herself as a pear-tree, hardy as few writers ever are. (Majestic were these old strong frames of the passing generation, built not to spend fast, but to live so tranquilly, kindly and usefully.) Sometimes Aunt Mary stepped out, in her shroud and fillet, when she happened to be making some visit of inspection, to see that the Concord household was going well. (Or to put Lidian in her place. "You must remember, dear," said Aunt Mary, "that you are among us but not of us.") Her visits were a divided joy; she trampled on the common humanities all day long. But she was very amusing at the tea-table. Oh, no, she never took tea. "Can you get a little shells?" The cocoa came, and she took it because it was soothing, and put a little tea in it to make her lively; and, if there was a little coffee, that was good for getting rid of the taste. Aunt Mary believed in medicine; she never threw any away, and if she found a drop of laudanum here, and a pill or two there, a little quinine and a little antimony, she mixed them up and swallowed them all together.

No easy flute, Aunt Mary, but a clanlike instrument, a bagpipe from which none but a native Highlander could draw music. As Elizabeth Hoar said, she thought much more of her bonnet and of other people's bonnets than they did, and she sent Elizabeth from Dan to Beersheba to find a bonnet that did not conform, while Mrs. Hoar, whom she severely taxed with conforming, was satisfied with anything she found in the shops. But she had a force of temperament like Dr. Johnson's, impressing her company, as he did, not only by the point of her remarks, but also, when the point failed, because she made them. And what a nose for character she had, what a taste for strength and distinction! She was a realist. She could remember the founders of the oldest families in Boston as retail merchants, milliners, tailors, distillers, as well as ministers, doctors, lawyers, and no one better than she knew a great man from a successful money-maker. She had made up her mind years before that her nephews were not to be mere good husbands and neighbours: they must be known of men as Rabbis and Fathers. They had somehow, one and all, slipped out of the pulpit; and William had left New England. But she couldn't deny that Waldo, in spite of all his notions, had a mind of his own. And Charles was a Romeo.

A noble sight, Charles and his betrothed, Elizabeth Hoar: she so calm, so patrician, so erect and slender, with her dark eyes that spoke of the gods and the muses, he so human, so handsome, with the senses of a Greek and a nature whose victories came as easily and naturally as Homer's verses. None so perceptive as Elizabeth, with her thousand silences and delays—hesitant Elizabeth!—with so fair a mind in discussion, such a feeling for the finest nuances of equity: she lived by laws so subtle they could never be stated. For himself, Charles was afraid of one thing only—of degenerating into a householder. As if there were any danger! He might turn into a tree, or flow into a stream, or lose his susceptible self in a hundred Ovidian forms; but lead the base life he could not. Not he whose ear tingled with Milton's melodies, who shunned nothing, dodged no corners, evaded no look or word.

"Put me by the world-wheels," said Charles. "If I wouldn't give them a twirl!" His brother was very proud when he gave his lecture on Socrates at the Concord Lyceum. Proud again when the gallant Charles stood up in that great company in Boston and declared he would rather see the town in ruins than that Harriet Martineau should be debarred from perfectly free speech! (For Harriet Martineau was touring the country, with guns mounted fore and aft, in the cause of Abolition.)

No gayer companion than Charles for a walk or a reading of Sophocles. No one better understood the severe taste of the Greeks or found more pleasure in these lofty and removed studies. His recitations from *Samson Agonistes* were of a diamond clearness: it was worth all Milton's labour to have given such joy and manly satisfaction to a lover in this distant time. None readier than Charles to see in Burke the poet rather than the partisan; none quicker for Shakespeare, "reading the world off into sweetest verse." And to live with him was like living with a great painter. The effect of the grey oak-leaf on the snow pleased him well; and each natural event, the finding of the mayflower, of the indigo-bird, of the cuckoo, was an epoch in his life.

Through what orbits of speculation these brothers travelled together! (In the two years of life that were left for Charles.) The same persons and facts were known to them both, and an occult, hereditary sympathy underlay their intercourse. But all Concord was like this: Emerson felt that he belonged to it in every fibre. The same names of the same families, the Bloods, the Willards, the Flints, the Barretts, the Wheelers were all about him, tenon'd and mortised to the farms his fathers had known six generations before.

Here in Concord were the men that make republics: Greeks like Charles, Romans like Samuel Hoar. A Cato, this father of Elizabeth, this pillar of the town, this leader of the Middlesex Bar. Rich, but of a Spartan plainness, with a face like Dante's and a grave military air, temperate, open-handed, severe and methodical in his logic but reverent and courteous, a solitary man, given to long and retired walks, with a strong, unaffected interest in crops and weathers, trees and birds, and the common incidents of rural life, with an influence, too, at the bar that was reckoned despotic, yet one in whom so rare a spirit of justice visibly dwelt that if you met him in a cabin or a forest he would still seem the public man, answering as sovereign state to sovereign state. He had no fine words; the useful and the practical superabounded in his mind. The engagement of Elizabeth and Charles was a contract; and, if you had read to him a page of Swedenborg or Plotinus, he would have waited to the end and answered you out of the Revised Statutes. Not by talent or magnetism but by presence alone—by direct statement—he won all victories: by demonstration of superiority, not by conflict. It might have been said of him, as Clarendon said of one of his contemporaries, that "he had a strange power of making himself believed, the only justifiable design of eloquence."

Emerson had found a circle, or the nucleus of a circle, that would call out in time all his natural faculties. A few persons prepared to understand him, who embodied in some degree the ideas he wished to utter, who would serve him as models and stir him to formulate these ideas, pique and provoke him, expect him to do his best, nourish the courage and insight his nature contained. And behind these Concord friends stood all the demigods

of the world of letters, the mighty host of the ages
who beckoned and led him forward. For the present, he proposed to consult the gods—to muse and
jot in his notebooks. When he had any news to
offer, the world should hear it.

It was always a pleasure, in the meantime, to
receive his friends in the orchard. One day a committee came and told him that a runaway pig was
ravaging the neighbouring gardens. It was the custom of the town to appoint newly married citizens
to the office of hog-reeve for the year. Would he act
in that capacity? With the greatest pleasure! Then
another committee came, from the Horticultural
Society: they wished to examine his pears. He received them with modest pride—he had sent a few
specimens to the Cattle Show. But they hadn't come
to congratulate him. They wanted to look at the soil
that produced such poor specimens of such fine
species. (And he thought—he had really supposed. . . . Then his were *not* the best pears in Concord?) A third committee came and asked him to
speak on the two-hundredth birthday of Concord.
A great privilege, this; he would have to do his
utmost.

Two or three of the minute-men were to sit
on the platform beside him. Veterans of '75; if
they had survived from Thermopylæ they could
scarcely have been more venerable. With such listeners, on such an occasion, it would never do to
make up a speech out of books. The town records
would yield something, and Aunt Mary's anecdotes:
but what a chance for a fresh version of the fight!

So he drove from house to house, with Grandfather Ripley, just as in the old days, and questioned the veterans. There was Abel Davis, seventy-nine, and old Master Thaddeus Blood, and Jonas Buttrick, the son of Major Buttrick who led the attack at the bridge. Jonas was only eleven at the time, but the fight took place partly on his father's farm, and he must have seen something as he dodged about. If only Grandfather Ripley had allowed him to talk! But, truth to tell, the Doctor, who was irritated by a narrative published in Lexington, had written his own *History of the Fight at Concord*; and the last thing he wished to hear was any detail that might put him in the wrong. Affecting it was to see old Thaddeus Blood searching in his memory for the facts: "It is hard to bring them up. . . . The truth will never be known"—while the Doctor cannon-aded him with questions, pursued him up and down, extorted the old man's assent to the facts as he had described them. "Leave me," said Thaddeus, "leave me to repose." All Emerson could get was a few touches, but they brought the scene before him. He had felt for another hour the thrill of the Revolution.

Good neighbours for a man of letters, all these Concord folk, high and low, standing on their own legs, like that barefooted yeoman, driving his oxen, who replied to the supercilious professor's question whether all the people hereabouts went without shoes and stockings—"Wal, some on 'em doos, and the rest on 'em minds their own business." Not a bad idea for a poet, minding one's business, a failing none too common in the scrivener's trade. One could say one's say in Concord, and Emerson was resolved to say it. "Henceforth," he wrote, "I design not to utter any speech, poem or book that is not entirely and peculiarly my work. I will say at public lectures, and the like, those things which I have meditated for their own sake, and not for the first time with a view to that occasion. If, otherwise, I select a new subject, and labour to make a good appearance on the appointed day, it is so much lost time to me, and lost time to my hearer. It is a parenthesis in my genuine life. I am my own dupe, and for the sake of conciliating my audience I have failed to edify them, and, winning their ear, I have really lost their love and gratitude. Possessing my liberty, I am determined to keep it, at the risk of uselessness (which risk God can very well abide), until such duties offer themselves as I can with integrity discharge." He could call Concord to witness. It was not his voice alone, but the voice of Massachusetts:

"Mind your own business."

Exactly that!

CHAPTER VII

A NEW kind of pulpit had been as it were invented for him. Some years before, in 1826,
Josiah Holbrook at Millbury, near Worcester, had
established a village Lyceum. Thirty or forty farmers and mechanics had joined in the venture, and
Holbrook himself had delivered a course of lectures on scientific subjects. His example had been
followed by others, and already almost a hundred
Lyceums existed in Massachusetts. A convention
had been held in Boston to organize them at which
Everett and Webster had been present, and soon
the remotest village had its centre of culture. There
were local museums everywhere, libraries, cabinets
of minerals, natural history collections, a hall and
a platform—above all, audiences, of every trade
and age. The renaissance in the capital had spread
through the provinces, and all New England was
waiting for a voice.

What could have been more opportune? Emerson had had enough of preaching: he wished to say
what he thought and felt at the moment, with the
proviso that to-morrow he might contradict it all.
But he wished to have the stimulus of a stated task.
He wished to have a connection with the world:
there would always be a danger of stagnation in
this village existence. Besides, he delighted in
speaking: nothing would have pleased him more

than an offer of a chair of rhetoric, and here was
a pulpit that made other pulpits tame and ineffec-
tual. No need for a cold mechanical preparation,
a decorous delivery, no stiff conventions that prescribed a method. Everything was admissible,
philosophy, ethics, divinity, criticism, poetry, all
the breadth and variety of conversation. What an
opportunity for painting in fire his thought—for
being agitated, to agitate! Here he could lay himself out prodigally on the subject of the hour, here
he might hope for nectar and enchantment.

To the road then, without delay! he said to himself. You have drawn all values to you; then ra-
diate and communicate all. Combine the largest
accumulation with bounteous imparting. Pass on to
the many the results of your studies, in art, literature, poetry, morals, manners. Be their mediator,
civilizer, inspirer. Give them something better
than political speeches and cheap wit and lectures
on Popular Science. Convert for them the dis-
honoured facts they know into trees of life, by sug-
gesting the principles that classify the facts. Be
Adam in the garden again, new-naming the beasts
in the field and the gods in the sky. Make them
drunk, drive them mad, this multitude of vaga-
bonds, hungry for eloquence, hungry for poetry! It
is they who have called you, and you, poet, have
only to respond and say: The people and not solitude is my home. Never your land, your stocks,
your income, but that power to help and charm the
souls veiled under these whiskered and smooth vis-
ages—that is your rent and ration.

Almost at once, after his return from England, Emerson had begun giving lectures in Boston. He had preached for a while, half-heartedly, in the parish of East Lexington; then he had gradually ceased even to go to church. He spoke on Great Men, on Trades and Professions, on Human Culture, on the Philosophy of History. But he was soon lecturing at the country Lyceums, too; and he found them a stringent test for the wares of a man of letters. Could he hold stout farmers upright on their benches or stop the gossip around the door by a mere discussion of art or manners? Not always, by any means. At times the audience was cold and unresponsive and his best efforts were drowned as it were in ice-water. But usually he found the experience exhilarating. Very gay were the country college commencements at which he often spoke: the students with the ribbons of their rival societies, the crowds gathering in wagons and buggies and chaises, the peddlers and gingerbread vendors, the barrels of cider and beer, the medley of rustic accents. Pleasant, too, were those evenings in country meeting-houses when the snow sparkled under the moon and the whole neighbourhood came stamping in, smothered in shawl and muffler, when the sleigh-bells tinkled up to the door and the dim oil-lamps flared under the low ceiling, and the boys and girls gathered round the stove giggling and munching apples.

Emerson was already widely known as a speaker when he rose one August day in 1837, in the old meeting-house of the First Parish of Cambridge, to deliver the annual oration of the Phi Beta Kappa Society. He was rapidly working out the thoughts that thronged his mind, but to-day he had a special word to utter. "The American Scholar" was the stock theme of these Phi Beta Kappa orations. Buckminster, Everett, Edward Tyrrel Channing had all used it before him, but for Emerson it seemed a focus for half the perilous stuff that was burning his soul.

He rose and faced the assembly. All Harvard was there, the old Unitarian war-gods, Palfrey and Andrews Norton, and Henry Ware, and the young men (two named Holmes and Lowell among them) for whom his speech was to seem the Declaration of America's Intellectual Independence. The hall was packed with listeners. He stood there, slender, motionless, serene, with the air of one who heard nothing but the voice within him, indifferent to the movement of the crowd. For a strange division at once took place in the audience—it became more and more marked as the speech went on. The older faces grew grimmer with every word, while the younger lighted up with eager approval. This speaker had come to bring not peace but a sword, and the words he uttered to-day were to mark the birth of another generation.

"Our day of dependence," he said, "our long apprenticeship to the learning of other lands, draws to a close." And then he went on to speak of Man Thinking. The business of a scholar was not to be a mere thinker but one who shared all the experience of mankind and then served as the delegated intellect. His duties were comprised in self-trust, for, as all minds were united in the One Mind, he descended into the secrets of all by descending into his own. "The poet, in utter solitude remembering his spontaneous thoughts and recording them, is found to have recorded that which men in crowded cities find true for them also. The deeper he dives into his privatest, secretest presentiment, to his wonder he finds, this is the most acceptable, most public, and universally true. The people delight in it; the better part of every man feels: This is my music, this is myself."

He spoke of the education of the scholar. Of the influence of Nature first. Nature was the opposite of the soul, answering to it part by part. Its laws were the laws of his own mind, so that "Know Thyself" and "Study Nature" became at last one axiom. Then books were the next great influence, not to be valued as such, but as means of inspiration. "I had better never see a book, than to be warped by its attraction clean out of my own orbit and made a satellite instead of a system." The one valuable thing in the world was the soul, but the soul must act from its own sight of principles. To accept the view of others was to lose one's own. "Man Thinking must not be subdued by his instruments. . . . But when the intervals of darkness come, as come they must,—when the sun is hid, and the stars withdraw their shining,—we repair to the lamps which were kindled by their ray, to guide our steps to the East again, where the dawn is." The third influence was the world, for action was essential to the scholar. "The world—this shadow of the soul, or *other me,* lies wide around. Its attractions are the keys which unlock my thoughts and make me acquainted with myself. I run eagerly into this resounding tumult. I grasp the hands of those next me, and take my place in the ring to suffer and to work, taught by an instinct that so shall the dumb abyss be vocal with speech. . . . So much only of life as I know by experience, so much of the wilderness have I vanquished and planted, or so far have I extended my being, my dominion."

Then he spoke of the office of the scholar: "To cheer, to raise and to guide men by showing them facts amidst appearances. . . . He is the world's eye. He is the world's heart. He is to resist the vulgar prosperity that retrogrades ever to barbarism, by preserving and communicating heroic sentiments, noble biographies, melodious verse, and the conclusions of history. Whatsoever oracles the human heart, in all emergencies, in all solemn hours, has uttered as its commentary on the world of actions— these he shall receive and impart. And whatsoever new verdict Reason from her inviolable seat pronounces on the passing men and events of to-day,— this he shall hear and promulgate."

There was much else in the speech, on the difficulties that stood in the way of the scholar, on the tameness and timidity of the American mind ("taught to aim at low objects") ; but the final burden was an emphasis on the present. "I ask not for the great, the remote, the romantic; what is doing in Italy or Arabia. I embrace the common, I explore and sit at the feet of the familiar, the low. Give me insight into to-day, and you may have the antique and future worlds. What would we really know the meaning of? The meal in the firkin; the milk in the pan; the ballad in the street; the news of the boat; the glance of the eye; the form and the gait of the body; show me the ultimate reason of these matters; show me the sublime presence of the highest spiritual cause lurking, as always it does lurk, in these suburbs and extremities of Nature . . . and the world lies no longer a dull miscellany and lumber-room, but has form and order."

Never had such a voice been heard before in New England. There were sentences that thrilled the young people like martial music. "Not he is great," said the voice, "who can alter matter, but he who can alter my state of mind. They are the kings of the world who give the colour of their present thought to all Nature and all art." And again: "If the single man plant himself indomitably on his instincts, and there abide, the huge world will come round to him." The poet, the artist buried in all these hearts had received the corroboration for which it was thirsting; for what was the "American scholar" but the gifted individual? They could trust their instincts now, these rebels against the law of a commercial world—believe in their times, their country, believe that their dreams had meaning, believe that in them, and not in the gods of matter, lay the real hope of society.

At a stroke, Emerson had become the prophet of the new age. It was not so much his ideas that

people received as a certain electric shock that
energized their latent power and knowledge. What
had been vague in their minds became suddenly
clear, doubts were transformed into certainties,
half-hearted hopes into vigorous resolutions. An
invisible authority had come to their support, the
authority of their own unconscious natures. And
they felt themselves no longer "pinched in a corner, cowards fleeing before a revolution, but re-
deemers and benefactors, advancing and advancing
on chaos and the dark."

Other addresses followed, one to the senior class
of the Harvard Divinity College in which Emerson bade farewell to the "Mythus" of Christianity
and spoke of a faith that should "blend with the
light of rising and of setting suns, with the flying
cloud, the singing bird and the breath of flowers."
A compound of folly and atheism, the Dean of
the college called it; and for twenty years thereafter Emerson was never again asked to speak at
Harvard. Then he gave an address on "Literary Ethics" to the students of Dartmouth College, a prose poem on the resources and the
discipline of the scholar, asserting that all literature was yet to be written. "The man who
stands on the seashore, or who rambles in the
woods, seems to be the first man that ever stood on
the shore, or entered a grove, his sensations and his
world are so novel and strange. Whilst I read the
poets, I think that nothing new can be said about
morning and evening. But when I see the daybreak,
I am not reminded of these Homeric, or Shake-

spearean, or Miltonic, or Chaucerian pictures. No; but I feel perhaps the pain of an alien world; a world not yet subdued by the thought; or I am cheered by the moist, warm, glittering, budding, melodious hour, that takes down the narrow walls of my soul, and extends its life and pulsation to the very horizon. . . . There is no event but sprang somewhere from the soul of man; and therefore there is none but the soul of man can interpret. . . . The whole value of history, of biography, is to increase my self-trust, by demonstrating what man can be and do. . . ." In all these speeches he was amplifying and applying the ideas he had tried to make clear in a little book called *Nature*, the fruit of three years of thinking and revising, which he had published in 1836. The soul was divine, he had said, and identical in all men. The scholar, the poet, the artist were merely those into whom, through a special discipline, more of the divinity flowed than flowed into others. They were only the most favoured of a race of potential supermen.

It seemed as if all New England had been waiting for these words. The young men and women crowded about the speaker, and one by one they began to drift to Concord. Margaret Fuller came, with a letter from Harriet Martineau. Margaret's guns were heavy, and she sailed straight for Emerson with a terrible speed, as for a walled fortress, the most formidable and provoking on the American horizon. The walls were high and thick: so much the better. Margaret was prepared for a siege. She meant to interrogate all the contem-

porary sphinxes, to drink at every source of insight
and power. And there was no dodging Margaret.
One could shudder at that bony face, those blinking
eyes; one could say to oneself, "We shall never get
far." No use! She had had it out with herself as a
child and resolved to be "bright and ugly"; and
who could resist that tide of superabundant life?

A Ceres, a Minerva. An avalanche of tropical
femininity. In vain Emerson protested; in vain the
voice cried within him, Stand from under! He had
always disliked queer people and people with lan-
tern faces. They shocked his nerves, they offended
his taste. They had no right, he felt, not to be
comely. And Margaret was so overwrought. Her
good people were too good to be true, her naughty
people were so naughty they couldn't be eaten.
There was simply no keeping her to the positive
degree. And that female mysticism, what a trial
it was, that romantic pother about birthdays, seals,
ciphers, coincidents, dragons, stars, heliotrope,
purgatory. She said she had an affinity with the
planet Jupiter; she believed that the month of September was inauspicious to her; she recalled that
her name, Margarita, signified a pearl; she
coupled her friends with the carbuncle, amethyst,
onyx; she was convinced that when she turned her
head to one side she had second-sight, like Saint
Francis. A pest, these auguries, presentiments, divi-
nations—a syrupy, florid flood that overwhelmed
you. And she taxed Emerson with "inhospitality
of soul"! She insisted that he "ought to know
how to be silent and companionable at the same

moment"! She grieved because they "met as strangers"!

But there she was; and stayed; and came back. Stayed for days, a week, a fortnight. And lo, what had become of that fantastic schoolmarm? You began to notice a peculiar swaying grace in her motion. You looked at her twice, you listened for ten minutes to that nasal voice, and a vaguely sumptuous apparition rose before you. Even her costume —was it bombazine or a modest alpaca?—had undergone some indescribable metamorphosis, and you could understand the rumour, going about Boston, that this Aspasia, of whom every one was talking, adorned herself with a pagan magnificence. It was certainly true that her eyes in some moods were visible at night, and her hair apparently lightened and darkened. Was this exotic creature really the daughter of Timothy Fuller, the plodding Cambridge lawyer? She was more like a Spaniard or a Turk.

She stormed Emerson with the frankest intentions. She meant to extract his secret and form an alliance that would be stimulating on both sides. She had read him and heard him and studied his tastes; she set out to pique and amuse him, and she made no concealment of her wish to please. She gave Emerson lessons in German pronunciation. She brought portfolios of engravings, and beside her, under the lamp, he couldn't but pore over those designs from Raphael, those etchings of Piranesi, those reproductions of Greek and Italian sculpture. Was she still inordinate? What of it?—

with all that amplitude and generosity. What of it, if she showed him how lifeless he was, what a poor Laplander burrowing under the snows of prudence and pedantry? No fear that Margaret would betray, like all the rest, under a thin garb of new words, the old droning, cast-iron opinions. She had read at the rate of Gibbon; she had raged through the history of art and philosophy; she sympathized too fast with all forms of life ever to be narrow or hostile. She was a living sketch, however crude, of the Goethean universality. And all that pathos of sentiment, those riches of literature and thought and her own invention, that march of character threatening to arrive at the shores and plunge into the sea of Buddhism and mystic trances, consisted with the lightest satire and a boundless fun and drollery.

What wit she had, what a store of illumined anecdotes! "Attica," she said to Emerson, "is your province; Thessaly is mine. Attica produced the marble wonders of the great geniuses, but Thessaly is the land of magic." (And indeed it was.) She spoke of her childhood, her scheme of life as a girl of fifteen: she had risen before five, walked and practised on the piano for an hour before breakfast, read Sismondi in French till eight, Brown's Philosophy till 9:30, Greek till twelve, practised again before luncheon; then two hours of Italian, a walk or a drive, and singing—eleven o'clock to bed and to write in her diary. "The demons," she remarked, "are not busy enough at the births of most men." They had not been idle at hers. Then she poured

herself out on the Zeitgeist. ("My voice excites
me," she said, "my pen never." And yet she had
just made a translation of Eckermann and was
planning a life of Goethe.) She felt that since the
Revolution there had been little in the circumstances of this country to call out the higher sentiments, that the effect of continued prosperity was
the same on nations as on individuals: it left the
nobler faculties undeveloped. "The superficial diffusion of knowledge, unless attended by a deepening of its sources, is likely to vulgarize rather than
to raise the thought of a nation. The tendency of
circumstances has been to make our people superficial, irreverent, and more anxious to get a living
than to live mentally and morally." (How often
Emerson had thought all this himself!)

Then she spoke of her work and her friends. She
was teaching in Bronson Alcott's school in Boston:
three classes, elementary German, Dante and
Alfieri, Lessing, Goethe. She had pupils outside,
one of them a blind boy, to whom she had read
aloud the whole of Shakespeare; and one evening
a week she read to Dr. Channing, who wished to
keep up with the new German authors. But her
friends were Margaret's lifework. She referred
calmly to the girls whom she had formed, the
young men who owed everything to her, the com-
rades she had long left behind her. ("I now know
all the people worth knowing in America, and I
find no intellect comparable to my own.") The
chambermaids confessed to her; how could the
schoolgirls resist her? (She understood them so

well.) Or the soul-sick boys at Harvard? She
looked upon life as an art and every person as an
artist: she could forgive anything but the apostasy
of a commercial career. Whole romances of life
and love had been confided, counselled, thought
and lived through, in her cognizance and sympathy; and she was perfectly true to this confidence. She poured a stream of amber over everything, clean and unclean, that lay in her path, and,
while her talk was a comedy in which dramatic
justice was done to everybody's foibles, she never
confounded relations, but kept a hundred fine
threads in her hand, without crossing or entangling
any of them.

There was Caroline Sturgis, and Ellen Hooper,
and James Freeman Clarke, who had gone to Kentucky with his Unitarian gospel. (To the Western
forests, where the stagecoach ploughed through
swamps of fallen timber and clay roads gullied by
rain. What landscapes!—enormous tulip-trees and
massive trunks of the sycamore, wild mountains,
wilder streams, rude cabins, scenes for Salvator
Rosa. Clarke was afraid of falling into routine in
Boston: in the West he would have to originate
his methods and prove that his faith was adapted
to human needs.) Clarke was a friend of Margaret's: he wrote to her regularly and returned each
year to keep in touch with New England. And another friend was William Henry Channing, the
doctor's nephew, a young minister, too, a Christian
Socialist, with as many doubts as talents. (You felt
in Margaret's presence, Channing said, as if you

stood bare before a disembodied spirit. You communicated without reserve thoughts and emotions which even to yourself you had scarcely named.) And another was Frederic Hedge, with the face of a wise young frog, with a steely ring in his voice, and a mountain of learning. (At eleven he had been ready for Harvard—had read half the corpus of Latin literature. And he had visited Germany as a child, had drunk at the very spring of the new philosophy.)

But how could one keep track of Margaret's friends? She had watched the unfolding of their powers with the warmest sympathy. They were all disgusted, she said, with the vulgarity of a commercial aristocracy, and so became radicals; they were disgusted with the materialistic working of "rational" religion, and so became mystics. And she had the utmost faith in their corporate endeavours. "If they have opportunity to state and discuss their opinions, they will gradually sift them, ascertain their grounds and aims with clearness, and do the work this country needs. I hope for them as for the leaven that is hidden in the bushel of meal, till all be leavened. The leaven is not good by itself, neither is the meal; let these combine, and we shall yet have bread."

Emerson's own thoughts and hopes, exactly. He too had heard this rare thrilling prophecy from bands of competing minstrels. Hedge he already knew, and George Ripley, brimming over with German philosophy and talking about a community at Brook Farm. And other friends of Margaret's had heard his voice in the darkness and were straggling out to Concord.

John Sullivan Dwight, for one, the sunny, beaming Dwight, slender, shy, sensitive, who had just abandoned the pulpit. He had written the first American review of Tennyson and published a capital translation of Goethe and Schiller; but his great passion was music. As a boy of fifteen, he had first discovered his bent following a band about the streets of Boston that was playing the "Hunter's Chorus"; and now with his popular lectures he was creating a want for something better than hackneyed glees and psalm-tunes. He was labouring to build up a public for Mozart and Beethoven, assembling the musicians in Boston, communicating his enthusiasm. But he loved to walk in the country—to watch the fireflies and gather the arethusas. And he said that the interest in Beethoven in Boston had begun at the same moment as the interest in Emerson, that Emerson had braced people's minds and procured an audience for every kind of art.

And Jones Very came, the tall, angular mystic with the wasted face and the burning eyes, from Salem. Very was instructor in Greek at Harvard, but he was so much concerned for the salvation of the souls of his students that the college authorities concluded he was mad. He went of his own accord and placed himself in the asylum at Somerville; he was sane enough, however, to write while there an essay on epic poetry and two papers on Shakespeare that had much in common with

Emerson's own thought. He was writing sonnets, too, of a rare spirituality, and he was among the first who found their way to Concord. Never had a man so fully accepted the doctrine of the unconscious. He did not feel at liberty even to correct his verses for the press; as they had come to his mind, he believed, so they ought to be printed. He considered it an honour to wash his own face (the temple of the soul) ; he never rested his arm on the mantel of his own will; he performed every slightest act, he said, "in obedience to the Spirit."

Emerson took charge of the publication of Very's *Essays and Poems* and sent Carlyle a copy. For Carlyle, too, he acted as publisher and editor, reprinted *The French Revolution* and the *Miscellanies*, and wrote a preface for the American *Sartor Resartus*, which had not yet found a publisher in England. There was even a chance that Carlyle might come to Concord. He was desperately poor, and Emerson had promised him a large return if he undertook a lecturing tour in America. For Carlyle had aroused the young people almost as much as Emerson. They were spoken of as two sides of the same rising sun.

For Emerson himself was busily writing now, shaping his thoughts into essays. He would sit in his rocking-chair, his portfolio on his knee, and the volumes of his journals on the table beside him, copying, combining, re-writing entries from the latter, and, as he wrote, in his large, flowing hand, dropping the pages on the floor. Now and again he would take a stroll in the garden, or knock off for the day and carry his books to Walden. A German book, for instance. It was lumpish and opaque in the house, but once in the woods he would find the sense transparent, and when he came home towards evening he would set to work again with a lighter heart.

For his essays he liked to choose themes that were central in human experience: Character, Manners, Art, Politics, Friendship. To focus on one of these points all the force of his mind, his observation and reading, was to build his inn on the highroad where every traveller passed.

And then there were other subjects, such as Compensation and Circles and Spiritual Laws, that gave him a chance to express, in a kind of prose poetry, the deep joy he felt in the workings of Nature. That old idea of Compensation, for instance, which had haunted him from boyhood and of which for years he had been collecting illustrations. He had found them everywhere, in the sciences, in mechanics, in history, in his own daily experiences. When he uttered the word Compensation, they seemed to run to meet him, charming in their variety and unanimity. Darkness and light balanced each other, heat and cold, and the systole and diastole of the heart. One could see the law at work in the animal kingdom, where no creature was a favourite and every gift was paid for by a defect. And so it was with man. If the government was cruel, the governor was always in jeopardy; if it taxed too high, the revenue yielded nothing; if the criminal code was sanguinary, juries would not convict; if the law was too mild, private vengeance came in. How many proverbs affirmed the law, how many fables described it! The borrower ran in his own debt; the dearest labour was the cheapest; the wise man paid as he went along; the great man was willing to be little. The spirit was always equal to itself; everything in Nature contained all the powers of Nature, and the whole by necessity appeared, counteracting any excess, when the part appeared. And this doctrine was not fatalistic. There was a deeper fact in the soul than Compensation, for the soul itself was life, a vast affirmative. The gain of rectitude was not bought by any loss, for in virtue and wisdom the soul properly existed. So far as it followed its laws it added to the world, "planted into deserts conquered from Chaos and Nothing."

And the Over-Soul, the flowing river of Nature, the "Eternal One" that passes into one's thought and becomes wisdom and virtue and power and beauty. Man lives in division, in parts, and yet within him lies the soul of the whole. "When it breathes through his intellect, it is genius; when it breathes through his will, it is virtue; when it flows through his affection, it is love." And he who trusts himself, who finds his own centre, becomes its channel.

This was the master-idea that bound the essays together. What was history but the record of this general soul? One looked within oneself and found "the Foreworld, the Age of Gold, the Apple of Knowledge, the Argonautic Expedition, the Calling of Abraham, the Building of the Temple, the Advent of Christ, the Dark Ages, the Revival of Letters, the Reformation." For the life of man passes through all these phases. And if one reconstructs in imagination any moment in history one actually lives that moment. What man has done, man can do again; for what we are able to conceive, that we are able to carry out in action. History exists for the sake of the individual, solely to make him conscious of his own resources, of his own creative power. And he finds this power through absolute Self-Reliance. His intuition lets him into the One that yields all truth and strength. We have only to follow the clue that Nature gives us, follow the line of our talent; in one direction all space is open to us. We are like a ship in a river: we run against obstructions on every side but one, but on that side the obstruction is removed, and we sweep serenely over a deepening channel into an infinite sea.

Was this the world of "ideas," of things as they ought to be? Was it only the fortunate man who found his line so easily? But what a fillip it gave to the will of Emerson's readers to have it assumed that all men are fortunate!—to be asked to sit— even they!—at the table of the gods, and live for an hour with the makers of space and time. (My friends, you show me by every word you utter, by the light in your eyes, your gait, your every movement, that the life we know is a germ—nothing less than a germ—of life as it might and will be. Even here in Concord. Massachusetts, Connecticut

River, Boston Bay—do you think them paltry places? Does your ear love foreign names? But here you are, and, if you tarry a little, you may learn that here is best. Your heart dilates in beholding the force and grace of the ancients, the Greeks and the Romans. You respond because that force and grace already exist in you—as the flower in the seed.)

Emerson had planted himself on his own instincts, and the world was coming to him. So much the more need to retire at times into the solitude of solitudes—to walk out at night and look at the stars. He would hear the voice of the wind, so slight and pure and deep, as if it were the sound of the stars themselves revolving. Then he lost himself in wonder—mute, bottomless, boundless, endless wonder.

CHAPTER VIII

NOTHING so fearsome as too much solitude. Left alone for a few days, he crept about as if in expectation of a calamity. There was much to be said for society too, and cities: to be isolated was to be sick, and so far dead. Rightly thought Goethe, that dealing habitually with men and affairs was essential to one's health. For one thing, society educated one's will, which never acquired force in solitude. It was true that if he stayed in the city he seemed to lose all substance and became surface in a world of surfaces: everything was external there, and he thought of his hat and coat, and all his other surfaces, and nothing else. But a periodical raid was another matter. He could do his thinking alone, but he had to go to market to get his facts.

On Saturday, as a rule, Emerson left his study and set out for the Athenæum or to see what friends he could muster. Away with his grey clothes: did the black suit need a brushing? Down came the silk hat from the shelf in the closet; then three long hours in the stage that lumbered past his door. But the passengers were a foretaste of the wide world, and the stage drove through the slums of the North End. How picturesque were the crowds on the sidewalks, how much more enlivening than the clean-shaved and silk-robed procession in Washington and Tremont Streets! He knew instantly, as he passed them, whence all the fine pictures had their origin; he felt the painter stirring in him. These unrestrained attitudes and manners recalled to him the force and eloquence of form and the sting of colour. No suggestion here of those depressing college anniversaries at Cambridge, those hurrahs among the ghosts, those yellow, bald, toothless meetings in memory of red cheeks, black hair and departed health. They were real crowds, wholesome and heart-warming; they restored one's flagging sense of the infinite wealth of humanity.

Then quick to the pavement!—and off he strode, tall, erect, light-footed and strong of limb, with his long neck and his bright blue eyes peering about, one shoulder slightly higher than the other. (You would have had to run to keep up with that man as he swung along, carrying his little satchel.) Where was he going today? To the Sculpture Gallery, perhaps, for a look at Michael Angelo's "Day and Night"? To a concert of Ole Bull? (A benign influence, that sorcerer, with a sleep as of Egypt on his lips in the midst of his rapturous music, even for a man without an ear.) Or perhaps to the foreign bookstore and reading-room that Dr. Nathaniel Peabody and his daughter Elizabeth had opened in the front parlour of their house in West Street? (Not to one of those literary clubs, be sure, where they still discussed the question, *Who wrote Junius?*) An embarrassment of riches! One trod rather proudly the streets of a town like Boston: Vasari had not felt more stimulus in the air of his darling

Florence. These pavements, too, had a history:
no accident, Boston, no mere crossroads, tavern or
army-barracks, grown up by time and luck to a
place of wealth, but a seat of men of principle.
How natural that the desire for glory and honour
should spring out of it!—so that all who possessed
talent were impelled to struggle, and labour by
every means to be foremost.

To the Sculpture Gallery, then, at the Athenæum: Margaret would be waiting for him there,
under that sunny roof, in those airy chambers.
There were the casts, selected by Canova, the
Laocoön, the Discobolus, the head of the Phidian
Zeus, and so many others—Greece and Italy
brought bodily to Boston. And there was the Brim-
mer Donation of French and Italian drawings,
prints of the Sistine frescoes, prints of Correggio,
drawings of Guercino, one apple from every tree.
And pictures ascribed to Rembrandt, Poussin,
Rubens, painted by God knows whom, obscure
nameless persons, yet with such skill and mastery
as to bring connoisseurs in doubt. What colour!—
a tonic that made him brisk and gay. Rome rose
again in his memory, and Paris danced before him.
(But how wronged they were, these paintings, dis-
crowned and disgraced, by being crowded together
in one apartment!—like so many men, lowered by
juxtaposition. One picture at a time! Let the eye
conspire with the painter, carry his work out far
and wide, see more than he has done, see what he
meant to do, enjoy the unity of the hour!)

A glowing companion, Margaret, in these adventures. A dubious guide, no doubt, too personal, too idiosyncratic, too bold an Ariadne. But why should he follow her clues when he had his own? (He thought of his own attempts at drawing as a boy, the heads he had sketched in his notebooks. Colour was to the eye what dancing was to the body, but form appealed to him more. And sculpture more than painting, the archaic grandeur of the age when the Greeks were at one remove from the Egyptians. He loved those block-like images, before freedom had become too free.) And how honest Margaret was, and what sympathy she felt with the artist in his protest against the deformities of common life! For months, thanks to Margaret, his world had been coloured with the genius of the Italians. She had made him warmly aware of so much in his nature that was still quiescent.

As a good child of Boston, he wished to see the best in every kind—let nothing pass, unseen, unheard, that was excellent. Fanny Elssler's dancing, for instance: could he ever forget this graceful silvery swimmer? The variety of her attitudes, the winning fun and spirit of her little coquetries, the beautiful erectness of her body? Or that slow, prolonged salaam?—she seemed to have invented new depths of condescension. What cheer and exhilaration the spectacle imparted! The sport and triumph of health, the virtue of organization. Such grace as hers, he knew, must rest on occult foundations of inward harmony.

But Dr. Peabody's shop was the likeliest haunt in town. They had all the new foreign books there,

George Sand, Schleiermacher, Manzoni; you
could stop and chat for a while, then carry off the
latest German or French review. And there you
were sure to meet the illuminati, talking and strolling about, or browsing over the counters: Dr.
Channing and Washington Allston, perhaps, the
veterans, or George Ripley, or Hedge, or those two
grave suitors of the Peabody girls, Horace Mann
and the shy Nathaniel Hawthorne. Ripley was
collecting translators for his *Specimens of Foreign
Literature,* and Hedge was full of German meta-
physics. There was always something in the wind
at Dr. Peabody's. A boon, that house, for a country
scholar for whom a new person was ever a great
event.

One could linger there by the hour, then saunter
off with some other casual visitor. Washington
Allston, for instance: how appealing this old man
was, so fragile, so quaintly courteous, with his
glowing eyes and his silvery curls! Yes, and that
legendary mission—to restore the grand manner of
the sixteenth century, as his friend Coleridge had
put it. A painter in the great line, as one couldn't
but feel, a boulder of the European ledge, a spur
of the Apennines of Titian and Michael Angelo,
cropping out here in this remote America, unlike
anything around it, and so far from reaching its
natural elevation. He rose at ten o'clock, it was
said, each morning, left his poor little house, with
a pitcher of water in his hand, hurried through the
dusty streets to his bleak little studio, sat down and
smoked and contemplated his picture, then painted

for a while and laid aside his brushes, and contemplated his picture again till dark. "Belshazzar's Feast" was the picture—that accurst, that baleful picture!—and for twenty years he had worked on it, in vain. He had started it in London, in the days of his renown; the subject had grown hateful, the mechanical labour was too great for him, he had had to change the perspective, and now he was white and feeble and the picture still unfinished. (His townsmen had bought it in advance; the newspapers constantly talked of it; the public was agape for it. Could he disappoint the world?) He had put aside everything else for the sake of that picture, commissions, new attempts, peace of mind; but how winning the old man was, as he rambled across the bridge to his house in Cambridgeport! A poet too: he would take you into the studio, and place you before the picture, and recite to you in an undertone lines that had taken shape in his mind as he painted.

Boston might not be nobly mad, either for learning or philosophy, art or association; but who could think ill of a town that harboured such souls as this? Not Emerson, and the times were crescent. No doubt Allston had starved there, had fed upon himself, withered away in the wind, he in whose veins the South had run so warm. His friend Dana was right: his spirit had risen and soared, but without force, for Boston had afforded him "no combat with other intellects, no strife for mastery, which gives vigour and development to the mind." But the scene was changing fast—with all those bubbling wits at Dr. Peabody's! And Margaret's "Conversations," in that same engaging house. For Margaret was holding classes for the ladies of Boston, in Mythology, Ethics, Literature, "What is Life?" Why should their minds be so woolly, so wanting in precision and clearness? So vague, so cold, so provincial, in a world so full of delights? What pursuits were they fitted for, how could they use their means, what were they born to do, and how should they do it? Coals for Margaret's fanning! Too many local interests! They should fix their minds on the broad, the objective, the tangible—"serious without being solemn, playful as well as deep." The ladies were disturbed to be told that in Christian times heathen Greeks should be envied, and they found it difficult to talk. But Margaret stirred them up, and they were soon aglow. They shook the films from their eyes; they melted, they laughed, they could scarcely express their rapture; and they showered their love and gifts at the sibyl's feet.

Who could withstand that verve, that haughty assurance? Those endearing perceptions, that all-attaching eye? It was easy to laugh at Margaret; but who could dispute her vitality? Had she not given tongues to the dumb and grace to the awkward? And Boston was full of these voices, if one knew where to find them. There was Father Taylor, for one, the apostle to the sailors, a master of wild rhetoric, an unconscious artist, a dancing drunkard of his wit, and Emerson delighted in him. Occasionally, in the days of his pastorate, he had had this minstrel in his pulpit, and he could always count on a thrill when he threaded the crooked old waterside streets and dropped in at the Sailors' Bethel. What teeth and eyes this man had, like a jaguar's, or an Indian's! What authority, wilful and despotic, as he rode on the waves of the sunny ocean of his thought! He would weep and grieve and pray and chide in a tempest of passionate speech, and never break the perfect propriety with a single false note.

A man with a way and sweep like a frigate's way, that takes up the centre of the sea and paves it with a white street! (Another Robert Burns, this Father Taylor. No corpse-cold Unitarian. Mighty Nature's child!) And Sampson Reed was always ready for a chat. (The Swedenborgian druggist, who had written *The Growth of the Mind*.) A grand poet, Swedenborg, a stark Scandinavian berserker with an iron training; and who could discourse on the subject better than Reed? But he wouldn't admit it was poetry; he meant you to take it all for literal fact. . . . "But really, Mr. Reed, those devils: you don't imagine . . . ?" But he did: those devils were solid flesh and blood.

One personage caught Emerson's fancy above all the others. On a June day in 1836 he turned in at the Masonic Temple, where Bronson Alcott's school was in its third year. He had met Alcott before and felt the attraction of this tall, blue-eyed prophet with his corn-coloured locks and his open, courtly manner; but the school was a revelation. The beautiful spacious room, the Gothic windows, the busts of Shakespeare and Plato, the well-chosen pictures on the wall, the gracious master presiding from his desk in the corner were very different from the dark, formal classrooms that he had known as a boy. But what struck the visitor most was the conversation in progress between the master and the pupils. With what absorbed attention these diminutive Bostonians listened and responded! No suggestion of painful tasks, routine, irritation, severity. This teacher, with his dialectic method of query and answer, was a Socrates indeed, for whom questions of thought and taste were independent of age. He was like the sun in April warming into life a hive of torpid bees.

Emerson had found a friend, the reasonable creature he had always longed for. He had heard much of this dreamer who thought the world was to be redeemed by education and who had aroused such furious opposition in Boston. A strange story was Alcott's. The son of a Connecticut farmer and mechanic, he had known the rigours of a primitive country school and had been set to work at fourteen in a clock-factory, the pride of a neighbouring town. He had wandered to the South as a peddler, with a small tin trunk in his hand and the hope of discovering a school in Virginia or the Carolinas where the rudiments he had learned at the rod's end would provide him with the work to which he felt predestined. He walked, he travelled about with horse and wagon, selling almanacs and tinware, thimbles, scissors, picture-books for children, spectacles, razors, buttons. Then, finding the

South apathetic, he returned to Connecticut, where
his uncle, Dr. Bronson, directed an Academy,
and there, and at Germantown and Philadelphia,
he opened schools and began to develop his
methods. (No corporal punishment. Gymnastic
exercises. No parrot-spelling of columns of unknown words. No treating these children as buckets
to be filled with the barren knowledge of the
world, but a veritable leading-forth of the innate
disposition.) At last he had come to Boston for the
great venture of his life. He had stirred up a storm
of abuse, with his heterodox conversations on the
Gospels; for who was he to brush aside so lightly,
with his pagan-Greekish talk of the beauty of the
natural instincts, the hallowed Puritan dogma of
original sin? ("The blissful moments," said Alcott,
"are those when a man abandons himself to the
Spirit. The highest duty is musical and sings itself.
And children are so attractive because they are
still under the sway of instinct.") But he had found
a powerful ally in Dr. Channing, who shared these
"intimations," and he seemed to be winning his
way.

A true comrade-in-arms. Emerson was entranced
with him. He could read his Plato now with new
eyes, for here was a Plato in the flesh. What was
it the sage had said?—that "education should be
conducted with a serene sweetness, never by force
or violence, but by gentleness, accompanied with
persuasion and every kind of invitation." Alcott's
way, exactly! And behold, from his face too, as
from the face of those divine ancients, there shone

a pleasing mildness; and over his whole external form was diffused that air of dignity and ease, of affability and modesty, which, according to Plotinus, true wisdom, deeply possessed, gives to one's manners. None of those smug arts, beloved of the worldlings of Athens and Boston, but the grace of the Muses. And what a gift for awakening aspiration and contemplation! He had, it was true, some rather odd ideas, as, for instance, that the human head was going to slough the body: the trunk would perish and the brain would unfold a new and higher organization. (He could hardly expect women to like such notions.) And he talked high and wide, and expressed himself very happily, and forgot all he had said: he seldom finished a sentence, but revolved in spirals until he was lost in the air. And his writing was vague and trite. He had never wrought his fine clay into vases, or his gold dust into ingots; he played with his thought too much, without subduing it; he used too many phrases about "the Spirit" that he ought to have left to the Unitarian Association. But who was more candid than Alcott? Who liked one's bluntness better? And how he loved life and the present hour! No skulker, ready to nestle into any cast-off shell and form of the past. An apostle and a pilgrim. If Boston refused to hear him, he would take his staff and go among the people, walk through the country, discoursing to the school-teachers and holding conversations in the villages.

Such were the rewards when Emerson left his study and slipped into town for the day. His mind, in Alcott's company, kindled and burst into flame. With men like this walking the streets, who could complain of the dumbness, the pomposity of Boston? Then why not improve the occasion and form a club? Hedge would enjoy it, the ever-liberal Hedge, who was publishing his translations of the new German authors, and Orestes Brownson, French-and-Indian Brownson, who had opened a radical church for mechanics and labourers, and Theodore Parker, of course, that blue-eyed Friar Tuck of theologians, with his pug nose and his hearty grip, who was able to carry a barrel of cider in his hands, yes, and with twenty languages on the tip of his tongue. (Persian, Coptic, Syriac, Dutch, think of it!—and all wrapped up in the frame of a Yankee farmer. A glutton of learning, for all his ruddy face: he could scarcely be brought to admit that Hedge was "learned in spots." And a real bringer of good tidings. What New England pulpiteer had ever before praised the Lord for the voiceless fish, "moving with the flapping of the sea," for the "bunchy and calumniated toad" and the frog, "shaking the bog with his hoarse thunders"?) One could certainly count on Parker, that hierophant of Nature and muscular man. And George Ripley, and John Sullivan Dwight, with his cult of Mozart and Beethoven, and James Freeman Clarke, on his annual visits from Louisville. (He found it so "flat" out there, beyond the mountains. But he had carried Boston with him; he was toiling away at Greek, geology, mineralogy; he had started a magazine, *The Western Messenger*.

And the leaves of the cottonwood-trees were "always in motion.") Good timber for a club. Unitarian ministers, for the most part, and mostly from habit and inertia, in their early thirties, with little taste for preaching—(not Clarke, not Theodore Parker!)—and bursting with profane passions for poetry, for music, for painting, philosophy or the Church of Rome. (John Dwight was the type cf them all, Dwight who awoke on the Sunday after his ordination and remembered that he had prepared neither of his sermons for the day. Too much Mozart in his cosmos, together with a "certain want of fluency in prayer.") Every rustic manse within walking, running, racing distance of Boston would contribute a rill to the stream of good talk. Why stick at home and read Sir William Jones's life, or the life of Gibbon, to shame oneself into an emulating industry, when all these cordial souls were so eager to shame one another?

Why indeed? Whatever your studies might be, they would certainly thrive better for a little airing. Did your reading grow stale as you frowsted over your fire? How quickly the faded colours revived in the presence of that fellow-student who showed such a lively interest in your speculations. There was nothing like matching wits to restore the price of thought. A club then, by all means. The Symposium, perhaps. Or the Transcendental Club. A little starchy, this word, a little cold and stiff. The Greeks would never have liked it: their thought needed no Transcendental bush, and they lived the *thing* as naturally as they breathed. But

the word was a good flag to fly in the face of all
this Boston Whiggism. Was man made to live like
a peddler, with his hand ever on his pocket, cau-
tious, calculating? Or to nourish himself on the
thin porridge and cold tea of Unitarianism? Or
to chop logic with John Locke? Or to take his revelation ready-made from a book bound in black
cloth? Man, enthusiastic man, possessed by a god?
Away with all this "evidence of the senses"! . . .
Transcendentalism! . . . Let them say, if they like
—with a wave of the hand—that it means "a little
beyond." A little *within,* good friends, a little
within!

The neophytes assembled, first four, then a dozen
or so. Now at Willard's Hotel in Cambridge, now
at Brownson's house in Chelsea, or at Ripley's, or
in Emerson's study in Concord. The neophytes assembled and took their seats. Was the air a little
frosty? Was the talk a little staccato? Were the
voices a little sepulchral? Were the pauses long
and frequent? They could only meet, these minds,
by soaring up in the fog, fortunate if, in the course
of an anxious evening, two of them came within
hailing distance of each other.

Alas, it was all a pale, frail mist! One doesn't
learn to loosen one's tongue in a lonely country par-
sonage; and the subjects—for instance, the Highest
Aim—were not exactly enlivening. How chagrined
the philosophers felt as they munched their russet
apples, when the dish was handed round at the end
of the soirée, and they vanished into the night!
What wild comets of thought had whirled through

their heads! What daring and extraordinary things they were on the point of saying!—and just as their blood was up it was time to go. That infernal Boston frigidity! They ought to have called it the Lonely Man's Club. (With a seal: two porcupines meeting with all their spines erect, and the motto, "We converse at the quill's end.")

But they stuck it out. They had made up their minds to be genial, cost what it might. One evening Father Taylor came to the rescue: with his green spectacles thrown up on his forehead, he burst into a stream of indignant and sorrowful eloquence on the indifferentism of the Churches and the lukewarm spirit of the day. And occasionally they happened on a topic that warmed them all like wine. Did property fulfil some natural need of man? Should they speak as they felt in the pulpit, or speak with reference to the fears and the sleep of others? (It was easy to settle that question.) Or the Union, the Constitution: how soon would Americans realize that individual character and culture were sacred, that these mass-obligations were trivial beside them? Or the state of affairs at Harvard? It was shocking to see how State Street voted the college down. Everything was permitted in Cambridge that pleased the respectables, while that which the college existed for—to be a Delphi uttering oracles to elevate and lead mankind—*that* it was not permitted to be or to think of. (Every generosity of thought was suspected at Harvard: not a poet, not a prophet, not a demon, but was gagged or driven away.) But one topic especially stirred the club: the American Genius, the causes that hindered its growth. On this titanic continent, with nature so grand, why should genius be so tame? One had only to think of Bryant—chaste and faultless, but uncharacterized. Or Dr. Channing's preaching, the sublime of calculation. Allston was thin, and Greenough was thin, and Irving and Prescott and Bancroft. Not one drop of the strong black blood of the English race! No teeth and claws, no nerve and dagger. A pale, diluted stream.

There was the topic of topics: the lukewarm spirit of the day, as Father Taylor called it. Who cared whether Bryant wrote good poems or not? Whether Greenough made a good statue? The great poems had been confessions of the faith of races, the great statues had been worshipped. No necessity of the people called these Americans out. And alas, why look for art where society was unbelieving, honeycombed, hollow? When it tingled and trembled with earnest, beauty would be born. And why rail and complain in the meantime? Why not take some positive step, why not start a quarterly journal? With Alcott's title, *The Dial?* (He had used it for his private diary.) And Margaret Fuller as editor? (For Margaret herself had been present at some of the meetings, and what a gift she had for inspiring confidence! She had fused the chilly philosophers into a glowing company; she had felt the moods of the speakers, gathered their rays to a focus, seized their balloons of thought and pulled them back to the earth. And who knew as Margaret knew it the silent army of the younger generation, that throng of eager souls, in college and village, lonely, constrained, obscure, who had given in their adherence to the spiritual revolution?)

Trust Margaret to sound the reveille! Trust Margaret to fill *The Dial* with the burning thoughts of the young!

CHAPTER IX

IT was 1841, and Henry Thoreau had joined the Concord household. As a steward, an adopted son, a master of rural arts—chiefly, perhaps, to give Emerson lessons in gardening. He had his little room at the head of the stairs and worked, when he chose, about the yard and barn, banked up the fruit-trees against the winter and the mice, looked out to see when a pale was loose in the fence or a nail dropped from its place, set up the stoves and put the shutters to rights. There was never such a man for locks and hinges and door-knobs, or for making the chickens behave.

It was all in the family, for Emerson had known Henry from his boyhood. He had helped him to get a scholarship at Harvard, for Henry's father, the pencil-maker on Main Street, was always short of money. And then he had had a surprise! Henry had come back to Concord the walking incarnation of all his own ideas. He had steeped himself in the Greek and Roman sages, he had hunted out the Elizabethan poets, Fletcher, Drayton, Raleigh, whom Emerson especially loved. But this was incidental. He proposed to live without following any profession, live for the sake of living and keep alive by whatever means might offer. Live like a monk, if need were, live like a workman; earn his dollar a day by carpentering, gardening, painting. But live for his thoughts, his perceptions, his journal and his flute.

Emerson set to work, with this stern instructor, digging and hoeing in the garden. Not for long, to be sure; he found himself sadly untuned. The smell of the plants drugged him and robbed him of energy, and he soon awoke from his dream of chickweed and redroot and made up his mind that writing and practical farming could never go together. But lessons in the art of walking, in the art of observing and exploring, were another matter, and Henry knew the country like a fox or a partridge; and, although he had no walks to throw away on company, he could always spare an afternoon for Emerson. He was not an easy companion, for he wanted a fallacy to expose or a blunder to pillory, he required a roll of the drums, a sense of victory, to call his powers into exercise. He would say, and wait for Emerson to contradict him, that nobody dared to go to the Concord Post Office with a patch on the knee of his trousers. Or that nothing was to be hoped from him or any one if this bit of mould under his feet was not sweeter to him to eat than any other in the world or any world. But only as long as the village was still in sight: in the swamps and pastures he forgot the limited human race. And then what an air came over him, what a light shone in his eyes, and what magic Henry performed with the jackknife and spyglass and microscope that were tucked away in his pockets with his diary and pencil! Snakes coiled round his leg, fishes swam into his hand, a sparrow even alighted on his shoulder. He would name the plants that ought to bloom this day, and there they were, as if his voice had evoked them. He would hazard a guess that the spot where they were standing had once been an Indian camping-ground; then stoop and dig in a circle and uncover the blackened stones of an ancient fireplace. Emerson could easily believe him when he said that if he awakened from a trance in the depths of the forest he could tell the time of year within two days by the plants that were growing about him.

He was writing too, as diligently as Emerson: crowded little poems, in the manner of the seventeenth century, with a certain intricate melody. But his journal was the greatest delight—pastoral as Izaak Walton, it seemed to Emerson, spicy as flagroot, broad and deep as Manu. What prose Henry wrote, how acute were his senses! Half the wisdom of the ancients seemed to have been born again in this Concord Pliny. He was very severe with himself and shaped his rambling thoughts into formal essays with infinite toil and a good deal of hesitation. But when Emerson read his paper on "A Winter Walk" and "The Natural History of Massachusetts," he was ready to account Henry the king of American lions.

They had not been friends very long when an opportunity came for them to work together in a more congenial way. Emerson was asked to take charge of *The Dial*. The magazine was not prospering, in spite of heroic efforts, and Margaret was unable to carry it any longer. There were scarcely one hundred subscribers. Some readers complained of the lack of a definite aim; others, that it savoured too much of the old order of things. The practical reformers were annoyed by its airs and graces, and those who cared for style were annoyed by the reformers. Margaret's idea had been to allow all kinds of people to say their say, without too much regard for their manner of saying it; and Emerson had winced at the barbarous form of some of the compositions. But Elizabeth Peabody had agreed to take over the management and find another printer; and if Henry would only canvass for new subscribers and Emerson would select the contents, they might make the paper a success in spite of all.

So *The Dial* came to Concord, and Henry read the proofs (and enlarged the list of subscribers to two hundred and twenty). Margaret had not been mistaken in promising the richest harvest of contributions. Her own paper on Goethe and her "Short Essay on Critics" were the best she was ever to write. There were Alcott's Orphic epigrams and Dwight's papers on Music, poems by Christopher Cranch and William Ellery Channing (the doctor's nephew). There were sonnets by Jones Very and James Russell Lowell (who had spent a few months in Concord not long before). And Ripley and Parker, of course, and James Freeman Clarke had much to say. But the greatest surprise was the number of unknown writers who rallied about the paper as if they had found their natural home at last. There were fragments of private diaries, each with a note of distinction, comments on works of art revealing some personal taste, sketches of village life, confessions, dialogues, soliloquies. *The Dial* was plainly a comfort and encouragement for dozens of lonely souls who felt themselves without support in the world.

Too "spirit-like" in expression. Carlyle was undoubtedly right. "Too aeriform, aurora-borealis-like. I can do nothing with vapours," he had written, after reading the earlier numbers, "I can do nothing with vapours but wish them condensed." Too much unbalanced intellectuality. But Thoreau was solid enough, and Parker and Dwight and Channing. And what unsuspected wealth *The Dial* revealed in the depths of this dumb New England! What reserves of thought and feeling! A chilly, misty dawn of some golden summer to follow.

What interested Emerson most, for it seemed to give most promise, was the poetry. He published some of the verses he was writing himself, *The Sphinx, Wood-notes, Saadi,* and a few of his own essays; and he made a point of printing as much of Thoreau as possible. He reviewed the new books that struck him as most significant, Borrow's *Bible in Spain,* Tennyson's Poems, *Two Years Before the Mast,* by his old pupil Dana, and Browning's *Paracelsus.* And he and Henry selected for publication passages from the Eastern Scriptures, the Fables of Bidpai, the Chaldæan Oracles, the Analects of Confucius. (All unknown in America.) Then, at the end of the fourth year, as *The Dial* seemed to have made no further headway, the editor closed his desk. He stored the remaining copies in the attic. (Where they lay for thirty years. In 1872 they were sold to the ragman.)

Concord, congenial Concord! It was good to exchange ideas with artists and teachers, people of the city and the world. But how much he learned from his country neighbours too! From the labourers, for instance: to refresh himself with the bone and sinew of society he had to avoid the so-called respectable classes as carefully as a good traveller in a foreign land avoids his own countrymen. Now and then, at least. Take a group of villagers laying a new bridge. How close they were to their work! They sympathized with every log and anticipated its every stir with chain and crowbar. And how grand were their postures, their air, their very dress!—like figures of Michael Angelo. No other cultivation but that of war could have made such forms and carriage.

He lingered by a blacksmith or a truckman. No fear these men would speak because they were expected to speak: they were realists, not dictionaries, and they only uttered words that stood for things. The style of the Boston scholars was so trite and poor because language was properly made up of the spoils of actions, of trades, arts, games, metaphors borrowed from natural and mechanical processes, from the street and the field and the market. That was Plato's secret: if he loved abstract truth, he drew his illustrations from sources disdained by the polite, from mares and puppies and pigs, from potters, horse-doctors, butchers, fishmongers and cooks. Everett and Bancroft should certainly have lived in Concord. They would never have poured out such floods of empty rhetoric if they had spent a few minutes in the square each morning listening to the drovers and teamsters. What rattling oaths, how beautiful and thrilling! They fell like a shower of bullets. What stinging phrases, and that fiery double negative! No pale academicisms there, but a strong, salty speech, brisk and laconic, words so vascular and alive that they would bleed if you cut them, words that walked and ran.

Where could he pass an hour better than on the Mill Dam, dropping into the grocery and the Squire's office, or chatting with Sam Staples on the steps of the courthouse? Or walking along beside Edmund Hosmer as he ploughed his cornfield? Sam alone, with his liberal experience, as hostler, barkeeper, constable, deputy sheriff, as jailor, auctioneer and real-estate agent, was a veritable Sancho Panza for any Don Quixote of the pen. And Edmund Hosmer was a Caesar, an Alexander of the soil, conquering and to conquer. A victor, this faithful, sweet-tempered man, the hero, in his old weather-worn cap and blue frock bedaubed with the slime of the marsh, of six thousand daily battles, and standing, with Atlantic strength and cheer, invincible still. (Sometimes, when Edmund Hosmer was not too tired, he would drop in for an evening in Emerson's parlour, and what weight and actuality he contributed to the talk! Especially when Alcott was there, the wingéd Alcott, like an

astral body without visible hands and feet.) And
a master was Abel Moore, that musician who could
make men dance in all sorts of weather. Trees bore
fruits for him that Providence never gave them,
and grapes from France and Spain yielded pounds
of clusters at his door. He could turn a bog into a
meadow with a stroke of his instrument or cover
a sand-hill with peach-trees and vines, and he the
plainest, the stupidest-looking fiddler that ever
drew the rosin over his bow.

They shamed one's slight and useless city limbs,
these soldiers of the soil—shamed the slackness of
a scholar's day. A glance over Abel Moore's fence,
a half-hour in the field with Edmund Hosmer, was
a tonic for Emerson's will. And these men, too,
spoke the language of Nature. They challenged his
mind, they drove his notions into a corner and
obliged them to render up their meaning in a
phrase, at the point of a pistol. They made him
study the low tone, and he never forgot in their
presence that the roots of the great and high must
still be in the common life.

A capital place, Concord, for the study of human
nature. He could find every human type there.
Take Cardinal de Retz's *Memoirs:* it was easy to
identify all his principal characters, playing simi-
lar parts in the village comedy. There was M. de
Rohan, whose only talent was dancing and who
knew that his element for rising in the world was
the ballroom. And that old granny of a M.
d'Angoulême, and Beaufort, who was only a private man and affected neutrality; and Mazarin,

with his genius for going about the bush and giving to understand (like Mr. E—— of Bangor, who never finished his sentence—"you take the idee?") In the country church one saw the cousins of Napoleon, of Wellington, of Wilberforce, Bentham, Humboldt. A little air and sunshine, an hour of need, would suffice to call out the right fire from these slumbering peasants. The more silently they sat in the pews the louder their faces spoke—of the plain prose of life, timidity, caution, appetite, old houses, musty smells, retrograde faculties "puttering round" in paltry routines from January to December. The old doctor was a gallipot, the bookbinder bound books in his face, and the landlord mixed liquors, in motionless pantomime. Emerson could scrutinize every breed in the germ and verify all the impressions his reading had given him.

Why should people talk so much of the broadening effect of travel? You made an immense conquest of humanity by studying one man thoroughly. And Juvenal was right: "A single house will show whatever is done or suffered in the world." All history—Parthia, Macedon, Rome and the Netherlands—repeated itself every year in Concord. At one end of the village scale were the clowns and sots who made the fringes of your tapestry of life and gave a certain reality to the picture: old Sol, old Moore, who slept in Dr. Hurd's barn, and the denizens of Bigelow's and Wesson's barrooms. At the other end was the courthouse, where the greatest men in the country appeared and spoke, Chan-

ning and Everett and Choate, Wendell Phillips
and Webster: the village got a handful of every
ton that came to Boston. And there were shows and
processions, animal-trainers and conjurors, revival-
ists and reformers, tourists and politicians—not to
mention the Penobscot Indians who always came
back with the summer. You had only to mix your
impressions with a little imagination, and the
whole panorama of human life unfolded before
your eyes.

A little imagination! Sometimes, at night, as
Emerson lay awake, he listened to the endless procession of wagons creaking past his gate on the
great road from Boston to the mountain villages
of New Hampshire and Vermont. All the wealth
and goods of the Indies, of China and Turkey, of
England and Germany and Russia, were in those
wagons, streaming through Concord. Easy for him
then to remember that the whole world was to be
found in any least part of it, that the stars and celestial awning that overhung his own walks and discourses were as brave as those that were visible to
Coleridge as he talked, or Ben Jonson and Shakespeare, or Chaucer and Petrarch and Boccaccio
when they met. One had only to make much of
one's own place, and it became in actuality all that
one's fancy desired.

It was true that the world came to you if you
were ready to receive it, if some fact in your experience gave you the key. The more facts, the
more keys: that was the beauty of living close to
the concrete. Housekeeping was a universal school,

where all knowledge was taught you, and the
price of your tuition was simply your annual expense. You wanted your stove set up, and this want
entitled you to call on the professors of tin and
iron in the village, inquire the cost of production
of cast and wrought metal, the kinds of iron they
had, the secrets of the trade. You wanted soap
or vinegar, manure, medicines, and you played the
chemist; you were a politician with the selectmen
and the assessors, a naturalist with your trees, hens,
wood and coal. You opened, in short, a shop in the
heart of all crafts and professions. And besides,
the familiar household tasks were agreeable
to the imagination. Were they not the subjects of
all the Greek gems?

Emerson was open, in Concord—how easy it was
to be open!—open at every pore to the common
life. To the spring sounds in the village evenings;
to the winning, artful-artless ways of the young
girls in the shops, buying a skein of silk and gossiping for half an hour with the broad-faced shop-boy
(each laying little traps for the attention of the
other, and each jumping joyfully into the traps);
to the casual talk of pot-hunters and wood-choppers and cattle-drivers, and the local worthies ex-
changing dry remarks round the grocery stove; to
the amphibious, weather-beaten, solitary fishermen on the river, floating in their flat skiffs and
consoling themselves with rum; to the farmer who
found in Plato so many of his own ideas; to the
Social Circle that met on Thursday evenings—doctor, lawyer, trader, miller, mechanic, solid men,

yielding solidest gossip, like the circle in *Wilhelm Meister* of which every member was a master of some indispensable art; to the Indians on the river —they could give you a new tea every day, and a new soup, lily-soup, hemlock tea, tea from the snow-berry, and cut a string from spruce-root, something no white man could ever do; to the County Fair and the barkers—(here they are, gentlemen, the Newtown pippins, the very pippin that demonstrated to Sir Isaac Newton that the world fell, not Adam); to old George Minott up there on the slope, in his little hip-roofed cottage, with his cow and his corn and his "crook-necks"; to the carpenters and the tricks they could play with saw, chisel and plane. (Real creators, those fellows, like Phidias or Columbus. Their hands and their brains were channels through which the energy of the universe flowed into human life.)

Best of all were the walks. The little walks and the long walks: a dash to the top of the ridge across the road where he saw Wachusett and Monadnoc on the shimmering horizon, or a stroll to the Estabrook region, with its old straggling orchards and clearings and cellar-holes, seventeenth-century farms, abandoned for generations, lapsing back into forest. (Where apples grew that were never found in the market, the "Beware-of-this," the "Bite-me-if-you-dare," apples bursting with cider.) Or the shorter walks in the wild garden at Walden. For Emerson had bought a woodlot, a wild, rocky ledge along the pond, with a populous grove of chestnuts, oaks and hemlocks sweeping

down to the shore. Some of the trees were old, but
an undergrowth of maples, pines and birches had
sprung up to the water's edge. At first he had spent
whole days there, with pruning-shears and hatchet,
cutting paths and opening vistas. And there, above
all, he liked to stroll and linger, bathing, reading
on the bank, jotting in his notebooks.

Hours like these were as centuries, loaded, fragrant. His spirits rose as he closed his gate behind
him, and the moment he entered the pastures he
found antiquity again. In the fields with the lowing
cattle, the birds, the bees, the waters, the satisfying
outlines of the landscape, he could not have said
whether it was Tempe, Thessaly, Enna, or familiar
Concord. A mile to the pond, now by the road, now
by the gulley along the track, and books, affairs,
petulance and fret were forgotten. Every bird,
every plant, every spring, every light from the sky,
every shadow on the earth detained him as he wandered hither and thither.

What health, what affinity he found there! Before him was the pond itself, blue and beautiful in
the bosom of the woods and under the amber sky,
like a sapphire lying in the moss. Overhead floated
the summer clouds, here soft and feathery, there
firm and continental, vanishing in the east into
plumes and auroral gleams, with an expression of
immense amplitude in their dotted and rippled
rack. No crowding in that upper air, but a boundless cheerfulness and strength: how they seemed
to enjoy, those clouds, their height and privilege
of motion! The chickadees, the robins, the blue-

birds, perching on the iron arms of the oaks, the chestnut-trees with their towers of white blossoms, even the waterflies on the pond were full of happiness. The very look of the woods was heroic and stimulating, and trees, birds, clouds and insects seemed parts of the eternal chain of destiny.

A symphony indeed for a man with musical eyes. Emerson had often regretted that he had no ear, but what others heard, as it seemed to him, he saw. All the soothing, brisk or romantic moods that corresponding melodies awakened in them, he found in the carpet of the wood, in the margin of the pond, in the shade of the hemlock grove or in the infinite variety and rapid dance of the treetops. The thrilling leap of the squirrel up the long bough of pine, the stems of oak and chestnut gleaming like steel on the excited eye, the floating, exhaling, evanescent beauty of the summer air were enchantment enough for him. The names of the reeds and the grasses were a lively pleasure, the milkweeds and the gentians, the mallows, the nymphæa, the cardinal-flower, the button-bush, the willow with its green smoke. What poems these names often were: Erigeron, the Old Man of the Spring, so called because it grows too early, the Chimaphila, Lover of Winter, the Plantain, called by the Indians the White Man's Foot because it follows man wherever he builds a hut. And the odorous waving of the flowers charmed him. It was like returning to some ancestral home to rejoin these vegetable demons: his heart seemed to pump through his body the sap of this forest of verdure. He ceased to be a person; he was conscious of the blood of thousands coursing through him. As he opened with his fingers the buds of the birch and the oak, as his eyes followed the thistle-balls drifting in space, covered with their bright races, each particle a counterpart and contemplator of the whole, he felt himself dilating and conspiring with the summer breeze.

Was there ever a more abandoned lotus-eater? But was it not for this idleness that all his affairs existed? Why should he hurry homeward? Allah never counted the time the Arab spent in the chase! Had he not come back to his own, made friends with the elements?—and why should he part with them now? The mind loved its old home, and he tasted every moment; the active magic reached his dust; he expanded in the warm day like corn and melons. Lying there on the bare ground with his head bathed by the blithe air, he was happy in his universal relations. The name of his nearest friend sounded foreign and accidental; he was the heir of uncontained beauty and power. He hesitated to move a finger, to lift his book, lest he should disturb the sweet vision.

He felt as if he had drunk the soma-juice with the morning-moving deities of the Rig-Veda, as if life were all an eternal resource and a long to-morrow, rich and strong as yesterday. Goethe had known this mood: "When the healthy nature of man works in its entirety, when he feels himself in the world as in a large, beautiful, worthy and solid whole, when his harmonious well-being assures

him a clear, free joy, then would the universe, if
it were conscious, exult as arrived at its aim and
admire the summit of its own being and becoming." And there were other times and other spots
—how many!—autumn, winter, night, the river.
Those Indian summer days, for instance, when
heaven and earth flowed with magnificence and he
could almost see the Indians under the trees in the
wood, when Florida and Cuba seemed to have left
their seats and come to Concord, when all the insects were out and the birds came forth, when the
cattle lying on the ground seemed to have great
thoughts and India and Egypt looked through
their eyes. Winter days, when the leafless trees became spires of flame in the sunset, and the stars of
the dead chalices of the flowers and every withered
stem and bit of stubble rimed with frost contributed to the mute music. Winter evenings, when
from every grey or slate-coloured cloud over the
whole dome depended a wreath of roses, and the
long slender bars swam like fishes in the sea of
crimson light, and the stars emerged with their
private, ineffable glances. And days and nights of
paddling up the river. What colours were in the
water then, as the paddle stirred it, the hue of
Rhine wine, jasper and verd antique, gold and
green and chestnut and hazel; and what sorcery
as he returned in the evening when the moon was
making amber of the world, when every cottage
pane glittered with silver, and the little harlot flies
of the lowlands sparkled in the grass, and the
meadows sent up the rank smells of all their ferns

and folded flowers into a nocturnal fragrance. Summer nights on the moving water, summer noons at Walden! Everything invited him to repose, to the dreams of the Oriental sages.

Yes, he was "adjacent to the One" at such moments as these. Moments, hours of perception, when the solitude of the body was the populousness of the soul, when he felt himself in active touch with that force, known of old to the Buddhists, which sleeps in plants, awakens in animals and becomes conscious in man. His mind became rampant as the tropical growth; he melted into the earth and felt all its organs at work within him. He had left his human relations far behind him, wife, child, friends, and returned to matter, to the rocks, to the ground, and he seemed of one substance with air, light, carbon, lime and granite. He became a moist, cold element. Frogs piped, waters far off tinkled, dry leaves hissed, grass bent and rustled, and he had died out of the world of men and existence. The trance of how many sages! —gymnosophists reclining on their flowery banks, hermits of Ceylon, Chinese philosophers in bamboo groves, charmed by the plashing of bright cascades. A swoon, an awakening; for, coming back to himself, he seemed to have traversed all the cycles of life. How truly Pythagoras had expressed it!—"One mind runs through the universe." And that other saying of the Greeks: "The soul is absorbed into God as a phial of water broken in the sea."

CHAPTER X

THE reformers thronged the roads. The Chardon Street Convention in Boston had assembled a thousand messiahs from the woods and mountains. Dunkers, Muggletonians, Agrarians, Abolitionists, Groaners, Come-outers. Every village crossroads in New England had contributed a voice and a scroll.

They roamed about the countryside in long gowns and with hair over their shoulders, and many a strange apparition haunted Emerson's house. The vegetarians came, for whom the world was to be redeemed by bran and pumpkins; and those who would not eat rice because it was raised by slaves; and those who would not wear leather because it was stolen from animals; and those who rejected vegetables the roots of which grew downward (and food that fire had polluted). And they sat at Emerson's table and criticized or abstained. ("Tea? *I?* Butter? *I?*") They made his Thanksgiving turkey an occasion for a sermon; they lectured him over his mutton on the horrors of the shambles. They even invaded his study, these portents of the times, formidable, unanswerable. He sat there glued to his chair, all thought, all action, all play departed, paralyzed. They somehow took the oxygen out of the air, and he twisted like the eel in the exhausted receiver.

The Phrenologists came too, and the Mesmerists, and the Homeopathists, and the Swedenborgians. And the Rat-hole Spiritualists whose gospel came by taps in the wall and thumps in the table-drawer —wizards that peeped and muttered. (A pistareen a spasm, or nine dollars for a fit.) What quaint phantoms were abroad in this morning of time! But among these maggoty souls there were other and more appealing figures, perplexed, ardent, hopeful, inarticulate. Edward Palmer, for instance, the journeyman printer: touching it was to hear of his little group of six youthful apostles who met one evening in Boston and talked over his plan for the abolition of money till all were convinced that nothing could contribute more to the brotherhood of man. (He had wandered all over the South, with a light in his eye, paying for his night's lodging with papers and tracts.) There were others, like those two young clerks who had forsaken their counting-houses and gone off to a hut in the woods: they had worked away through the winter, reading and writing (in mittens), as best they could for the cold, and had barely escaped with their lives. New types, desires that had never been voiced before in prosaic America. What were they seeking, these young men, what were they feeling, thinking, for what were they groping?

For modes of life, perhaps, familiar enough in history, or in other parts of the world—in China, in India, in Paris, in the cells of the Thebaid, in the studios and taverns of Moscow, Rome or London; for careers and social customs, outlets, disciplines, that a simple colonial society had never dreamed of providing, had not been able to provide. And withal they shared the faith of the Age of Revolutions, a faith like that of the first Christian Age in the immediate perfectibility of man and society. (The Communists were on the march: every month some new colony was arriving from Europe, setting out to build its Eden in Ohio and Missouri.) No more compromises, no more adjustments, no more half-hearted acceptances of the merely customary. Trade was selfish and fraudulent, education mere word-mongering, politics a swindle and the Church a lie. On all hands the young were seceding from the social organization, discarding the forms that existed and seeking forms of their own.

No need to stir from Concord to see how the tide was turning. The village hummed with these plans. Brook Farm was an accomplished fact. Some time before, George Ripley and Margaret Fuller had discussed the project in Emerson's study. It was charming, refreshing, engaging; and yet, at the name of a society, all his repulsions had played, his quills had risen and sharpened. He had wanted to be convinced, to be thawed, to be aroused by this new dawn of human piety to a mania better than temperance; but instead he had sat aloof, his voice had faltered and fallen. Was this the cave of persecution that might become for him the palace of spiritual power, this room as it were in the Astor House hired for the Transcendentalists? Should he raise the siege of his own hen-coop and march baffled away to a pretended siege of Babylon? Could he work better than at home in that select, but not by him selected, confraternity? Toiling in the barnyard and the peat-bog, in a blue frock and cowhide boots, certainly had its points, but it was the last form of activity to stimulate the mind. He had expressed himself very freely to the brave Ripley, but he had greatly enjoyed his visits to the community. Who would have dreamed that such grace, such a gay abandon, could have been evoked out of the old dry shell of Puritanism?

And now another plan was in the air. The dauntless Alcott had conceived the boldest scheme of all. He had passed through many vicissitudes, this God-intoxicated man. Boston had rejected him at last; his school was gone; his book had been remaindered and sold for trunk-linings. He had come to Concord, with his wife and children, and hired himself out as a wood-chopper. (Alcott, even so, who should have been maintained in a prytaneum. Alcott, who had so little genius for labour, preach it as he might: it cruelly wasted his time, it depressed his spirit to tears.) Then comforting news had reached him, as he toiled away at the chopping-block: the star that had sunk in the New World had risen in the Old. A school had been established in London, named in his honour and manned by his disciples. Alcott House, no less! The disciples had urged the master to visit them, and Emerson had collected a purse to cover his expenses. He had filled the purse himself, in fact— ten golden sovereigns and a bill of exchange on a firm of English bankers; and at last he had dispatched the pilgrim with a handsome letter to Carlyle.

Then what should begin to appear at the little Post Office window? Pamphlets, bundles of them, more than Concord had ever seen before. Pamphlets, periodicals, prospectuses, broadsheets, advertisements, and all stamped with the head of Queen Victoria. Alcott's new associates. There were Communist Manifestoes and Phalansterian Gazettes, plans for Syncretic Associations, Hydropathic Societies and Health Unions, Appeals of Man to Woman, treatises on the Necessity of Internal Marriage. Alcott had discovered an England that was never mentioned in travellers' books and had hastened to send the happy tidings back to his friend in Concord.

A letter presently followed. Alcott was coming home. Not alone: the masters of Alcott House, Charles Lane and Henry Wright, were sailing with him. The school had been driven to the wall, and they had all decided that the spirit of England was "hostile to human welfare, and her institutions were averse to the largest liberty of the soul." (In America, Alcott wrote, "is that second Eden to be planted, in which the divine seed is to bruise the head of evil and restore man to his rightful communion with God.") Emerson was troubled. How had Alcott pictured to these confiding Britons the paradise to which he was leading them? He dispatched a hasty reply: You must show it to your friends, Alcott. I say merely this: they can safely

rely on your theories, but they must put no trust
whatever in your statement of facts. . . . Alcott,
the ever-candid, carried out these instructions. And
now his victims, not to be deterred, were already
on their way.

Six months later, in the little red house at Fruitlands, Alcott lay down upon his bed and turned his
face to the wall. The Con-Sociate Family was a
failure. How happy they had been, driving over
in the big wagon from Concord, on that rainy June
day, happy for all the rain, with the bust of Socrates on the front seat and the children laughing
and chattering behind! Dreams of the Pythagorean
life, of the school at Crotona, had swept the philosopher's brain as he hastened the horse. What
dreams!—the morning walks in the grove, the
searching discussion of doctrines and disciplines,
the chaste repast of honey, maize and salad, the
domestic labours and economies, the pure white
garments, the gallant hospitalities, the bath and the
evening meal and the quiet sleep. Once more the
Grecian sun was to rise over the earth, amid
the gracious meadows of Massachusetts, rise over
a world redeemed by serenity and wisdom.

Emerson had watched the calamitous venture
with a more than benevolent eye. For himself, he
could only build on his own ground, unaided, his
house of peace and benefit, good customs and free
thoughts. But that was not Alcott's way, and there
was always something right about Alcott's undertakings; so his heart and his purse were open to the
rashlings—a deed for their land was made out in

his name as trustee. They had chosen an enchanting spot for the community: a steep slope near the village of Harvard, with a view that spread over miles of well-tilled farms and well-pruned orchards. The house was amply stocked, with comely maple furniture, cupboards full of copper and brass, a library of a thousand volumes in the front entry. (What books! Pindar, Alcaeus, Mimnermus, Spinoza, Behmen, pagan and Christian poets, mystics, sages, the richest collection of its kind in all America—Lane's library brought from London.) At the foot of the slope was the twenty-acre field, redeemed from the "curse of ownership," where they meant to cultivate their grain, pulse, herbs and flax, and their upright, aspiring vegetables, not with the enslaving plough, that bane of the republic of animals, but with the spade, the symbol of the creative life. No manure—Nature was not to be forced. No polluting animal food within doors. No tea or coffee to disturb the poise of the physical organism. Bread made from unbolted flour, and shaped, to render it palatable, in the forms of beasts. The men bathed in the brook, the women in a shelter of clothes-horses covered with sheets: Alcott himself mounted the ladder without and poured the water from a pitcher over their heads. For the rest, there was much emblematic ceremony. When the first load of hay was driven into the barn, one member of the household made a little speech: "I take off my hat, not that I reverence the barn more than other places, but because this is the first fruit of our labour." Then all fell silent for a time, that holy thought might be awakened. And on May Alcott's third birthday, the child was escorted by the whole community to the grove and crowned with flowers, while Alcott read an ode composed by himself in honour of his daughter.

But how could such an Academe endure? The British apostles quarrelled. Wright found the lack of butter, tea and coffee "too hard for his inside" and the regular hours and clearing up of scraps "too desperate hard for the outside." Young Isaac Hecker, already on the road to Rome, was unwilling to submit to a merely pagan discipline; and another member, a lady, was found to have eaten fish at a neighbour's house. (It was only the tail, she insisted, but out she went.) They had abjured the plough, but they failed to do the spading; and they would have had no crop if Joseph Palmer had not brought over his oxen from Leominster and set them to work at the last minute, while the rest of the Con-Sociate Family averted their eyes. They had planted their apple and pear-trees in the path of the north wind; and the men had drifted away on a lecturing tour when the grain was ready to be harvested. At last winter came and nothing was left but the stick of the beautiful rocket. (Nothing but Joseph Palmer and his yoke of oxen. Joseph Palmer remained; and for twenty years thereafter some fragrance of the original dream clung to this paradise lost. The house was a shelter for the hungry and the destitute; and two great iron pots, one containing baked beans and the other potatoes, always stood by the door ready for passers-by.)

Emerson had shared their hopes, and more than once he had come to the rescue of the innocents. (On that winter's day, for instance, when Joseph Palmer shovelled the snow off the road that led into Fruitlands and Silas Dudley shovelled it back again. The road crossed Silas's land—an endless cause of warfare, and for once neither of the old men would surrender; they had to send for Emerson to settle the dispute.) He had shared their hopes. How much he couldn't but say for all the reformers! It was true that their wish to obey impulse was guarded by no old, old Intellect, which knows metes and bounds. But that was their loss, not his, and what qualities they had, and how grateful he was to them for calling to his attention one by one all the problems of the time! The partial action of their minds in one direction was a telescope for the objects on which it was pointed. And they were enthusiasts, too: where else could one look for that virtue in the circle of American wits and scholars?

There was much to be said for the reformers. They were right in refusing to adapt themselves to usages that had ceased to have any meaning. They were right in revolting against employments and standards that stifled their genius and their conscience. Right they were in asserting—and how clear they made it!—that the cost of life was almost all for conformity. (Intellect cost very little, the heart, beauty. Then why struggle so hard for money? "Do you think," said John Hunter, engrossed in dissecting a tiger, "do you think I can leave my work for your damned guinea?") And they alone were attempting, however blindly, to redeem the grand promises of the Revolution, they, and not the Cotton Whigs of State Street. Were they even so wrong in their disbelief in the Government? (What a pother, this, about Government! These caucuses, these conventions, with every palpitating heart swelling with the cheap sublime of magnitude and number! One had only to look at Kansas, at Mexico, Cuba—was the capital enemy of the comfort of all good citizens anything but this ugly Government? The politicians fancied that the popular laws had to be maintained by force. A pity they couldn't revoke their Government for a week, to save themselves the trouble, and watch the result. The popular laws, the laws of natural right, the laws of natural expedience! O fatuous politicians! You would find the priests and the lawyers, the bankers and chambers of commerce, the innkeepers, the village grocers, you would find the very farm-hands in the fields and the fishermen on the river mustering with fury to their support!)

Much to be said, even for the vegetarians. Their ostentatious glasses of cold water, their dry, raw diet might well make one's blood run cold to see. No joyful signs that they had ceased to care for food in nobler cares. One might think intemperance better, with such a ruling love. But who argued so sourly for beef and mutton against these men of herbs and grains? The fat and ruddy eater who had just wiped his lips from feeding on a sirloin, whose blood was spouting in his veins and whose strength kindled that evil fire in his eye. It was not the voice of man one heard, but the beef and brandy roaring for beef and brandy. And were these to play the judge in their own cause?

How could Emerson shake his head and turn the reformers away?—the greatest heretic of them all? He could only applaud and envy (while his heart sank within him). When some zealot came and showed him the importance of the Temperance Reform, his hands dropped—what excuse could he offer? Then an Abolitionist described to him the horrors of Southern slavery. (Guilty, guilty! he cried.) A philanthropist told him of the shameful neglect of the schools by all good citizens. (Guilty, guilty again!) He heard of the poor, living on crusts and water, and he took to the confessional anew. He hadn't a leg to stand on. And he sat there, frigid, unhappy, convicted, labouring for speech.

That gulf, and those mendicant arms! That accusing bosom of his, that unanswering bosom! A yoke of oxen could have turned between every pair of words he was able to extort from it. Nothing to say, with so much that he ought to say? Who was the porcupine now? Who was on stilts? Was it true that he didn't belong to these people, that they didn't belong to him? They fled to him, each with a pet madness in his brain. They hastened to him with the utmost joy and confidence that they were the very souls his faith invited. Was he not the prophet of self-reliant action, the voice that arfirmed their desires and justified their refusal to conform to the stale prescriptions of society? Who but he had painted those entrancing pictures of a life in harmony with Nature, a free spontaneous life like that of the Golden Age? They had flocked to hear him lecture, they had pored over his essays; and who but they had set out to make his gospel real? Had he nothing to say to them now, no word of cheer for their means and methods, no hand but that of a friendly neutral to lend them in actualizing their dreams of a better day?

Disturbing, these importunate reformers, much more disturbing than the watchdogs of the established order who had barked so furiously at the prophet. What a power he had of begetting false expectations! He had blundered along for a time, assured by the surprise and joy of those to whom he communicated his results. Then he looked up for a moment, and the sympathy was gone or changed. The faces of all his friends were shaded with grief, and the bystanders accused him. (Come, soul, he said to himself, new solitudes, new marches! Jump into another bush and scratch your eyes in again! Pass on to new developments as surprising as your first, to fresh indirections and wonderful alibis that will dissipate the indictment!)

They had asked him to throw himself into their causes, to adapt his life to theirs. He was willing to try a few experiments, just to see if he could. Manual labour: to make it an "honest sweat," had he not arranged with Thoreau to teach him the real austerities of the hoe and the spade? He persuaded his wife to invite the Alcotts to join them and establish a new Fruitlands, *à quatre,* in Concord. He asked the housemaid and the cook to take their meals with the family. He breakfasted on bread and water. He adopted a vegetable diet. But the servants refused to leave the kitchen, and Mrs. Alcott declined to share in a second venture; and as for the vegetable diet, Emerson found that it dulled his wits more than it toughened his nerves. Reform was not for him.

For Emerson had watched the reformers. He had noted the effect their activities had upon them. They were bitter, sterile people all too often. Their eyes were so filled with abstract images that the poetry of every day, the light shining in a child's spoon, the sparkle in a mote of dust, they saw not at all. And what egoists they were, how detached from the collective forces that kept life sane! They became tediously good in some particular, and negligent and narrow in the rest. They shared the new light that promised the kingdom of heaven, and they ended with champing unleavened bread or devoting themselves to the nourishment of a beard. The more they tried to impose their will upon others, to transform the external world, the more they fell out of relation with their own souls.

Not for Emerson was the sociable satisfaction of scaling with others the silver mountains whose enchantments he had sketched. He saw the peaks from the valley, but the moment he began to climb the vision vanished. And to see, to paint, to feel was his proper task. He would listen to no more reproofs but steadily persist in his own native choices against all argument and example—defend them against the multitude, defend them against the wise. Defend them against his disciples. By no man's distaste was he to be chidden out of his most trivial natural habit. Even pie for breakfast!

CHAPTER XI

COME, quit the high chair, he said to himself, lie down and roll on the ground. Enough of this playing tame lion and talking down to people! And a truce to these disputations!

"I am tired of fools," as Aunt Mary said, with wonderful emphasis. Where were the spade and the hoe? Nothing like a bout in the garden for the sinking heart and the clouded brow, for the perturbation and fret of too much sitting. No harm if he worked at first with a little venom: that good hoe, as it bit the ground, avenged his wrongs, and he had less lust to bite his enemies. (Manual labour, at moments, had its value!) By smoothing the rough hillocks he smoothed his temper; by extracting the long roots of the piper-grass he drew out his own splinters. And before long he heard the bobolink's song and beheld the blessed deluge of light and colour that rolled around him.

No need now to run to Acton Woods and live with the squirrels. The cranks and the bores were forgotten.

To every reproach he knew but one answer, to go again to his work. He had no genius? Then he would work the harder. He had no virtues, he neglected his relations? He would only work the harder. He had lost the esteem of all decent people.

he must regain some position and relation? True as ever—he would work harder still. In his journals he had accumulated in the course of years a store of observations, reflections, perceptions. He jotted them down in various notebooks, paged and indexed according to their topics; then, when he wished to give a lecture, on the Poet, for instance, or Manners, he gathered together the material he had on the subject, arranged and combined it and added whatever suggested itself as he copied his entries out. The lectures were the basis of his essays, but they had to be re-handled. He condensed and pruned away the topical allusions, the anecdotes he had used to hold the attention of his audience; and he did what he could to organize his thought—not often with much success. Not for him was the laborious joy of the systematizer: he had often regretted it, but he had little power of construction. The sentence was his unit, at most the paragraph. For the rest, an apparent order was the best he could hope for, an order like that of his "grand old sloven," Montaigne.

He had published little: *Nature,* that first slim book, written in the old Manse, to the tune of the wind in the willow-tree that overhung his window (five hundred copies, many of them still unsold), the two volumes of *Essays*, the *Addresses* of 1844. A relatively slight performance for a man of forty; but why should he rush into print? The good of publishing his thoughts was that of drawing to himself like-minded men and of giving to men he valued, Carlyle, for instance, and Thoreau, Parker,

Alcott, one stimulated hour. A single book well done contained the whole of his history. It was rhetoric—was it not?—that took up so much room; and the great thing was to charge a few lines with a world of meaning. Each sentence should be an idea, and every idea one that had filled his whole sky when he first conceived it. Most Americans, he felt, were over-expressed, beaten out thin, all surface without depth or substance. The thoughts that wandered through their minds they never absorbed or made flesh of; they reported them as thoughts, retailed them as stimulating news to all and sundry. At a dreadful loss they played this amusing game. For himself, he could hardly ponder his discoveries too much, digest them and turn them over in his mind. The writing should be like the settlement of dew on the leaf, of stalactites on the cavern wall, the deposit of flesh from the blood, of woody fibre from the sap.

He knew and would know no such thing as haste in composition. Well said Simonides: "Give me twice the time, for the more I think the more it enlarges"; and he who found himself hurried and gave up carrying his point, even for once, wrote in vain. Goethe had the *urkräftige Behagen,* the stout comfortableness, the stomach for the fight, and he would have it, too! It was true that every writer was a skater and had to go partly where he wished and partly where the skates carried him. True that a thought he had once believed so happy often turned out to be nothing but empty words. While it glittered newly before him he fancied he had chipped off a scale of the universe; then he came again to the record a few months later and it seemed the merest tinsel. But certain things he could do to control his style, keep it hard and firm, hard but light and elegant as Landor's. He could cancel every "very," and every "intense" and "exquisite," avoid the fat of the language, and all such terms as "Yes, to a certain extent," "as a general thing." (Had he used "grim" too often? A mannerism, perhaps; and that would never do.) He could keep to the Saxon forms and eschew the ponderous Latinisms; he could make every word cover a thing. And what compensations there were for all his difficulties! A new phrase at times was like a torch applied to a train of powder—it awakened so many thoughts. And sometimes in making a sentence he felt himself launching out into the infinite and building a road into Chaos and Old Night.

But how control his moods? They never believed in one another. One state of mind was never able to remember, was unable even to conceive of another state. Life was a flash of light, then a long darkness, then a flash again. To-day the electric machine would not work, not a spark passed; and presently the world was all a cat's back, all sparkle and shock.

Mysterious, ungovernable, these periodic motions of the soul. There were fortunate hours when things sailed dim and great through his head, hours when the right words came spontaneously like the breath of the morning wind, when he could not sit in his chair for the joy that brought him bolt

upright and sent him striding about the room, when
he had not the composure to set down the thoughts
that thrilled him. His intellect was so active that
everything ran to meet it. He was like the maple
trees in the spring when the sugar flows so fast that
one can not get tubs enough to contain it. And then
came hours of pain, sterility, ennui, and he sat out
the day and returned to the necessities of the household doubting if all this waste could ever be justified. No child passing the house on his way to
school, no boy carrying a basket, but gave him a
feeling of shame and envy. He was on the brink, it
seemed, of an ocean of thought into which he could
not swim. And sometimes the ocean itself seemed
a mirage.

Was persistence enough, at such times, mere
brute sitting, day after day, in the face of his own
skepticism? It was true that the mood returned,
sooner or later, always, and life had a grip again
and the hours a taste. How cheering were those
anecdotes of old scholars and poets, Niebuhr, for
instance, whose divination came back to him after
years of eclipse, and George Herbert who, having
lost the muse in his youth, found himself later,
"after so many deaths," living and versing again.
He had known such minds himself, minds like
those pear-trees which, after ten barren seasons,
burst into a second and even more vigorous growth.
But was there no way of domesticating these high
states of contemplation and continuous thought?
The rich veins of ore were always there, could he
only command the shaft and draw them out. Writ-

ing was his metre of health, and success in his work was food and wine, fire and horse and holiday. Were there no tonics for the torpid mind, no rules for the recovery of inspiration?

Alas, neither by land nor by sea could one find the way to the Hyperboreans! But one thing was certain: his talent was good only as long as he worked it. If he ceased to task himself he had no thoughts. That was the value of the journal he kept so faithfully: every day he collected the disjointed dreams, the reveries, the fragments of ideas, the drupes and berries he found in his basket after endless and aimless rambles in woods and pastures. It was the hive in which he stored his honey, cell by cell, as the bees in his brain distilled it. A treasure, this journal, for a desultory mind; many were its uses. He could no more manage his thoughts than he could manage thunderbolts; but once he got them written down he could come and look at them every day and grow accustomed to their faces, and, by and by, discovering their family likeness, he could pair them and range them better and join them in the proper order. By this means, too, he could convert the heights he reached into a table-land. A fact that was all-important a month ago stood here along with one that was equally important a month before, and next month there would be another. Here they all occupied but four lines, and he could not read these thoughts together without juster views of each than when he read them singly. His journal was indispensable, for what was written was the foundation of a new superstructure, a guide to the eye for still another foundation. Every thought he expressed was a cube, and every cube a candidate for the mosaic of his essays. And if the results were precious, so was the habit. Work, of all tonics, was the most effective, and this was the most inviting form of work.

No doubt, but for work itself what were the best conditions? The free mind was the fruit of an austere law: it had to be reconquered day by day, it subsisted in a state of war and belonged only to those who fought for it. But how conduct the fight, how prepare for it? What were the omens, and how was he to read them? How coax and woo the strong instinct to bestir itself and work its miracle? The ancients were masters of this art: what was it Plato said about living out of doors and simple fare and gymnastic exercises, and Pythagoras, of the use of certain melodies to awaken in the disciple now purity, now valour, now gentleness? For every constitution there were certain natural stimulants, just as there were natural poisons, and the problem was to find these, to know them, and to regulate one's life accordingly.

For himself, he had such low animal spirits that he could not stand an extravagant, flowing life. He regretted it as much as he regretted the shortness of an American scholar's day. He marvelled at the constitution of the Germans, with their twelve, fourteen, sixteen hours of work. He loved in others the generous, spontaneous soil that flowered and brought forth fruit at all seasons. But he had to consult the poorness of his powers; he had to be content with moderate, languid actions. If he had obeyed his irregular impulses, established half the relations his fancy prompted, he would not have been followed by his faculties; he would certainly have died of consumption in six months. Parties disqualified him, and so did arguments. There were those who, disputing, made him dispute, and nervous, hysterical persons who produced the like symptoms in himself.

The one good in life was concentration, the one evil dissipation. What untuned him was as bad as what crippled or stunned him: domestic chores, even correcting proof-sheets, even packing a trunk. And talking about himself—how empty it made him feel! And being praised—a pest, the worst of all spoil-thoughts. (One turned around to look at oneself and one's day was lost in personal considerations.) And manual labour untuned him. (Did they fancy that the greatest of arts, the subtlest and most miraculous, could be practised with a pen in one hand and a crowbar or a peat-knife in the other?) Trifles? A grasshopper was a burden. It was all very well to talk of a life taken as it comes. Thoreau, with his tough grain, knew the weight of these feathers in the scale: he had found that the slightest irregularity, were it only the drinking of too much water on the preceding day, disturbed the delicate poise that composition demanded. Carlyle knew this too, with his room on the top floor, high above the orbit of all housemaids: he could hope there for six years of history. And George Sand knew it, humouring her love of heat. Was the steel pen a nuisance? Try the quill. For himself, he pounded so tediously on that string of the exemption of the writer from all secular tasks because his work needed a frolic health to execute.

Plenipotence of health; for health was the first muse, comprising the magical effects of air, landscape and exercise upon the mind. And silence was the second. How true was Fra Angelico's remark that "he who practised the art of painting had need of quiet, and should live without cares or anxious thoughts"! How like his own the experience of that old Chinese painter who wrote: "Unless I dwell in a quiet house, seat myself in a retired room, with the windows open, the table dusted, incense burning, and ten thousand trivial thoughts crushed out and sunk, I can not have good feeling for painting or beautiful taste, and can not create the Yu." Proclus was right. "How can the soul be adjacent to the One, except by laying asleep the garrulous matter that is in her?"

His own primal rule was to defend the morning, to keep all its dews on, to relieve it with fine foresight from any jangle of affairs. A stroll in the orchard first, in spring and summer, attuned him for the day. But he knew many other stimulants, many other provocative influences. A Greek epigram at times, a verse of Herrick, a glance at the mottoes in some novel of Scott, a page from the Neo-Platonists. Nectar, opium, these latter, as he let sail before him the pleasing and grand images of these gods and demoniacal men. He heard of rumours rife among the azonic gods, of demons with fulgid eyes, of the unenvying and exuberant will of the gods, of the aquatic gods and the Plain of Truth, the meadow, the paternal port. What pictorial distinctness!—as if the gods were present. "This is that which emits the intelligible light that, when it appeared, astonished the intellectual gods and made them admire their father, as Orpheus says." What rhetoric! These rare, brave words filled him with hilarity and spring. His heart danced, his sight was quickened, he beheld shining relations between all things. He was impelled to write, he was almost impelled to sing. (Read Proclus much and well if you wish to grow handsome!)

No need to tell this man the secret that beside the energy of his conscious intellect he was capable of new energy by abandonment to the nature of things. The perfection of writing was when the animal thought, and a little wine and good food furnished some elemental wisdom, and the fire, too, as it burned on a winter's day; for he fancied that his logs, which had grown so long in the sun and wind at Walden, were a kind of muses. Why should one spare any stimulant, any purgative, that brought one into a productive state, to the top of one's condition? How easily, alas, one lapsed into flesh and sleep!

Health, south wind, books, old trees, a boat, a friend—auspicious all; and the fair water that Demosthenes drank. There was inspiration for Emerson in any assertion of the will, in a glance at the first proposition of Political Economy: "Everything in the world is purchased by labour, and our

passions are only causes of labour." Then walking
had the best value as gymnastics: with the first step
over the threshold of his study he would suddenly
get a spontaneous perception of his subject more
just and searching than hours of toil had given him.
The sight of a man of genius filled him with a
boundless confidence in his own powers; and certain trifling expedients sometimes served. Writing
letters, for instance. When thoughts refused to
come and the gift of the happy phrase, the bright
image, seemed to have vanished forever, he would
begin to write to some friend, and behold, there
he was, floating off on the most cordial tide of expression. And the power of the fetish was not to be
despised. Handel always composed in court dress,
and Machiavelli, before sitting down at his writ-
ing-table in the evening, threw off the garments of
the day and arrayed himself in his robe of ceremony. Was there not some virtue in this association?
Some virtue in his own coat, made for him in Florence, which he wore when he wrote his essay on
Michael Angelo?

As a final stratagem, for perfect seclusion, he
would go to a hotel: in summer, some country inn,
in winter the American House in Hanover Street.
Even in Concord, even on his little farm, there
were always distractions, running feet in the halls,
a leak in the roof, a disaster in the garden. The day
was cut up into short strips, and the world seemed
to be in a conspiracy to invade him, to vanquish him
with details, to break him into crumbs and fritter
his time. Friend, wife, child, fear, want, charity,

all knocked at his door at the critical moment, rang alarums in his ear, scared away the muse and spoiled the poem. (And the carpenters, the masons, the tradesmen. Did they think a writer was an idler because he worked with invisible tools, worked to invisible ends?) Then a few days in Boston, at Nantasket Beach, in the mountains, made all the difference. No distractions there, no visitors. Not an insect's hum to shake the quiet hours.

The moment of inspiration—he was its reverent slave. He watched and hailed its aurora from afar.

CHAPTER XII

THE Alcotts had returned to Concord and settled in the Hosmer Cottage. Charles Lane followed. He had striven to the last to keep his land at Fruitlands from "falling back into individuality," and he could not forgive Mrs. Alcott: she insisted that her own family was all she lived for. Alcott himself, said Lane, had listened too much to his private affections. "Constancy to his wife and inconstancy to the Spirit" had blurred his life forever.

But still he had followed them to Concord. (Much demurring. He complained that Emerson was too personal, that he did not even profess to act on universal grounds, that his interest in Fruitlands had sprung from the "purest individual friendship." How could the world be redeemed as a world of *persons, persons?*) He clung to a desperate hope: could they not, even in Concord, make shift to carry on? They breakfasted round the fireplace, while Alcott prepared the potatoes, and the apples and water; and conversation of a useful and interior kind was mingled, as Lane said, with their physical increment. A singing-lesson followed, with pretty, simple songs, to the tune of Lane's violin. They had no dishes to wash, so the females, as Lane called them, could all remain. And Alcott sawed and chopped, and baked the bread.

It was only a shadow of Fruitlands, but Alcott and Lane were happy. They lectured at the Lyceum and spent their evenings at Emerson's house, debating. (What is Prophecy? Who is a Prophet? The Love of Nature.) Mrs. Alcott was used to it now: a good crying spell, and her spirits rallied. There was always a poorer family in the neighbourhood, with four small children and a drunken father. A cousin brought bundles of clothes for the little girls; and potatoes, apples and squashes were enough to live on. They could even carry baskets to the other family, and Alcott could chop the other family's wood.

Their library, meanwhile, had been sold and scattered to provide shipwrecked Lane with another nest-egg. Simonides, Pindar, Alcaeus, Behmen, Spinoza had found new homes on every shelf in the neighbourhood. (What a sowing of seeds!— each one to bear fruit in the coming generation.) Brook Farm was scattering too, and these other sansculottes were drifting to Concord. Isaac Hecker, the "baker-general," came, the rich young German from New York, with his pock-marked face: simple, smiling Hecker, reserved, observing. And his tutor, George P. Bradford, and Margaret's friends, visiting Elizabeth Hoar. (They had all had their "poem in *The Dial*.") There was Caroline Sturgis ("Z") who loved to walk in the moonlight, and Belinda Randall, who played Beethoven with such expression, and frosty Sarah Clarke, gentle, wise and just. And the Curtis brothers, George and Burrill Curtis. Some of them

came and went, some of them came and stayed; but
each of them brought some note that Emerson
would not have missed.

Isaac Hecker stayed. He rented a room at Mrs.
Thoreau's. He was greatly taken with Henry—
asked him to go on a walking-tour in Europe.
(They could walk to Rome and join the Catholic
Church together. Hecker was simple indeed if he
thought he had found a fishing-pole that was long
enough to catch Henry.) The Curtis brothers
stayed and returned to stay again. (The admired of
all Brook Farmers—the ever-attentive George, and
Burrill with the flowing curls and the face of
Raphael. What strollers in the moonlight, these,
what singers at Belinda's piano!) Graceful as two
young Greeks, they had fallen in love with the
Over-Soul and made up their minds to practise
Self-Reliance—not an easy task as Nathan Bar-
rett's farm-hands, for Nathan was resolved to "test
their metal." They slept in one room and worked
in the fields in the morning, spreading manure
(George of the masquerades, who had looked so
well as Fanny Elssler and Hamlet!) ; and they read
and wrote and botanized. They even hired a patch
of their own, raised vegetables and sold them in the
village; and when they came home from their
walks at sunset their arms were laden with flowers.

George Bradford raised vegetables, too, in his
garden at Plymouth: they understood him there
and allowed him to do as he pleased. He pushed
his own wheelbarrow to the public market, with his
peas and beans, potatoes and squashes and corn.

An oddish mode of life for so rare a scholar, but it gave him more pleasure even than his Greek. It was agreed in society, he said, to consider realities as fictions and fictions as realities; but now and again he returned for a week or a fortnight to resume his place with the idlers. He took an occasional pupil, Hecker, or a class of young girls, and he haunted Concord—the shrinking, affectionate George, brimming over with friendly devotion. Was Emerson's garden prospering? He liked to trim the fruit-trees. And a walk with George to Walden was a balsam unparalleled.

One of these young initiates had come to Concord to stay for the rest of his life. William Ellery Channing, the doctor's nephew and namesake. He had married Margaret Fuller's sister—the pretty sister, Ellen—and together they had taken the little Red Lodge on Ponkawtassett Hill, a mile up the turnpike. Ellen (as cool and *dégagé* as Margaret was volcanic) had opened a school in the village for little children, and Ellery was determined to work his acre of land.

A character, a true original, this Ellery Channing. He had published several pieces in *The Dial* —poems, "Ernest the Seeker"—and Emerson had been eager to meet him. But Ellery was always playing hole-and-corner, tearing back and forth to the Western prairies or hiding at "Aunt Becky Atkins's" in Newburyport. With the manners of a man of the world, the address of a merchant and features that suggested all the Boston families with which he was connected, Ellery was as much the social antinomian as Henry Thoreau himself. He had refused to take his degree at Harvard and had built himself a log-hut in the wilds of Illinois: he was resolved to have no commerce with the "bottomless stupidity" of the Bostonians. A poet, a botanist, a lover, as he said, of old books, old garrets, old wines, old pipes, an amateur in all things, he lived for the hour and chiefly for conversation.

No one so moody as Ellery. He was harsh and tender by turns, abrupt, disagreeable, distant, then cordial and generous. He struck up a friendship with Elizabeth Hoar, and for weeks he would not look at her in the street. Off-again, on-again Ellery! His fear of his uncle was comic. "He used to scold me," said Ellery, "and I stood in such dread of him! When I came back from the West I stopped at Lenox to see the Sedgwicks, and there, to my horror, was Dr. Channing—in Lenox, under my nose! He lectured me solemnly for coming home again, after all it had cost to send me to Illinois. Here I was back in Boston, or soon would be. . . . And all because I stopped to see the Sedgwicks!"

But who was a better crony for a walk? Ellery led like an Indian. Was Emerson piqued by the impatience of his countrymen, each one striving to get ahead of the rest? A stroll with Ellery soothed one's irritation. He would stop by a clump of golden-rod: "Ah, here they are! These things consume a great deal of time. I don't know but they are of more importance than any other of our investments." He spent his mornings (for the farm was

soon forgotten) conning old folios of his favourite
authors: there was never a man of more recondite
learning, with so many mottoes, conceits and allusions bubbling in his brain. His taste was so sound
that if he said, "Here's a good book," Emerson
knew he had a day longer to live; and if he preferred Herrick, as a true Greek, to Milton (who
reminded him of his uncle)—so much the better.
Herrick, poet of cherries and Maytime, with his
hen Partlet and his Julia's hair, was the right
touchstone for strollers in rural Concord. And
Ellery had such a wonderful respect for mere
humours of the mind. He caught the most delicate
shades of one's meaning, matched one's happiest
phrase with another and always returned to the
weather and politics when there was the least fal-
tering or excess on the high keys. Capricious, yes,
the April day incarnated and walking, soft sunshine and hailstones, east wind and flowery southwest by fits and starts. He complained of Nature
—too many leaves, too windy and grassy. And he
forgot one's existence for weeks, ceased to bow as
he passed, then called and hobnobbed again as if
nothing had happened. But a sensible, solid, well-
stored man was Ellery, for all his whimsies. He
despised dooryards with foreign shrubs. He said
that trouble was as good as anything else if you
only had enough of it. He admitted that even cows
had their value. They gave the farmers something
to do in summertime, and they made good walking
where they fed.

Concord was becoming a school of human nature, with all these poets and philosophers. (With Ellery and Henry and Alcott, the Society of Sunday Strollers and speculators-at-large was now complete.) A school of eloquence too, where Emerson could study his trade as a lecturer. Father Taylor made him an occasional visit and preached in the village church; and the leaders of the Abolition movement constantly spoke there—Garrison, Charles Sumner, Wendell Phillips. And Concord, as a county town with a courthouse, attracted all the bigwigs of the bar. Webster himself now and again filled the town with his presence, and Rufus Choate, that wild, extravagant man, with his grotesque imagery, his impetuous rush of speech.

A school indeed for Emerson, this Concord forum. He could scan here, at close range, every type and shade of oratory. There was Father Taylor, so sure in his generous humanity, rolling the world into a ball and tossing it from hand to hand, marching into untried depths with the security of a grenadier: he actualized, in his mania, the tripod and "possession" of the ancients. Temperate man that he was in other respects, he would certainly have liked the old cocks of the barroom a thousand times better than their temperate monitors; and he alone, when he came, brought together all the extremes of the village society. Poet and grocer, black and white, contractor, lawyer, farm-hand flocked to hear Father Taylor, and Emerson was always the first, although for so long he had ceased to go to church.

Garrison struck him as bald and dry in comparison, without the feminine element one found in men of genius. But there was always great body in Garrison's harangues, no falsehood, no patchwork, perfect sincerity and unity—a virile speaker, with his feet firm on a fact. Phillips, too, groped and groped till he found the stones beneath him. The politicians talked of the Union, the Constitution. (There were no such things in Nature.) Phillips always felt after the fact and found it in the commerce of New England, in the devotion of the Slave States to their interests. And a realist was Charles Sumner, the incorruptible, the friend of the poor, the champion of the oppressed. A stirring sight on the platform, the great-hearted Sumner, with his fine social culture and his statesman's breadth of knowledge. One night, at the Lyceum, he lectured on Lafayette; and Emerson felt that of all living Americans Sumner was best entitled to deliver that eulogy.

But the great event was always Webster's coming. A natural emperor of men, so easily great. One could go behind him, as behind Niagara Falls (as Elizabeth Hoar put it), and find the whole man still magnificent. He would roar, and his words were like the blows of an axe. His splendid wrath, when his eyes became fires, was good to see, so intellectual it was. He was perfectly fair in debate; he carried all his points by taking superior ground. No incendiary allusions, no puerilities, no tricks, no flourishes, no strut in his voice and behaviour, no academical play in his discourse: every speech he made was a majestic man of business.

His rhetoric was homely, fit and strong, and he hugged his facts. Each word he uttered had passed through the fire of his intellect, and the statement was always erect and disengaged. And what opponent could face the terror of those eyes? Easy it was to understand the story, how Webster had looked a witness out of court. He had set his great eyes on the man and searched him through and through; then, as the cause went on, and this fellow's perjury was not yet called for, Webster looked round again to see if he was ready for the inquisition. The witness felt for his hat and edged towards the door. A third time Webster looked on him, and the witness could sit no longer. He seized his chance and fled from the court and was nowhere to be found.

Tempestuous days when "Dan'l" came and stayed in Emerson's house. He brought with him the rumour of a multitudinous world, and it was vain to think of settling down to writing till the "steam-engine in breeches" was well gone from the county. But Webster and his audience were an object-lesson for Emerson. Had he ever doubted the power of the spoken word? It was credible in Webster's presence that a snowflake would go through a pine-board, if it were projected with sufficient force. He remembered that old experiment of the magnet and the filings of steel, how the energy of that subtle fluid passed into every one of the metallic atoms. Webster did something like this with a roomful of listeners, and a poet could do the same thing with a nation! There was Chladni's experiment, too: he strewed sand on glass and then struck the glass with tuneful accords, and the sand at once assumed geometrical figures. Then Orpheus was no fable! One had only to sing, and the very rocks would crystallize; sing, and the plants would organize; sing, and the animal would be born!—and the god in man.

Emerson had found another friend who shared this faith with a fervour he died too soon to express —a friend he was never to see, whom he knew only through letters. Carlyle had given John Sterling in London a copy of *Nature,* and Sterling had carried the book off to Madeira after sending Emerson a line: "You are the one man in the world with whom, though unseen, I feel any sort of nearness." He had left the Church, like Emerson, and thrown himself into the radical movement, with an all too impetuous belief—beset by a rapid consumption that drove him hither and thither, to Italy, the West Indies and at last to the Isle of Wight, where he was to die at thirty-eight, a comet that had filled the air with transient splendours. He had sat at the feet of Coleridge, then toiled, a romantic crusader, in behalf of Spanish exiles and the poor of London; but he longed to be a poet and he loved Montaigne (that "large-minded, clear and healthy man").

When his first letter came, Emerson dived into *Blackwood* and spelled out Sterling's biography in the unsigned poems and stories which he recognized as if by second-sight. A gallant, radiant creature, with a darting eye, frank, loyal, childlike, who seemed to have undergone all his own experiences, whose hopes and desires were his and who had heard his voice across what gulfs of prejudice! So he had two brothers-in-arms in England now. He even believed that in Carlyle's disputes with Sterling, on the value of poetry and art, on liberty as opposed to force, he would always have agreed with Sterling.

And now, with all these illuminati in Concord —Carlyle, too, still spoke of coming—a new plan drifted through Emerson's mind. Why not open a university, announce an annual semester, for the promulgation of all these living ideas? An informal sort of school, a Platonic Academy, with the best available instructors, drawn from all the professions? (Allston as professor of Painting, Greenough of Sculpture, and Bryant, Irving and Webster. They could even send abroad—for if America sent for dancers, singers and actors, then why not scholars, too?—and Carlyle, Hallam, Campbell could lecture on History, Poetry, Letters.) It was painful to see young men coming out of Harvard, ready for the voyage of life, and to see the entire ship made up of rotten timber, rotten traditional timber, without so much as an inch of new plank in the hull. Everett, who was president of the college, ridiculed the new philosophy—compared it to Virgil's thunderbolt, three parts fire, three parts of the twisted hail and three of empty air; and the students laughed at Garrison and Phillips—"copies of Luther in the pasteboard style." The Boston bankers, in league with the slaveholding South, and the dry disciples of Locke still ruled the college. But at least in Concord they could teach the superiority of knowledge to wealth and physical power.

A dream not to be realized for almost forty years (and then only as a phantom of this first idea). Emerson took no practical steps to achieve it. He merely drew up a list of possible instructors: George Ripley for Modern Literature and the History of Opinion; Hedge for the Philosophy of History; Theodore Parker, Paganism and the History of the Church; Alcott, Psychology and Ethics. For himself, Belles-Lettres and Rhetoric, Percy's Reliques, the plays of Beaumont and Fletcher. The school would front the world without charter, diploma, corporation or steward. Golden thoughts hovered in Emerson's mind as he talked it over with Alcott. Why should they not concert another Athens? Bring back the muse to the eye and cheek of youth? Set working the leaven of enthusiasm in this vast apathetic America? They could fire the artillery of sympathy and emotion. They could celebrate the spiritual powers in their infinite contrast to the mechanical powers of the time.

As a group?

He thought of *The Dial,* of Brook Farm and Fruitlands. Take it sadly home to thy heart, he said to himself again; there is and can be no coöperation. (In Massachusetts, in the eighteen-forties.)

CHAPTER XIII

A DUBIOUS business, lecturing. He felt as one turned out of doors, living on a balcony, living on the street. A profanation, too, these Peter Parley's stories of Uncle Plato, these puppet-shows of the Eleusinian Mysteries. But his debts were piling up: he had to make the plunge into this odious river of travellers, these wild eddies of hotels and boarding-houses, these dangerous precincts of charlatanism, that out of all the evil he might draw a little good.

Travelling was very instructive, if only its lessons were more immediately applicable! He could not use them all in seven transmigrations of Indra —hardly one of them in this present mortal and visible. On the road he had no thoughts, no aims, and seemed never to have had any; and he met too many people. It was all very well for Napoleonic temperaments, impassive, unimpressible by others, insensible to circumstances. He was not himself a pith-ball, yet nothing could have been stranger than the way people acted on him: their mere presence turned him to wood and to stone. If he talked with a man of sense and kindness he was imparadised at once, but the powerful, practical type disconcerted him and made him less than he was. He was forced to live in the country, if only because the streets made him desolate.

Strange how long one's novitiate lasted! As long as one continued to grow and did not inveterate, one was subject to circumstances and never quite controlled them. All the chemical agents acted with force on Emerson, and he came, as he felt, a greenhorn to every conversation. The young, the knowing, the fashionable, the political, the Pharisee and the Sadducee were able to strike him dumb: to human electricity no man was more susceptible. Hypersensitive hermit that he was, so much the more need for him to get an occasional shock, to run out into new places and multiply his chances for observation.

To Maine, for instance. Many and many a mile, through wastes of snow and pine-trees, the villages few and cold as the Tobolsk and Irkutsk of Siberia; and, staring into the white night, he dreamed he had committed some crime against the Czar and was bound a thousand versts into arctic Asia. But Maine was a great country: he looked at the merchants in the cars—independent, with sufficient manners and more manly force of all kinds than most of the scholars he had known. (A pity, but why deny it?) These Yankees were people who, if they once got hold of a rope's end or a spar, would make it carry them; if they could but find so much as a stump or a log, they would whittle out of it a house and a barn, a farm and stock, a mill and a village, a railroad and a bank. What enemies of labour, and therefore friends of man, making wind and tide, waterfall, cloud and lightning do the work, by every art and device their cunningest

brains could achieve! And here they were beside
him, bound for Bangor. (And sneering a little at
Maine, like all the Boston merchants. They said
they could buy the State and have eighty millions
left. But they didn't seem to consider that the
values of Boston were artificial values, the value
of luxuries, furniture, inflated prices of land and
lots and houses, whilst the values of Maine were
primary and necessary and therefore permanent
under any state of society.)

But what had all these things to do with literature? He thought of his æsthetic friends, with their
pale, sickly, etiolated, indoor minds. Writers, he
said to himself, must honour the people's facts.
(Shakespeare did, or they wouldn't be discussing
him now.) If they had no place for the people, the
people would have none for them; and, whatever
they had to say or do, if to them politics was nothing, navigation nothing, railroads nothing, men
and women nothing, they might have their seat or
sphere in another planet, but never in this. The
earth and sea and air, the constitution of things,
and all that men call Fate, were on the people's
side; and that was a reasoner not liable to a fallacy.
They should humble themselves, they who never
saw a grander arch than their own eyebrow, never
saw the sky of a principle that would make them
modest and contemners of themselves. How could
any writer afford, for the sake of his nerves and
his nap, to spare any action in which he might
partake?

Bangor! There was the committee of local magnates waiting at the station to escort him to his lodging. The owner of the best house had carried off the prize, but the whole town had been talking about him, around the stoves in the stores and over the fences. At home he was only known in connection with the cows, and his name was *moo;* but he was a great man in Bangor. And in York and Paris and Bath. And what amusing characters he met on the road! The stately chairman, for instance, who took pleasure in introducing the Reverend Ralph——. (We can do without the Reverend, Mr. Smith.) And the worthy W. W. who remarked, "Three things make the gentleman, the hat, the collar and the boots." (Ah, that Professor Teufelsdröckh had heard the word!) And the man in the coach with his contrivance for defending his own coffin in the grave from body-snatchers. He had devised a pistol to go off—*pop!*—from this end, and a pistol—*pop!*—from that end of the coffin; and he was plainly spending his life in the sweets of that revenge.

There were journeys to foreign lands, Philadelphia, Baltimore; for Emerson's fame was spreading, and they wanted to hear him now in those regions, too. Cosy rides in the Jersey ferryboat, where he found himself snugly ensconced in the warm entrails of an argument with a Presbyterian clergyman. Bear's meat like this was not to be had at home: he might have been in Scotland again, with all this Princeton brimstone. (But how these sects fattened on one another's faults! How many men got a living by calling the

Unitarians prayerless, or by showing that the Calvinists were bigots, while the poor devil who only saw faults in himself died in his sins.) The Catholic Cathedral in Baltimore was a great relief, with the pictures, the lighted altar, the swinging censer, with every whiff bringing all Rome again to Emerson's mind. How dignified, this shrine, where priest and people were nothing and for once an idea excluded these impertinences! He detested, for an hour, the Reformation and all the parliament of Barebones, the Protestant with his "private judgment," and his family pews and doctrinaires and schismatics. The Catholic Church, he felt, was the church of poets; it ignored the private man, it respected masses and ages, it harmonized with Nature which loved the race. Well he could understand the joyful adhesion of the Winckelmanns and the Schlegels—just as one seizes with delight the fine romance and tosses the learned Heeren out of the window (unhappily with the sigh that follows the romance—"Ah, that one word of it were true!"). It was lucky for his own Protestantism that he had no cathedral in Concord. He and Elizabeth Hoar would be confirmed in a fortnight.

The Philadelphians "listened with great pleasure to the chaste and beautiful lecture of the Boston essayist." (Or so the newspaper said.) A dull, timorous town, with a very lymphatic appearance; and Emerson looked eagerly for the stars at night, for fear they should disappear in the torpid air. But Furness, at least, was there, his old crony in the

Latin School, hero-worshipping Furness, best of
gossips, with a store of anecdotes about Channing
and Fanny Kemble. There was no pleasure like a
chat with Furness over the last ten years; no tie to
be compared with that of playmate from the nursery onward, a true clanship and key never to be
given to another.

New York was an outpost of home, with William living there on Staten Island. He had settled
at Dutch Farms (he had christened the village
Concord), as Judge of Richmond County. William
was no longer the isolated man that Emerson used
to fancy him; he seemed to be an important part of
the web of life on the island, as genial as possible
now, riding along in his gig or strolling with his
dogs: good company, in his Snuggery (as one
couldn't but call the house), or out for a ramble on
Todt Hill, where Emerson stopped for a moment
to cut a walking-stick. Henry Thoreau had come
down to tutor his son; but Henry was unhappy.
(Was there too much starch in the Judge's house?
A pity, really; Henry was a little narrow. Why
should he despise everything outside of Concord?)

Henry was very droll (with the mud of the Concord River still on his boots) discussing New York,
the Academy exhibition, the "Great Western," the
sidewalks ("no give to the foot"), the cabmen at
the ferry ("Want a cab, sir? Want a *nice* cab, sir?"
—"A sad sight," said Henry), the churches these
people bragged about, the pigs in the streets ("the
most respectable part of the population"), the im-
migrant labourers hustling off the ships, the Eng-

lish travellers on their way to the Astor House, to whom he had "done the honours of the city" ("mere herds of men," said Henry)—the whole town meaner and more pretentious even than Boston. But he liked the hum (from a distance) and the roar of the sea; and he had found a few things on Staten Island that were worth his attention. The sunsets were not bad, and they had a fine red honeysuckle there that ought to be transplanted to Concord, and he had heard of a certain tulip-tree—but of this he had some doubts. Homesick Henry! He could not have been more disgruntled. He was very touching when he spoke of the river at home, and the Cattle Show, and the inkstand that Elizabeth Hoar had given him. Concord and his own Romans and fellow-citizens!

He was not so wrong, either, when he talked of the editors and the magazines: Mr. Willis's *New Mirror, Brother Jonathan,* the *Ladies' Companion.* ("I couldn't write anything companionable," said Henry.) He needed the money badly, and he had rambled, he said, into every bookseller's and publisher's house in the city; and he found that he talked with these poor men as if he were over head and ears in business, and a few thousands were no consideration with him. But they proposed to him to do, as he put it, what an honest man could not— a "very valuable experience," said Henry. Let them stick to New York and the West for their contributions. One had other things on one's mind in Massachusetts.

So Henry went back to the Judge's house. "Literature" was not for him. He spent his evenings translating the *Seven against Thebes* and looking into Pindar. (And reading Quarles: "Not much straight grain" in Quarles, but "plenty of tough, crooked timber. . . . He never doubts his genius: it is only he and his God in all the world.") But Henry had neglected none of his opportunities. He had called upon Horace Greeley, the latter-day Franklin, who had just started *The Tribune* ("Now be neighbourly," said Horace), and William Henry Channing, who had started a magazine himself, called *The Present* (and was "sadly in earnest," as Henry remarked, "discussing the question, What to do for the race?"), and Lucretia Mott, the Quaker preacher in Hester Street. (What poise that woman had, in the hurly-burly of the anti-Abolition mob! Tar and feathers? Go ahead, my dears!) But the best friend he had made was Henry James, the "little, fat, rosy Swedenborgian amateur," as Ellery called him, "with the look of a broker and the brains and heart of a Pascal." A sterling man, James, said Concord Henry, so patient and so determined to have the good of you. He humanized New York.

Henry had missed nothing but the inessentials. (He had even talked with young Albert Brisbane, who had just come home from Paris and had taken a daily column in *The Tribune* to explain the doctrines of Fourier.) But for Emerson the inessentials had their charm. These crowds of passers-by —a lovely child, a heroic-looking man: could he only have stopped and told them how much they attracted him! There was Barnum's Museum, too. (The sea-serpent had an instinct to retire into the depths of the sea when about to die. He was sadly afraid of the naturalists, but his heart sank within him when he heard that Barnum was born.) Captain Rynders, the Tammany boss, was well worth a glance: a blackguard, of course, but was he a blackguard merely?—he was almost a consolation among so many palefaces. And fashion. Milliners with a skill and French with an accent that was not the accent of Boston.

Trifles, no doubt. But Bryant was no trifle. A "true bard, but simple," a tyrant over the young. People talked of the clever shopmen who advertised their wares on the Palisades and the rocks by the railroad: this man, more cunning by far, had contrived to levy on all American Nature. Not a waterfowl, not a gentian but Bryant had bribed to speak for him. What usurpation was this?—that who spoke of the autumn woods, of the gardens of the desert, of any feature of day or night in the country, was forced to remember Bryant. But he talked like a man whose great days were over when Emerson called to see him in his office at *The Evening Post*. He was free from all pretension, direct, plain-spoken, but suffering manifestly from want of culture, with no time for himself, no time for books or thoughts (weltering all day long in a foam of papers). He stared and rubbed his eyes when Emerson spoke of his poetry—said all such things were for boys and girls and the aged, that men in middle life had too much else to think of. And then he gave such a look—

Now my weary lips I close,
Leave me, leave me to repose.

But Horace Greeley, of course, was the great New Yorker. He was always following somebody, and every one followed him. He was following Dr. Graham at the moment, the high priest of brown bread: after bolting his food for thirty years, ransacking the table with his long arms, as if Time's chariot were after him, he had made up his mind— in silence and the tears of indigestion—that the gospel of "little meat" had much to be said for it. He was living in a Graham boarding-house when Emerson went to find him, and he dashed in with his coat-tails on the wind. (A sunny soul, this Greeley, with his round, honest face, like a ripe New Hampshire pumpkin! With the wrinkles in his coat, with the necktie under his ear, with his stockings round his ankles and his great ploughman's boots. And Brisbane at his heels.) Bang went the beaver on the rack. "Here's Brisbane—he wanted to meet you." And they all fell to. (Or Horace did. What manners! "Will you have a little salad, Mr. Greeley?"—"You can be fixing me some.")

So this was "neighbourly" Horace, still reaching for the butter, with his pockets bulging with seeds and papers and pamphlets! Could anything have been more encouraging in a Whiggish age than a farmer's boy in the city of New York, adopting every benevolent crotchet and maintaining it, and making the people sit up! Carlyle was right again: "The journalists are now the true kings and clergy." And Emerson could only wish long life to *The Tribune,* long life and a million readers.

Brisbane was eloquent too, when Emerson saw him again, at the Globe Hotel. (For who could utter a word when Horace had the floor?) He wanted Emerson to join him—"come in," with all his "party"; for he evidently thought of the Boston Transcendentalists as a sort of phalanx, much like Fourier's own. And what pictures he drew of the world when the Fourierists had redeemed it! What palaces, what concerts for all! What lectures and poetry and flowers! What perfections of tillage and architecture, gardens and baths! They were going to cover the planet with "groups" and communities. And all the poets and artists and Transcendental persons were to flock to Constantinople —(they were far too good for their Concords, New Yorks and Bostons)—for music, society and wit such as words could never describe.

It was very attractive indeed, this Attractive Industry, though Emerson thought he could mention a few real mischiefs—living for show, losing the whole in the particular, indigence of vital power —that would appear as much in a phalanstery as in a tub. And it figured man as a thing, a thing to be ripened or retarded, moulded or polished, turned into fluid or solid or gas at the will of the leader. (Why not send in a Christmas order for a pair of little girls like No. 91 in the catalogue, with a tinge more of the Swede and a tinge of the Moorish?) It was rather embarrassing for Emerson: Brisbane had misconceived him, misread his political theories—had not seen that he was a poet, of no more use in such a scheme than a rainbow or a firefly. He had to make endless disclaimers and explanations: "I am not at all the sort of man you supposed." (For Brisbane was painfully literal. He spoke of Transcendentalism as a known and fixed element, like salt or meal.) But how cheering, in spite of all, he felt, as he left the hotel, how cheering in a day of small and fierce undertakings, were projects of such friendly aims and such bold and generous proportions!

But for cheering no one compared with Henry James. He had redeemed New York for Henry Thoreau; he redeemed New York for Emerson, when the latter was most oppressed by the noise and the stress and the bustle. He tempered the acrid mass like a woman—James, with his heroic manners, with his nestful of bright little boys and that genial face, glowing with human kindness. No one could speak more nobly: "I do not wish this or that thing my fortune will procure, I wish the great fortune." Or more honestly: of woman, "The flesh said, It is for me, and the spirit said, It is for me." Or with more penetration, as that the blunder of the savants was in fancying that science was a finality, that science *contained* instead of *being contained,* whereas its life was wholly in its relatedness, its implication of the All. What animal spirits he had!—with his broad Irish "Bless your heart!" and "Glory be to God!" ("My dear Madam, God is working all the time in His shirt-sleeves with all His might.") How amusing when he talked of New York and the artists there ("poor, vain, conceited nobodies") and of Thackeray's visit and his speeches in society! The merest boy, said James; he could not see beyond his eyes, he was nothing but a sounding-board against which his experiences thumped and resounded. (But Emerson regretted he had missed Thackeray himself: he had made a good impression while he was here by blurting out his opinion in various companies where so much honesty was rare and useful. Besides, he had not attempted a book on America. Now Dickens. . . . All praise to Dickens for showing so many mischiefs at home that Parliament had not been able to remove. But what was the *American Notes?* A lively rattle: too short, too narrow, too ignorant, too slight and too fabulous. "Fixings," soap and towels, and all the other trivialities this trifler detected in travelling over half the world!)

James was a mine of ideas. What wrath, what exuberance, what witty and elegant billingsgate, half-humorous all the time! But his Swedenborgian theology was too much for Emerson. He said the latter had no conscience and lived by perception alone, said he was virgin-born, a vestal virgin, that his goodness had come by nature—no credit to him!—that he had never in all his days been tempted to steal, or commit adultery or murder—and how *could* he understand a "conviction of sin"? Good heavens, how soothed and comforted he said he was by Emerson's innocent look when he saw

him first—so destitute of all the apparatus of hum-
buggery, a literal divine presence in his house. And
Emerson couldn't understand, he couldn't and he
simply didn't! He wouldn't allow for "evil," he
wouldn't allow for "sin"!

Then what was the secret of Emerson's "personal
fascination"? His immense superiority to the common herd of writers? He locked himself up with
Emerson in his bedroom, swearing that before the
door was opened he would have it. (As if Emerson
knew or could tell him.) Then he gave it up in
despair. For all he could understand of the sphinx
of Concord, he might have locked himself up with
a handful of diamonds.

CHAPTER XIV

GREY clouds, short days, moonless nights. A drowsy sense of being dragged somewhere by the locomotive Destiny. Invisible, this locomotive, yet Emerson knew it must be hitched to the car wherein he sat. So much for these November weeks in Concord. A sufficiently dull routine: but what could he find in New York, inward or outward, to repay his breaking it?

Good days to potter along at home—to think of his imperfections and read some sneering reviews of his new book. He stood very stiffly on his cold and proud doctrine of self-reliance, and here he was shaking like a reed! Was there anything in these notices? Was he really a "treacherous marsh-light"? Were his theories "ancient errors disguised in misty rhetoric"? Was his taste so "false and flippant"? Was there anything in this letter from Dr. B. who said he was wholly mistaken?

Tell me, Lidian, am I right or wrong?

Said his wife: "This whole practice of self-justification and recrimination between literary men seems every whit as low as the quarrels of the Paddies on the railroad."

"But what will you say, Lidian, when my smart article comes out, in reply to Mr. A. and Dr. B.?"

"I shall feel the first emotion of fear and sorrow on your account."

"But do you know how many fine things I have thought of to say to these fighters? They are too good to be lost."

"Then there is some merit in being silent."

And again his wife remarked: "In the gossip and excitement of the hour, be as one blind and deaf to it; know it not. Do as if nothing had befallen."

He couldn't but venerate the oracular nature of woman. He acquired a sentiment gradually through the events of years, and he found her already dwelling there, as in her native home. He thought himself very fortunate, he who knew a lady with such sovereign sweetness of temper, who received the simplest detail of any statement with such happy, anticipating intelligence that it acquired at once importance, breadth and better intent from her welcome. Fortunate, with Ellen, five years old, and Edith, three, and Edward, squealing in the nursery. A house, he said to himself, is held up by magnetism: draw out the magnet, and the house falls and buries the inhabitants. And who was ever going to steal his magnet?

But what did the Koran say? "Paradise lies under the shadow of swords." His house had almost fallen once, when little Waldo died. There he was, spinning away stories without end, with his big, earnest eyes—how his horse went out into a long, long wood, and he looked through a squirrel's eyes, and saw a great giant, and the giant was himself.— "Mamma, may I have this little bell to stand by the side of my bed?"—"Yes, it may stand there."—

"But, Mamma, I am afraid it will alarm you. It may sound in the middle of the night, and it will be heard over the whole town. It will sound like some great glass thing which will fall down and break all to pieces; it will be louder than a thousand hawks; it will be heard across the water and in all the countries; it will be heard all over the world." What a calm, wise little creature, so calmly and wisely happy, who sat beside his father for hours together in the study and spoke of anything but chaos and interruption! He seemed too precious and unique to be huddled aside into the waste and prodigality of things. So gentle, so rich in hopes! And this little temple, which all the muses had seemed to love to build, was shattered in a night.

Three years ago. Emerson still heard the bell-stroke. He read Ben Jonson's story of the death of his son, who died of the plague in London, how he saw the boy in a vision, "of a manly shape, and of that growth, I think, he shall be at the Resurrection." That same preternatural maturity his own little statue assumed the day after death; and often it came to him now, to tax the world with frivolity. But life had worn on, with its endless poetry, its short, dry prose of skepticism—like veins of cold air in the evening woods, quickly swallowed by the wide warmth of June; with its pure repairs of all the rents and ruin it had seemed to give. And the new had stolen upon him like a star that rose behind his back as he walked.

He had three children now. There was Ellen at

the door! She wanted to be carried round the room, wanted to see the wings on the little Psyche, the bronze Goethe, the "Three Fates" over the mantel (with the shears and thread in their hands). And she wanted a pencil and a letter-back. (Vain to attempt to get rid of the children by going on with your work. If their purring and humming was not noticed, they began to squeal; if that was ignored, to cry; then, if you consoled them, they found the experiment succeeded and began again.)

There was Ellen asleep in her bed, with the air of one riding a horse of night—protected from all infusions of evil persons. Then she woke and began to fret, and presently put all sleep of her seniors to rout. The seniors grew very cross, but Ellen conquered all by the pathos and eloquence of childhood and its words of fate. She wished the morning would come. She broke out into sublimity: "It *must* be morning." She fell asleep; she rolled out of her bed; she pattered about the floor. "Oh, dear! Where's my bed?" Then she slept and woke again. "I'm so afraid! I wish I could sleep on the bed beside of you. I'm afraid I shall tumble into the waters—it's all water!" What else could papa do? —he jumped out of bed and laid himself down beside the little mischief, and soothed her as best he could.

Edith spent half her time looking innocent, and the other half looking dignified. Edith was a realist: let her mother describe as she might the joys of heaven—Edith would have none of it. She wanted to stay—and she looked around the room—

where there were "folks, and *things,* and a *door.*"

What was so interesting as the nursery?—every tear and every smile deserved a history, to say nothing of the stamping and the screaming. How touching the strewn toys became the moment the children left the room! How bewitching were all these experiments with grammar and language! A writer used ten words for one the children used, attempting by many words to suggest what he could not describe, while their strong speech was made of nouns and verbs and went straight to the point. No "telling" on the microscope, meaning no name of the maker. "Where is the wafer that *lives* in this box?" They carried the analogy through: *bite* made *bited,* and *eat, eated.* Ellen called the grapes "green berries"; and when her father asked, "Does it rain this morning?" Ellen replied, "There's tears on the window."

Nature's best feat, enamouring a man of these children!—like making him kiss the knife that is going to cut his throat—they fretting, mortifying, ruining him, and upsetting him at last because they want his chair, and he, dear old donkey, well pleased to the end!

Emerson could have listened forever to a lively child, with an almost reverent care. How few men spoke, as children spoke, not from their fears or their senses, but directly out of their souls! But Henry spoke this way, and so did Alcott, and Charles Newcomb, the quiet, retreating young man whom Emerson had met at Providence and who, after staying for a while at Brook Farm, had come to make him a visit. A subtle, inward genius, puny in body as a girl, yet with an aplomb like a general's, never disconcerted. He too, like all the young illuminati, had had his poem in *The Dial*; but, unlike so many of the others, who had lived a great deal in a short time, he had *not* come forth with a shattered constitution.

A captivating soul, wrapped in his great Gothic cathedral of fancies, Newcomb, with his strange eyes, his atmosphere of mystery and his cult of contemplation, who kept Fanny Elssler's portrait on his bureau between those of Loyola and Xavier and was filled with some mediæval dream of an absolute priesthood. Saints in a cloister who recognized each other, and still retired—that was his image, but there were other dear solicitations: he made Emerson feel the pertinency of the Platonistic word "all-various." No journal was ever like the one he kept, with intense solitude appearing in every sentence. A Patmos of thought!—soliloquies, an abridged, stenographic wit and eloquence. Emerson could hardly sit as he turned the pages, for Swendenborg rose before him, and all the gods out of earth and air and ocean. What power this young man had of illustrating refinements of feeling by means of household experiences!—"Bacon, at home in his reflections. When intellectual, then is he himself, as a childless woman, restless except when making bread, and is then happy and singing." What perceptions!—"It is not what the thought is, but how he stands to his thought, that we value in friendship." And Emerson marvelled

again at the unerring instinct with which, like an
arrow to its mark, the newborn fine genius flew to
the geniuses. Newcomb darted upon Shakespeare,
Dante, Coleridge, and let nothing intervene.

A journal to be read in the woods, in the arm-
chair of the upturned root of a pine-tree. Emerson
made a copy of the best passages, for Newcomb was
so sure to destroy the original. He said that Shakespeare was "the farthest bound of subtlety and
universality compatible with individuality, the subtlest of authors, and only just within the possibility
of authorship." And Newcomb himself was just
beyond authorship! He defied thought; he said it
made him old and harried and anxious. He could
ill conceal his dislike of a general remark; he spent
his mornings all summer at Newport walking, his
afternoons "in society," and never opened a book.
(Dear Swedenborg, Emerson said to himself, catch
this American sprig, and whip him soundly!)

For what was that maxim of Swedenborg's?—
"The perfection of man is the love of use." And
what did Shakespeare say?—

> Will Fortune never come with both hands full?
> She either gives a stomach and no food,
> . . . . or else a feast
> And takes away the stomach.

A continual surprise, this finding some stranger
who spoke the same mother-tongue as oneself: a
graceful young man, free as a palm or a pine-tree,
listening eagerly to one's theory of the world, yet
having a theory of his own. If only the fine tulips
made good timber! And if only the good timber had

a little more of the tulip! There was Hawthorne
over at the Manse—he had rented it within a year
of Dr. Ripley's death: Hawthorne pacing up and
down under the ash-trees of the avenue. An Apol-
lonian creature, noble in every movement, with his
great shipmaster's frame and his haunted eyes,
Hawthorne, "in the sea of life enisled." But with
never a word for Emerson. They met, in the slush
and snow, trudging along to the Post Office. They
skated together on the river, with Henry perform-
ing geometric dances and Bacchic leaps on the ice,
Emerson, head foremost, pitching along, and the
grave Hawthorne, shrouded in his cloak, like a
floating statue, unweariable. Emerson besieged him
at the Manse, plied him with questions, dragged
him into the study so that no one could interrupt his
interrogation; and Hawthorne sat there mute as a
Salem figurehead. (Or only looked his answers.)

Emerson had met his match—a real Sphinx,
with a subterranean self buried fathoms deep in
the desert sand. What strange thoughts were stir-
ing in that vaulted skull? Thoughts very unlike his
own, but with what horizons!—the first he was ever
to meet that were not for him. Carlyle, Wordsworth, Coleridge—he had understood them all; but
this tragic soul was beyond him. (These eyes that
spoke of the Fates, of the fore and after, of the
whence and whither of all things, like the bird
that flew through the hall of the Saxon king.) He
remembered that day in Sleepy Hollow, when
Hawthorne had just arrived in Concord: there
were muses in the woods and whispers on the

breeze, and he emerged from the green shade and saw this apparition seated on the bank, with Margaret lying beside him. They had met by chance, they said, and were talking about autumn, and the pleasures of being lost in the forest, talking about the crows and the experiences of early childhood and the sight of mountains from a distance. They seemed to be sympathetic; but what had he surmised, as he joined in the conversation? That Hawthorne distrusted Margaret and scarcely liked her? There was something else. A shadow, a breath, a reminder as it were of some vast Cimmerian universe that lay outside his own solar track.

(Not for you, Emerson, not for you to enter!—you whose sun traversed the remotest sky. A God, a God your severance ruled. Did he fear you a little, perhaps, you whose iron orbit no lesser soul could resist? Had not Ellery Channing's gait, air, voice, the turning of his eyebrow, his very thoughts come to resemble yours? Had Henry been able to resist you? His manners, the tones of his voice, his modes of expression had unconsciously followed yours for many years. How many others there were who found themselves unable to withstand your power! One could almost foresee the day when Concord would be populated with little Emersons. Wise Hawthorne, to keep you at a distance!—for who knew better than you that genius can be fatal to genius? He was friendly enough with Henry, went botanizing with him, hunting for Indian relics, paddling up the river: he had bought Henry's boat, the boat of the famous "Week"—too sad for Henry to keep, now that his brother was dead. He went fishing with Ellery, camped with him, talked with him, laughed with him. But when you appeared the clouds rolled over the face of the moon.)

How inviting, too, the Manse had become, with Sophia's magical touch! Emerson would never have known it, when he dropped in of an evening. The grimy ceilings had vanished, the timbers blackened with smoke, the dust and the cobwebs, the prints of the Puritan divines that had once stared down from the walls. What a change from the days when he wrote his first little book there! Yellow wall-paper, new books, cheerful pictures, fresh paint and the gayest of carpets, and Sophia herself under the astral lamp. It was she who had thought of this purple vase, and the flowers, and the bronze jar with the ferns. Clever Sophia, with her Latin, Greek and Hebrew, and with all she knew about history, and the way she painted and modelled!

He stole in softly. He found them there, so happy, in the midst of all this freshness, in the beams of the great star that hung from the ceiling, Sophia with her sewing, Hawthorne reading aloud. Shakespeare? No, Spenser, this time: the tales of Gloriana and the Knights. (The paradisal forest rose before him, and the wild hills of Ireland, the fairies, dwarfs and giants, the struggles of the soul, the shapes of evil.) Hawthorne's poet—lovelier than a butterfly's wing. Hawthorne was fresh, too, fresh as the night-blooming cereus. By what sorcery had he kept this dew of youth? How had he escaped the dust and roughness of the world, and the world's fatness—he with the giant's strength?

Emerson went again, in the afternoon, in the stillness of late September, when the thump of a falling apple was the only sound. Hawthorne was in the garden; he was bending over, examining the yellow squashes and the "crook-necks" basking there in the warm sun, and he spoke of their beautiful forms, urn-like, vase-like. He said that no sculptor had invented anything more graceful, that, if he could afford it, he would have a service made of delicate porcelain, wrought into the shapes of squashes gathered from his vines. He loved this old garden; he had spent whole days there, watching the vegetables grow, the swelling of the pods, the clambering of the bean-vines up the poles, the bursting of the little corn-hills, incidents filled for him with the tenderest meaning. How could one live so near this man and never get to know him? Could they take a little walking-trip together? Would that loosen his tongue?

Hawthorne was not unwilling, so they set out together for the Shaker Colony at Harvard. They were both in high spirits, and the talk flowed for once. They could easily have filled much longer days with matter, old collectors that they were who had never before had a chance to show each other their treasures. Walking was a luxury in that rich autumn light, and the borders of the road brimmed over with bursting grapevines, wild apples, purple gentians and the red fruit of the thornbush.

They might have picked up all sorts of stories, had they cared to knock at some door for a glass of milk—pathetic private histories, threads of romance, the blush on the cheek of some girl when the mail-stage failed to come. But they had too much to say as it was: they could even dispense with the jokes at the taverns (where Hawthorne liked to sit and watch from his corner). They made their twenty miles by way of Stow, and set off to see the Shakers the following morning. The Sisters gave them breakfast, while Cloutman and Seth Blanchard described the community—described it to Emerson, at least, for Hawthorne was rather Jovian. They were peasants, with a squalid contentment; but here was the model farm Emerson had longed for, inventions the neighbouring farmers saw and copied. And here was a kind of Socialism in action, and what noble arcades of grapes! No man allowed to join just for a living, no man turned off only because he was poor.

What sketches one might have made of this genuine Connecticut life transplanted to Massachusetts! (There was even a touch of Alcott in these simple Shakers.) It was not for Hawthorne, however: theology bored him, and Brook Farm had destroyed his interest in all communities. A great gift, Hawthorne's, never to see or hear what didn't belong to him; nothing appealed to him very much but the fringed gentians by the road. But they talked about Landor and the possible advantage of being disappointed in love. (Wasn't that sentence of Landor's worth a divorce?—"Those to whom love is a secondary thing love more than those to whom it is a primary.") And they talked about Scott. (Some greatness, after all, in defying posterity and writing for the hour. Some greatness in being a harper.) And they passed through Acton towards twilight and listened to the frogs.

A rich democratic land, this Massachusetts, Emerson said to himself: in every house well-dressed women with an air of town ladies, in every house a piano and a copy of *The Spectator*. (And a daughter who read Willis. And the houses in Acton, he had to admit, seemed to be filled with fat old people who looked like old tomatoes, their faces crumpled into red collops, fatting and rotting at their ease.) Hawthorne had missed nothing that befitted those deep-sunk eyes; but he spoke of sleep. The world, he said, should recline its vast head on the first convenient pillow and take an age-long nap. It had gone distracted (he was thinking of the reformers) through a morbid activity; it was preternaturally wide-awake, and yet tormented by visions that seemed real to it now, visions that would assume their true aspect and character were all things once set right by an interval of sound repose. How else could humankind get rid of its old delusions? It would then reawake as an infant out of dewy slumber.

What a skeptic Hawthorne was! What depths of doubt were these!—deeper than Emerson had ever sounded—and *he* could have told a tale or two himself. Well, sleep was good at the Manse: a Prospero's isle, Hawthorne's enchanted ground.

His guests, he said, felt a slumberous influence upon them. They nodded in their chairs, or took a more deliberate siesta on the sofa, or stretched out among the shadows of the orchard, looking up dreamily through the boughs; and Hawthorne rejoiced in this, rejoiced to be able to welcome his friends out of the dusty glare and tumult of the world to share the transparent obscurity that floated over him. Rest in a life of trouble, rest for these weary and earth-worn spirits, with their careers of perpetual action, harassed and impeded, staggering under the burden of their gifts. A proof, this powerful opiate, he said, that they had left their cares behind as they passed between the gateposts of his avenue. And what better could one do for any man than to throw the spell of a magic spirit over him?

CHAPTER XV

IT was 1847, the year before the year of revolutions. Emerson was forty-four, and a new occasion had presented itself for extending his travels across the sea. For some time he had felt the need of a special stimulus; he had reached one of those dead points when the stars stand still in one's inward firmament and one requires some foreign force to prevent stagnation. His energies had ebbed, he had no thoughts, and America had come to seem of a village littleness. And now the Mechanics' Institutes, rising through the North of England, were urging him to come and lecture to them. Carlyle was urging him, too. Why shouldn't he go?

"In March, many weathers"; and in life many. He had often looked with longing eyes towards Europe. He had had his dreams of living there, perverse dreams, he felt, but very inspiriting. He had dreamed of Valencia, Florence, Rome, Berlin, but of Oxford and Cambridge especially; he had read with the frankest envy Aubrey's anecdotes and the letters of English scholars. Their life was a complete circle of means and ends; and they had an audience, no poor, scattered following like his own, no mere handful of uncritical men and women, but a dense, compact body of instructed minds. What precise, what powerful demands were made upon them, and how these demands stirred them to labour and concentration! If he languished himself at times, if his thought remained so often vague and cloudy, was it not because so little was expected of him? The needs he addressed were so very far from conscious; he felt no sort of team-work between himself and his listeners. (What was it the old lady said, that she never understood a word he uttered? —but she liked to go and see him just the same, standing up on the platform, looking as if he thought everybody else was just as good as he was. Pleasant enough, but not exactly stimulating. If she had only been able to catechize him a little, make him define his ideas, he would not have been quite so much "up in the air.") It was very hard to go beyond your public. If they were satisfied with your poor performance, you could scarcely make it better. But when they recognized what was good and delighted in it, you aspired and burned and toiled till you achieved it.

Yes, he had envied the thinkers of England, the richness, the calm assiduity, unhasting, unresting, of their lives. (Eupeptic studying-mills, cast-iron men, whose powers of endurance compared with those of the Americans as the steam-hammer with the music-box.) Their lot could never be his, but he envied it none the less—in hours like these. When his own tide was in flood it was easy to feel that his duty was at home: he could well defy these lingering looks *behind*. But when the tide ebbed, towards evening, on rainy days—that was another story. In America the people meant that men of thought should be ornamental merely. There was Everett, for instance, with his Liberty and his Dying Demosthenes, and in practice wearing the slave-holder's whip in his buttonhole; and Eliot with his *History of Liberty* and his votes for South Carolina; and Sparks and Felton who carried Demosthenes clean for slavery. Bancroft, Emerson said to himself, would never have known George Fox had he met him on the street, the same George Fox he had eulogized so well. (Historical democrats, all these men, interested in dead or organized, but not in organizing, freedom.) Was it true that deep convictions, realistic visions of a more enlightened society, were not to be entertained by a race that was busily settling a continent? They were pretty souls, these American men of thought; they gave such a fillip to the emotions on the Fourth of July! And they slept away the rest of their days, becalmed. No strong wind filled their sails, and they lost their incentive. For no commanding cry came from the void.

Alas for America, the ungirt, the diffuse, the profuse, procumbent! Alas for this great, intelligent, sensual, avaricious America, with its restless, rickety, hysterical population! A puny and fickle folk, a country of small adventures, short plans, daring risks, but not of patience, not of combinations, not of long, persistent, close-woven schemes, demanding the utmost fortitude, faith and poverty. A country without an aristocracy, governed in barrooms, in which every village brawler, every clamorous partisan made known what he called his opinion as loud as he could scream. American books—what were they? Tents, not pyramids. American reformers—slight and wearisome talkers, not man-subduing, immutable, all-attractive. Even the American physique: the head alone was finished, the face alone alive, the body only blocked, the trunk and limbs inferior and appearing to exist only to support the head. And how poor and pallid were most American lives! Otis talked too much. Webster had no *morale*. Choate wanted weight. Alcott was unlimited and unballasted. Staid and timid mostly—no fiery grain. How hard to find a man!

Alas for America, with its levity and facility! Eager, solicitous, hungry, rabid, busy-bodied America, attempting many things, vain, ambitious to feel its own existence. What immense resources it had, land, men, iron, timber, gold!—and all a village squabble and capacity. No passions, only appetites; hesitation and following; no form, no terrible and beautiful condensation. A lack of the male principle: plenty of village attorneys, saucy village talents, but no great captains. Too easily pleased, these Americans! As soon as they learned to read and write and cipher they set up for themselves as leaders of opinion, and they wrote away without check of any kind, played whatever prank they chose, indulged whatever spleen or oddity, and even felt complacent in doing so; and thus the finest wits came to nothing. Provincial Cæsars, one and all, easily filling their measures and lying on their oars with the fame of the villages!

Alas for America, this Lilliput! And these Americans, free-willers, fussy, self-asserting, buzzing all over creation! How different from the Asiatics for whom everything was writ on the iron leaf and who would not turn on their heel to save themselves from famine, plague or sword! Fatalistic, yes; but it gave a grand air to the people. Job was right when he said that "wisdom is not found in the hand of those that live at their ease." Or those that disparage books, O fellow-Americans, and denounce severe culture, and magnify the mother-wit swagger of bright boys from the country colleges! Make the most of your ignorance, your un-learning and inspiration, you that are superficial and can make much of nothing else! And you, Mr. Know-All, look at the great writers, look at the great scholars, the Lessings and Goethes and Johnsons, and despair! You are up to Nature and the First Cause in your consciousness, but you have no concentration; and that wondrous power to collect and swing your whole vital energy into one act, and leave the product there for the envy of posterity, *that* you cannot approach!

Alas for America! An air loaded with poppy, and all running to leaves, to suckers, to tendrils, to miscellany, dispersion and sloth. A wilderness of capabilities, of a many-turning, Ulyssean culture; an irresistibility like Nature's, and, like Nature, without conscience. Everything speedy, everything new and slight. Shingle palaces, shingle cities, picnic universities. Leather not tanned; sulphuric acid, half-strength; knees, instead of grand old oak, sawed out of refuse sapling; for stone, well-sanded pumpkin-pine! An art scarcely more than the national taste for whittling: no independent creation of the sort that requires an artist charged in his single head with a nation's force. And hearts too soon despondent. Young men, young women, at thirty and even earlier losing all spring and vivacity: let them fail in their first undertaking, and the rest was rock and shallow.

Emerson had other moods. If now, as so often before, his estimate of America was low, it rose again as often to heroic proportions. He had felt so many times the greatness of his opportunity. It was something to be the Hesiod of a dawning nation, the Ennius, the Venerable Bede, up so early before the break of day. But the country seemed sadly naked in these hours of depression, naked, unatmospheric. Boston was mean and petty beside life in Concord, and Concord was so limited, so lonely, so insular! Pathetic was the sight of Edmund Hosmer creeping into one's barn, just on the chance of a little conversation. It was true he had often scoffed at travel—as if there were any country where they did not scald the milk-pans and burn the brushwood! As if every traveller were not a mere impertinence when he came among the diligent in their places! As if one could ever hope to find in geography the aliment the mind was seeking! A foolish American passion, this running about in the hotels and theatres of Europe.

He still scoffed at travel. A mark, this gadding abroad, this European complaint, of youth, of an endless novitiate, a proof that America was not ripe for the reign of heroic instincts. What could any one expect of travel but confirmation of his simplest sentiments at home? Still, even this, at the moment, might have its value; and he wanted a bath in the currents of the world's thought. There were facts of science he could only obtain in England, new theories which, for want of a learned class at home, he had never heard of till years after they were published. And he wanted to know the greatest of his contemporaries, know them not merely through books: at a spoken word, at the touch of a hand, a whole new view of the world passed into one's mind like lightning. He would see his own society in relief, in contrast with other societies; he would see the utmost that social man had accomplished—an aristocratic system with as few abatements as possible—model men, the distinctions that were flouted too easily at home. Above all, the scholars, the mighty workers of England: he would meet these giants and measure himself beside them. (And find an audience, too, the most exacting, one that would rouse and frighten him.) Carlyle was undoubtedly right. He would get an "immense quantity of food for ideas."

Carlyle! What wealth of being that name signified! How the sight of that man's handwriting had always warmed his heart at the Post Office window! A redeemer of life, Carlyle, seeking no reward, warping his genius to no dull public, writ-

ing for he knew not whom and finding his readers
at last in the valley of the Mississippi—readers
who brooded on the pictures he had painted, un-
twisted the many-coloured meanings which he had
spun and woven into so rich a web of sentences,
domesticated in so many remotest heads the
humour, philosophy, learning, which, year by year,
in summer and in frost, this lonely man had lived
in the moors of Scotland! A true man of letters,
Emerson said to himself, one who made good the
place and function of Erasmus, of Dryden, Johnson, Swift, to one's own generation, who sustained
the dignity of his profession of author in England.
It was true that he mixed himself a little too much
with his erring and grieving nations and saddened
the picture. Health belonged to the author, too,
Goethean health and cheerfulness! And his aims
were sometimes paltry; he would draw weapons
from the skies to fight for some wretched English
monopoly or prejudice. And the slam-bang style,
that grotesque, apocalyptic strain, was far from
the Periclean. (O Carlyle, the merit of glass is not
to be seen, but to be seen through; and every crystal and lamina of your glass is visible!) But what
rules for the illumination of windows could ever
apply to the Aurora Borealis? And what life he
endowed the world with, this worshipper of
strength, heedless much whether its present phase
were divine or diabolic! He scorned all paper
formulas, all "Pantheism, Pot-theism, Mydoxy,
Thydoxy." ("Did the upholsterers make this Universe? Were you created by the Tailor?") And

right he was in believing that every noble creature contained, if savage passions, also fit checks and grand impulses within him, and had his own resources, and however erring would return from far.

Again and again Emerson had sent his friends to that king's house in Chelsea—Alcott, Margaret Fuller, Henry James, Hedge, Theodore Parker, that the best of America might meet the best of England. The shrewdest comments had come back from the lover of heroes, shrewd, humorous, benign: "The good Alcott, with his long, lean face and figure, with his grey, worn temples and mild, radiant eyes, all bent on saving the world by a return to acorns and the golden age. . . . A kind of venerable Don Quixote, whom nobody can even laugh at without loving! . . . Let him love me as he can, and live on vegetables in peace; as I, living *partly* on vegetables, will continue to love him! . . . Margaret Fuller: a true heroic mind, altogether unique, so far as I know, among the writing women of this generation. . . . Such a predetermination to *eat* this big universe as her oyster or her egg, and to be absolute empress of all height and glory in it that her heart could conceive, I have not before seen in any human soul. Her 'mountain *me*' indeed:—but her courage too is high and clear, her chivalrous nobleness indeed is great; her veracity, in its deepest sense, *à toute épreuve*. . . . Theodore Parker, a most hardy, compact, clever little fellow, full of decisive utterance, with humour and good humour, shining like a sun amid multitudes of watery comets and tenebrific constellations, too sorrowful without such admixture on occasion! ... Frederic Hedge, one of the sturdiest little fellows I have come across for many a day. A face like a rock, a voice like a howitzer; only his honest kind grey eyes reassure you a little." A joy to have one's friends seen by such eyes, eyes that had seen Daniel Webster, too: "That amorphous crag-like face; the dull black eyes under their precipice of brows, like dull anthracite furnaces, needing only to be *blown;* the mastiff mouth accurately closed:—I have not traced as much of *silent berserker-rage,* that I remember of, in any other man." A joy to have those thirsty eyes of Carlyle, those portrait-eating, portrait-painting eyes, fall full on the great forehead one had followed about in one's youth from courthouse to Senate! And now Carlyle had fixed his eyes upon *him.* "Come if you dare," he had written; "I said there was a room, house-room and heart-room, constantly waiting you here, and you shall see blockheads by the million. *Pickwick* himself shall be visible; innocent young Dickens reserved for a questionable fate. The great Wordsworth shall talk till you yourself pronounce him to be a bore. Southey's complexion is still healthy mahogany-brown, with a fleece of white hair, and eyes that seem running at full gallop. Leigh Hunt, 'man of genius in the shape of a Cockney,' is my near neighbour, full of quips and cranks, with good humour and no common sense. Old Rogers, with his pale head, white, bare and cold as snow, will work on you with those large blue eyes, cruel, sorrowful, and that sardonic shelf-chin. . . ." Who could resist such a branch of golden apples?

On a sunny afternoon in the following July, Emerson and Carlyle were strolling together at Stonehenge. The larks were singing overhead, and the wind was blowing the buttercups in the meadows. They clambered over the stones, counted and measured them, and talked of the flight of ages. Carlyle was in a gentle mood; he spoke of the old times of England, the acts of the saints, the men who built the cathedrals. Emerson and he had had their differences: they had found themselves worlds apart in their views of the nineteenth century, for more and more Carlyle had come to believe in the doctrines of work and force as ends in themselves. But this ancient sphinx of a temple put all these petty dissensions out of sight.

For nine months Emerson had been travelling in England, lecturing in Manchester, London, Edinburgh, Glasgow, observing, going to school. His journals were packed with notes, enough to make a book of English Traits; he had dropped his net into this teeming sea and drawn up what a draught of fishes! Carlyle still seemed the largest man in England, but he had basked in half the glories of the country. He had even seen Wordsworth again at Rydal Mount, very old now and sleeping on his sofa, but soon roused when the talk turned to the new French Revolution. (He was bitter against the French, bitter against Carlyle—"a pest to the English tongue," but a fine healthy old man, with his corrugated face; and Emerson still thought that, with all the torpid places in his mind, the something hard and sterile in his poetry, the want of grace and variety, Wordsworth alone in his time had treated the human soul with an absolute trust.)

With Carlyle his relations had been somewhat disappointing. "Well, here we are, shovelled together again!" Carlyle had said, standing in the door with a lamp, when Emerson arrived at ten o'clock at night. They had met with much affection and talked far and wide before going to bed, but in the morning Carlyle had changed. "What has brought you over to the old country?" he said. "Surely not to 'lecture.' Aren't there enough windbags in Lancashire?" He thought Emerson was a fool to waste his time palavering to Paisley weavers and mechanics; he had grown very cynical and sour; he bespattered the whole world with his oil of vitriol. They found they had little in common; but for Emerson his friend was still the bravest scholar in England, and he was glad to listen. Carlyle was all for murder, money and punishment by death, for slavery and every petty abomination. You praised republics, and he liked the Czar of Russia; you admired free trade and found him a Protectionist; you upheld the freedom of the press, and he wished nothing so much as to turn all the reporters out of Parliament; you stood for free institutions, he for a stringent government that showed people what to do and made them do it. But in all this he plainly revered realities; he anathematized decorum and respectability; he worshipped fortitude and enthusiasm. And, as Emerson said to himself, he had carried his life erect, made himself a power confessed by all men, taught scholars their lofty duty and scornfully taught the nobles. A hammer that crushed mediocrity and pretension. A divining-rod for all that was real and sound.

Macaulay was another story. In his talk what fire, speed, fury, talent and effrontery! The king of diners-out, but with no affirmative quality, Emerson thought: a historian whose sole interest was to glorify every sort of material advantage. (What a notable greengrocer was spoiled to make Macaulay!) But he had liked George Stephenson, the inventor of the locomotive: the man who created a material good brought something into the world —a very different thing from the philosopher who said that such goods as these were the ends of life. He had liked Tennyson too, when they dined together at the house of Coventry Patmore. For this musky poet of gardens and parks and palaces, so rich in fancy, so powerful in language, with a colouring like Titian, colour like the dawn, for "Ulysses" and "Œnone" he had long been thankful: a perfect music-box, Tennyson, for all manner of delicate tones and rhythms. And there he was at Patmore's, with his quiet, sluggish strength, a talking Hawthorne, Carlyle's "best man in England to smoke a pipe with." And in Edinburgh he had seen De Quincey, a gentle little elf, with an old, old face, shabbily dressed, with exquisite

speech and manners, who had walked in from the
country ten miles on the muddy roads and had *not*
spoken like the organ of York Minster. He was
quite serene and happy, like a child of seven, telling how he had been robbed by two girls in the
street, talking of Landor's *Hellenics* and of *Paradise Regained,* and how he had lost five manuscript books of Wordsworth's unpublished poems.
A few days later, Emerson dined with him at Lass-
wade, where he lived with his three daughters, and
De Quincey came back in the coach to hear Emerson lecture. As they entered Edinburgh, De Quincey grew very nervous, until one of the company
assured him that his old enemy, the landlady Mrs.
MacBold, had moved to another quarter of the
town.

Emerson had made up his mind to miss nothing
interesting or significant. Never in all his life had
he dreamed of so many dinners, breakfasts, recep-
tions (where he found himself the "parlour Ere-
bus" of old). He had gone to breakfast, of course,
at Samuel Rogers's, that museum of art and anecdote; talked with Disraeli, Prince Albert, Lord
Palmerston, Rothschild; spent an evening with
Dickens in John Forster's rooms; visited Turner's
studio, and Kew Gardens with Hooker; and Robert Owen had taken him through the Hunterian
Museum. And how many other personages he had
met, each of whom contributed to his gallery of
human nature!—Leigh Hunt, Thackeray, Mil-
man, the Duchess of Sutherland, Faraday, Mrs.
Jameson. A young fellow of Oriel, Arthur Hugh

Clough, fascinated by his lectures, had invited him to Oxford; and there he had talked with some of the younger writers, Froude and Matthew Arnold. Clough and Arnold had been much bewildered by Carlyle, and Arnold had written a sonnet in honour of Emerson's *Essays*.

He had gone to Paris for a month. Clough had come over too, and they had dined together daily at a *table d'hôte*. The Revolution of May had broken out, and the streets were full of soldiers; and one day, looking out of his window, Emerson had seen a crowd of furious horses dragging cannon towards the National Assembly. He had spent an evening at Barbès's *Club de la Revolution,* and another at Citizen Blanqui's Club, where the workmen in their blouses spoke with a fire and a deep sincerity that were good to hear; and on May 15 it looked as if the Revolution were going to succeed. But Blanqui and Barbès, who had reigned for a quarter of an hour, were fast in jail by night. Emerson had not really known the French before, and he found himself rapidly correcting his preconceptions. He heard Lamartine speak on the Polish question and Michelet lecture on philosophy. He saw Rachel in *Phèdre* and two other plays and was struck by the terror, the demoniacal power she threw into passages of defiance and denunciation, by the raging fire within her, by the intellectual cast of her manners and carriage. The gaiety and politeness of the people, the fountains and parks and gardens were an endless pleasure; and he said to himself that, if hard should come to hard, and he needed some refuge of solitude and independence, he would always remember Paris.

More lectures in London followed. A letter had appeared in one of the papers urging him to speak at a price sufficiently low to allow poor literary men to hear him; for "Emerson," the writer said, "is a phenomenon whose like is not in the world, and to miss him is to lose an important part out of the Nineteenth Century." So he read three lectures in Exeter Hall, on Domestic Life, Shakespeare and Napoleon; and now he had lingered on till July, with what a store of impressions! This island, stuffed full in every corner and crevice, with towns, towers, churches, villas, palaces; the number and power of the trades and guilds, the military strength and splendour, the multitudes of remarkable men and women; the old men, red as roses, with their clear skins and peach-bloom complexions; the vigour and brawn of the people (castles compared with Americans), their sound animal structure, their freedom and personal courage had filled him with an ever-increasing respect. A sensible, handsome, powerful race, a population of lords, he was ready to call them. The best of actual nations.

What manners, too, what talent turned into manners! He had caught many a glimpse, perceived many a trait, of that Aristocracy, that dim superior race, unrealized as yet in humanity, of which he had always dreamed. But that race was a race of gods, not lords, commensurate with Nature, all-comprehending, disdainful of the world. The Eng-

lish stood in awe of mundane facts; they confined
their aspirations to the means of dealing with facts,
and they valued only the faculties that enabled
them to do so. In America, he felt, as he turned
his face towards home—but he couldn't clearly express the feeling that filled him. Thin and pale the
New World danced before bloodshot English eyes.
But the New World was a faith, and he lived in
the light of it.

CHAPTER XVI

SUMMER days had come to Concord, those glowing summer days that made him sad because he could only spend them once. He sighed for the thousand heads and thousand bodies of the Indian gods, that he might celebrate this immense beauty in many ways and places.

It was good to be at home again, in pleasant Concord, in this kind New England, in this vast slovenly continent, with its high Allegheny pastures and the sea-wide, sea-skirted prairie where slept and murmured still the great mother Nature. Still asleep, Nature, though almost conscious, too much by half for man. A little *triste,* perhaps, with all this rank vegetation of swamps and forests, steeped in dews and rains. But what a poem! A dream never to be told to English ears.

They had laughed when he tried to explain it. Not for them were these mysteries of the unborn, these visions of the law of love and justice. Not for them, with their trim hedgerows and cultivated gardens, their indispensable mutton-chop and spinach, their sodden conceit of antiquity. Not even for Carlyle, great and good as he was, with his "windbags" and "donkeys" and "monkeys," and his "niggers" and "bladders" and "blockheads," his "vile Pythons" and "thick-skinned denizens of chaos," his "ninth parts of thinkers" and "Sanhedrins of windy fools," his "ugly universal *snoring* hum of the over-filled deep-sunk Posterity of Adam." Not for the grim Ishmaelite, he of the bad liver and the little faith! Let him scoff as he might at one's azure dreams, but what were the words of the Koran, the book of his own Mohammed?— "On the day of Resurrection those who have indulged in ridicule will be called to the door of Paradise and have it shut in their faces when they reach it."

Alas for those British jokers, with their damnable derision! Let them have their day's joke, as duly as their bread, they that parried earnest speech with banter and levity, that smiled the speaker down or changed the subject! Let them say, over their wine, that "all this about liberty, and so forth, is gone by: it won't do any longer." Let them keep their squalid contentment with conventions, their shop-till politics, their idolatry of usage; trample on other nationalities to reproduce London in Asia and the Antipodes; domesticate and dress the blessed soul itself in English gaiters. Let them glory in that island, that roaring volcano of Fate, material values, glutted markets and low prices. They had paid too much for their empire, they that esteemed a philosopher only as they esteemed an apothecary who brought bark or a drench, they for whom inspiration was only some blowpipe or finer mechanical aid. What said Macaulay, the voice of their governing classes?—that *good* meant good to eat, good to wear, material commodity, that the merit of modern philosophy was to avoid ideas and morals. Better sick-chairs! Better wine-whey for invalids! "Solid advantage" that reduced intellect to a saucepan! Not so spoke their sages of old, their Bacons and Miltons and Berkeleys, spirits of an endless leisure, basking in an element of contemplation beyond all modern atmospheric gauges! Let them have their laugh— even Carlyle, the brave and strong genius. For him there was only one joke in the end: that all this pettiness and rottenness and cant of the practical, that all these gladiators and causes, were going speedily into the abyss together.

Emerson had foreseen that, once at home again in Massachusetts, he would fall back into his old dream of America. The brawn of the English had made him feel like an invalid. He had seen proofs of sense and spirit. He liked the English, as good as they were handsome: they had everything, they could do everything. And yet the hope of this vast free country, with all things still untried, rose again in his mind. Hope and faith were better than all this resignation to the *fait accompli!* For the rest, the crudeness of America, the gruff Jacobin manners of the American populace, no longer disturbed him so much. He thought of the pirate forbears of the English race, the ferocious dragoons of Hastings. Out of Druids and berserkers were Alfred and Shakespeare made, with all their animal vigour. Could a strong nation develop without strong wild will? These bad manners, he told himself, were a screen of porcupine quills by which the germ of genius was concealed and guarded; would not Jacksonism itself, heedless of English literature as of all literature, redeem America in the end from imitation? Let the children of darkness advance, root out in the coarsest way the hollow dilettantism of American culture that the generations to come might frame their own world with greater advantage!

He could not but wish that Carlyle had stayed in the Scottish hills, a lonely seer, kept free of that cynics' world of London. For what had those young men told him—Clough at Oxford?—that Carlyle had led them all into the wilderness, led them out and left them. He had cast aside the sham kings, only to embrace the real kings, however bestial; and he had railed at Emerson for addressing the intellectual canaille, the kings-in-essence-on-their-own-account. Canaille? Perhaps. Why quarrel over epithets? But they numbered among them Carlyle's dearest disciples, and they had left the lost leader, the "crabbed, sulky piece of sorrow and dyspepsia," and flocked about Emerson himself, flocked about the gymnosophist, "sitting idle on a flowery bank." Carlyle had turned in his sleep, astonished, in his smoky Babylon, and reopened his Plato. Was there something in this gymnosophy, after all, this idleness, these azure dreams? Was there really something in the world besides "work" and "nigger-driving"? Too late, counsellor of empire-builders, too late!

But what was this on the parlour wall? Guido's

"Aurora," the good Carlyle's gift to the Concord household. What profound health these Hours had, how firmly they trod the clouds! Masculine force in every part of the picture, no convulsion, no foam, no ado; the most flowing grace and ease, like a strain of Mozart. A token of old friendship, the best of friendships, Carlyle's. And what did this letter say, this last letter from Chelsea, that, potatoes having vanished in England, they had tried American meal, "with considerable despair"? That it left a bitter taste in the mouth and made the throat smart?—a serious matter, since now their staff of life was Indian corn. How to cook mush rightly—that was the problem: and was there some pellicle or hull that ought to be rejected when the meal was made? A question for the Concord oracle! (To be sure, Carlyle, the corn is kiln-dried here, to keep it from becoming musty on the voyage, and this accounts for the bitterness. Try this barrel of cobs from the Concord barn! You will find them not only sweet, but with a touch even of the taste of nuts in them.)

A sample of New England, this virile New England which, like Greece, owed its power to the genius of its people. There was no prosperity here, no trade, no art, no city, but, if you traced it home, you found it rooted in the energy of some individual. Here was Henry Thoreau, for instance, like Indian corn himself, even to the taste of the nuts. Henry had taken charge of the house in the master's absence. He had had the same little room at the head of the stairs; and how the fruit-trees had thriven under his hands, and the tulips and the roses! And Edward, Edith and Ellen! No one could tell such stories as Henry—Homeric tales of battling ants and turtles, of squirrels, hawks and muskrats. He stirred up the fire at tea-time and made the corn pop in the old copper warming-pan. He fashioned pipes of grass, onion-tops, willow-shoots and the stalks of squash and pumpkin. Knives and pencils vanished mysteriously and issued again from Henry's nose and ear; and he took the children camping, took them out to the swamps where the high-bush blueberries grew. They scrambled up together to the top of Wachusett and set to work building a house of boughs, and Henry showed them how to cook and how to live on berries, beans and meal.

None so thoughtful as Henry, with such a conscience: he always did much more than he bargained to do. He had planted a pine wood on Emerson's knoll at Walden, where his bean-field used to be. A little brusque, pugnacious about trifles, a lover of contradiction: he would praise wild mountains for their domestic air, snow and ice for their warmth, wood-choppers for their urbanity and the wilderness for resembling Rome and Paris. He would come to the house and say with little preface what he had just observed, deliver it all in a lump, scowl at any comments and take himself off without another word. He was ill, at home again now; and Emerson sent him a bottle of wine. Had he opened it? Not Henry; and as for taking his arm,

Emerson would as soon have taken the arm of an elm-tree. Well said Mrs. Hoar, that he "talked about Nature just as if she had been born and brought up in Concord"; and Elizabeth, that she loved Henry but could never like him. He was the best of talkers, and one never had the least social pleasure in his company. But how sensitive he was, and how considerate!—just like his brother John. (For John had made a bluebird-box and set it up on the barn, a dozen years before. A melodious family had lived there ever since, singing John's praises.)

One could safely sail for England with such friends as these to defend the Concord household. Who cut this wood, for instance? Ellery Channing. And who built that great rustic Æolian harp up in the boughs of the tree? And that summer-house in the yard? Alcott, with Henry's help. An out-of-doors study, fashioned from limbs of pine, cedar trunks and gnarled branches of oak, gathered by Alcott in his perambulations in the woods—with even a second story. Henry had described it in one of his letters, had said that when he was driving the nails in the roof he felt as if he were "nowhere doing nothing." It was Alcott's idea, of course, and quite spontaneous—no mere work of the brain, no fruit of calculation—with the eaves curving upward to make it more beautiful and the roof lined with moss, in defiance of all the laws of gravity and decay. When it was almost finished, some one said, "It looks like a church"; so off came the Gothic porch. And the countless doors and windows, and the mosquitoes, made it useless for study. With prophetic eye Emerson's mother called it "The Ruin" on the very day it was finished.

But how like Alcott! Nothing could have been more pathetic than this wandering emperor making his round of visits from house to house of those who did not exclude him. What a difference a little success would have made with Alcott, and who deserved it more? His problem of earning a living accused all New England: a huge satire on the social order, the plight of this man, with his courtesy, his refinement, his unalterable sweetness. All other souls were slow and mechanical beside him. No one ever heard Alcott sharp or angry. No one ever heard him raise his voice to beat an opponent. He had no shop-condescensions that others stooped to; yet because he could not earn money by his pen or his talk, or by school-keeping or bookkeeping or editing, because he was ahead of his contemporaries, higher than they, he was condemned to die by the unanimous opinion of all New England judges. They did not condemn him to hemlock, or garroting—they were too hypocritical for that. But they doomed him just the same by refusing to protest against this doom, by not combining to save him and give him employment that would be fit for him and salutary to the State. They would certainly have heard of his death with pleasure and felt relieved that his board and clothes were saved. Alcott was much too good for their Beacon Street and Park Street, and their lawyers' offices and wharves and sterility and *leave-all-hope-behind!*

Too good for their boot-factories and bonnet-factories and pasteboard and eye-to-profit! Alcott, with his idleness and conversation, his "abandonment to the instincts" and his "rural affairs," his Cowley and Evelyn and Pythagoras! And his curved sticks, "every curve in the geometry of beauty." They said that all the young men who followed his influence were lost to popular success. No doubt, and so much the better.

As if beautiful manners were not as meritorious as hard work! And courage: who but Alcott was the first man to visit Garrison in the Leverett Street jail and renew his pledge on the day when *The Liberator* was mobbed! Trust Alcott to defy all Boston, with his cane in his hand—and the utmost philosophic composure. They called him shiftless, insensible to the primary claims of life. But his magnanimity was unparallelled among men of his class. A lover of truth, Alcott, to such a degree that he gladly heard his own from the lips of others. They wished to know if his coat was out at the elbow, or if somebody had not heard from somebody else that Alcott had a new hat, they for whom intellect was a sort of bill of exchange, easily convertible into fine chambers, wines and cigars! Let them sneer away, these clever souls, and assert their superiority; let them beat him down, he so childish and helpless, not apprehending or answering their remarks aright, they such masters of their weapons! But wait till Alcott recovered himself, recaptured his own thought. They would see him then, like an Indian, seizing by the mane and mounting a wild horse of the desert, and overriding them all!

Alcott was very different from the vulgar mono-maniacs of reform, Alcott with his wise love of all real facts, of street faces, and of the broad-shoul-dered farmer, the domestic woman, the kitchen, the season as related to man. No fine heroic action, no poetic passage made any impression on him, for he expected heroism and poetry in all. How could Boston understand him, with this want of eleva-tion, this absence of ideas, this sovereignty of the abdomen reducing everything to the same poor-ness? One fancied that in the houses of the rich, with the temptation to servility removed, there might be some generosity. But no, one sent these men to Congress and they originated nothing; whatever the question might be, they instantly ex-hibited the vulgarity of the lowest populace, a lack of all perception and natural equity. They had no opinions of their own; they cringed to their at-torneys who told them the opinion of the insur-ance-offices. As if one could have an aristocracy without real elevation of ideas! Alcott was too much for these people. To make anything of such a man, they would have had to find him in a book a thousand years old, with a legend of miracles appended.

The best of all company, this dervish by the river: none so exciting, he made one think so freely. And how young he was, for all his grey hairs—as Henry said, just on the threshold of life. Very few visitors ever saw him rightly, for Alcott was like a piece of Labrador spar, dull enough till you turned him to the angle where his colours appeared and he became a jewel; but then he seemed to take up all Time and Nature like a boy's marble in his hand. It was true, he was not exact, not severe with himself; if only he could have been locked up in prison and obliged to define his thought, to render a separate account of his memory and his fancy, his instinct, his analysis! Amusing was Henry's description of him, "rallying for another foray with his pen, in his latter years, not discouraged by the past, into that crowd of unexpressed ideas of his, that undisciplined Parthian army, which, as soon as a Roman soldier would face, retreats on all hands, occasionally firing backwards; easily routed, not easily subdued, hovering on the skirts of society." But his wit was deeper than the serpent's. They had laughed in the old days, those Boston wiseacres, when he made his refractory pupils punish *him*. But the method worked! They had laughed again at his trust in human nature when Alcott gave ten dollars to the confidence-man who had asked for five. But the confidence-man could not endure the strain—he sent the money back. One bitter winter night, when the Alcotts' pile of wood was almost exhausted and they had a baby in the house, a child came begging for fuel. "Give half our stock," said Alcott, "and trust in Providence." The next knock on the door that night was the lumberman's. He could not get to Boston for the drifting snow: would they take his load to oblige him and pay him later? Somehow, as Mrs. Alcott said,

the bread they cast upon the waters always came
back buttered.

Alcott was giving Conversations in Boston. His
subject was "The Times." He had forty or fifty
listeners, Garrison, Lowell and Emerson among
them. He began by reading aloud from Pythagoras. Sin, he said, was to be driven out by diet, and
then he developed another idea that was destined
to have a sturdy life in the future: the blonde and
blue-eyed type belonged to the nations of light, to
the realm of goodness, while those with dark eyes
and hair belonged to the night and evil. One evening, a dark, demoniac man remarked that the great
philosophers had taught standing. "I teach; I sit,"
said Alcott: men of the light, the angelic type,
always sat, when uttering their wisdom. When the
Conversation drifted too far away, Emerson would
come to the rescue; he called on the persons present
to express their feelings. And he would not allow
them to harass Alcott by asking for definitions. "If
this were a class on logic," he said, "and that were
the professor's chair, it would be another matter.
But in a free, general conversation, the object
rather is to draw forth remarks."

Emerson would have paid a regular tribute, if
need were, to keep such a royal family in the neighbourhood. (If only to share the expenses of their
own almoner's department. And people could say
what they liked about Alcott—he had always preferred himself a great tendency to a small revelation.) He helped them to buy their house; he paid
for his tickets in gold when Alcott gave one of his

Conversations; he would leave twenty-dollar bills under some book on the table, or behind a candlestick, when the grocer was pursuing them. (Confident that no one would notice it, except perhaps Louisa: they were too much in the habit of carrying their breakfast or their dinner to other families.) It was useless to put money into Alcott's hand: he would only come back smiling from Boston with a huge box of sumptuous writing-paper. But no sight was more reassuring than Alcott in his orchard, so tall, so benign, laughing away so merrily, with his bright, eager glance, piling his russet apples. Adam on the sixth day, with the world all before him where to choose!

One member of the old Concord circle had vanished forever. Margaret Fuller was dead, drowned at Fire Island, and Henry had hastened down, on behalf of them all, to recover the remains. Emerson joined with James Freeman Clarke and William Henry Channing in writing a Memoir: Margaret and her friends, he thought, were an indispensable line in American history, and he wanted to leave some record of his gratitude to that eloquent, constant soul with whom he had shared so many high adventures. He read her faded letters, he plunged into the past and recovered and lived again the glowing days of *The Dial*. Spontaneous, genuine, solitary thought: that was the note of the young in those years of discovery. Margaret's note, above all; and in her Emerson felt he had lost his audience.

Sarah Ripley at the Manse could never take her

place; but a wonderful person this Mrs. Ripley was, Aunt Mary's old friend, George Bradford's sister and the widow of Emerson's uncle, Samuel Ripley of Waltham. The best classical scholar in Concord and one of the best in America, but the last to display her learning or to seek praise or influence. Tall and spare, with her clear blue eyes and her radiant, serene expression, with her plain black robe and her silvery hair, the mistress of six sciences and five languages, the mother of nine children, she was always the centre of interest whenever she appeared in company.

She was Emerson's oldest friend. She had supervised the studies of his boyhood, urged him to correspond with her in Greek, excited his pleasure in Virgil, Rollin, Tacitus, for Sarah's love of learning in those early days was unique even in Boston. She was so "indifferent to trifles" that once, to try her, Mary Emerson had placed a broom in her hand and bidden her carry it through the streets to her lodgings. Sarah had carried the broom across the Common as far as Hancock Street, "without hesitation or remark." As a schoolmaster's wife in Waltham, handsome, gay and burning with enthusiasm, she had taught the boys their Greek and differential calculus, washed, ironed, made the clothes for her children, and the hired man as well, laboured away at Klopstock, chemistry, botany, and "broken Morpheus's head with Italian dramas"—surrounded the while with "cribs, cradles, guards, dolls and playthings."

She had travelled once as far as Waterford,

Maine, and once to New York, where she saw
Lafayette. But she had the world within her when
at last she came to Concord, and her books and
Nature were joys that never grew stale. At the
Manse she rose at half-past five to get breakfast for
her daughter, who went off to Boston to school.
Then she passed the morning in the garden, gathering and preparing the vegetables and making
clothes, learning Spanish in the meantime, reading Darwin, or sitting with a friend in her little
sunny parlour, darning and talking of the flowers.
She spent every Sunday evening at Emerson's, with
Elizabeth Hoar and Alcott, perhaps, or Henry;
and she was charming then, so buoyant and responsive, with her quick movements and her constant
play of expression, as she glanced from speaker to
speaker.

Margaret was dead, but Concord had secrets of
self-renewal. And Henry and Ellery Channing
were fountains of life. A perfect companion,
Ellery, for a ramble to White Pond, that pretty
little Indian basin where Emerson could almost see
the sachem canoeing in a shadowy cove; or to
Flint's Pond, perhaps, or Nine Acre Corner.
Sometimes Henry joined them, and then the blue-
bird's warble and the murmur of the brook would
be drowned in the play of their talk: strokes of wit,
tags of rhyme, and the Latin names of the flowers,
for Linnæus too was one of the gods of Concord.
They thought of those "herborizations" at Up-
sala, when the master summoned his class for an
excursion into the country and they gathered plants

and insects, birds and eggs, and returned in the
evening, marching through the streets of the town
with flowers in their hats, to the sound of drums
and trumpets. Less pomp attended their own perambulations, but they were not less joyous. They
lingered over every pool by the roadside, stopped
to examine the buds of the marsh-marigold, tossed
stones into the river and watched the circles and
dimples and lovely gleaming motions of the water,
for time meant as little to them as it meant to old
weather-beaten Goodwin, fishing from sun-up to
dusk on the bank. They discussed the labours of
the farmers whose fields they passed, and the religion of the Indians, so much clearer and fresher,
as Henry said, than the desiccated theologies of the
paleface, and Shakespeare and Carlyle, Ebenezer
Hubbard's pears and the architecture of Palladio,
while Ellery's dog Peter, with his cheerful tail,
capered through hedge and bush. Nor was the day
complete till they had stripped and had their swim,
now on the leafy little beach at Fairhaven Bay, now
from some willowy ledge at Walden.

For a longer journey, to Sudbury, for instance,
they could set out in Emerson's Jersey wagon, stopping wherever they chose: the good mare Dolly
could be trusted to stand patiently for half a day
at a tree while they roamed about in the woods and
pastures. There was nothing like Sudbury meadows on a sunny morning to remind one of Izaak
Walton's gentle Lea. The mere sight of Sam
Haynes, fishing at the mouth of the Pantry Brook,
was enough to set the rhymes running in one's head,

rhymes as sweet as Carew's or Suckling's, sweet as the notes of the redwings and bobolinks that flitted over the fragrant marsh. From afar came the faint sound of the bells of Framingham. They pushed on to the hill for a glimpse of Marlboro. What a spectacle of rustic plenty and comfort, what ample farms, what mountains of pumpkins, what spacious houses, with squashes ripening between their Grecian columns! Gates's, where Dr. Channing used to retreat, was no longer an inn; but they could picnic in the chestnut grove.

Now their goal was the Three Friends' Hill overlooking Concord, when the odour of grapes filled the breeze and the freedom of an orchard was dearer far than the freedom of all the Romes. Now it was the Goose-shore swimming-place on the Assabet, or Baker's Farm, that sumptuous park —if only its owner had known his wealth!—with lawns and slopes and terraces like another Lord Breadalbane's; or Conantum, named by Ellery from its ancient master, Eben Conant, a noble seigniory fit for some Yankee Montaigne. Shakespeare himself had not sung a lovelier prospect, and what bard was to save this present beauty from oblivion? If Ellery could only have written as he talked, if, writing, he had not been so shamelessly indolent and slovenly, New England would have had its Virgil, for his mere presence turned the day into the most melodious of eclogues.

An art, walking, like any other, with strict qualifications: endurance, plain clothes, old shoes, an eye for Nature, good humour, curiosity, good speech, good silence and nothing too much. No loud singing, no story-telling, no vain words (Emerson said to himself) profaning the river and the forest. With a loved and honoured companion his sentiments appeared as new and astonishing as the lightning out of the sky: every thought rushed to light, rushed to body, and society was already revolutionized. With Alcott alone he never got very far, for Alcott would stop at the first fence and soon propose to sit down or stroll home again. He believed the world existed for talk alone, though he listened as well as he talked: he was always ready to stretch out on the bank at Walden while Emerson read aloud from the proofs of his new book. With Henry walking was another matter. No graceful idling then, but a strenuous chase, for walking was Henry's work. One stepped along more quickly, submitting to one's guide; and the tempo of one's talk, so often languid, soon grew as brisk as the biting autumn air. Even when Henry stopped to study some plant by the pathside one felt the relentless ticking of his brain. Always in action, that brain, hard, precise, clear as a clock.

Ellery too was hard, hard and cool, and Emerson liked him for it, he who liked dry light and hard clouds, hard manners and hard expressions. But Ellery could melt as well and waken to the most genial mirth. He was full of amusing notions. He suggested setting up in every village a magnified dollar as big as a barrel-head, made of silver or gold. Let Colonel Shattuck, he said, or some other priest be appointed to guard it; they would then have a local deity and could bring it baked beans and other offerings and perform rites before it. "If a girl is mad to marry," he remarked again, "let her take a ride of ten miles and see meadows and mountains she never saw before, two villages and an old mansion-house, and the odds are it will change all her resolutions. The world is full of fools who get a-going and never stop: set them off on another tack, and they are half cured." He was always laughing at the villagers and their stodgy ways, the passengers on the train squeezing their bundles and the member of the Legislature hastening to drain the last drop of gossip from the trumpery newspaper before he left the car to fodder and milk his kine. And he railed at Concord, he said he would rather have settled on the icy peak of Mount Ararat: it was absolutely the worst spot in the world. ("Think of the climate of Venice," he lamented, "of Cuba, the Azores, Malaga"—there was scarcely a field in Concord he had not watered with his tears.) Then he talked about landscape painting, the only art that was worth a moment's attention. He had much to say of the abundance of lemon-yellow in Nature, in the cistus, the potentilla, the yellow star of Bethlehem. (And what chemist was it?—M. Bouvières—who had spent his whole life producing a yellow pigment.)

So Ellery sauntered along, squandering his jewels as if they were so many icicles, sometimes not comprehended, sometimes not even heard. He was airy and capricious as the spring breeze.

Henry was bleak beside him, bleak as frosty November. (But what a tonic! Even his captious paradoxes kept Emerson's wits in motion. Was he rather inclined to dream and drift? Henry, with a volley of facts, brought him back to the earth.) As they lingered beside some spring, Henry would take out his notebook and scribble away, with a mind fixed upon what he called the particular and the definite. Then Ellery followed suit and tried to recall his impressions, but all in vain. He soon slipped the notebook into his pocket, or scrawled some sketch on the broken page, or contented himself with a few "ideal remarks."

He complained that Emerson was never in the least contented. "When am I going to be perfect? When is the really good rhyme going to be written?" That was the Emerson colic, the terrible Gorgon-face of the future that turned the present into a "thousand belly-aches." (Henry, he said, suffered from a like disease.) It was only because Emerson tried to induce him to work over his poetry. (Come, Ellery, it's not a question of French correctness. Hans Sachs and Chaucer, rather. No occasional delicacy of expression or music of rhythm can atone for stupidities. You bring me lame verses, false rhymes, absurd images. You are simply indulging yourself. Collins would have cut his hand off rather than leave, from a weak self-esteem, a shabby line in his ode.)

Think of a man with such lordly self-repose, such tenderness and fine perceptions, yes, and such

greatness of meaning, think of a poet capable of a
line like this—

> If my bark sinks, 'tis to another sea—

satisfied with warbling like a vireo that whistles
all day long in the elm and never sounds a tune!
Urgent, fiery glances, poetry like an exquisite nerve
communicating by thrills, but nothing finished—
threads of gold in a mass of the merest ore. But
Ellery despised art; he even sneered at Goethe,
thought him dubious, thought Sam Ward was not
quite in his senses because he seemed to value his
prints from Giotto. ("These idle gentlemen," said
Ellery.) In vain Emerson replied that Michael
Angelo, Ribera, Phidias, the sculptors of the Par-
thenon reliefs, had a drastic style that was starker
than a blacksmith's. In vain he said there was a
pleasure from works of art which nothing else
could yield. In vain, that Goethe was the pivotal
man of the old and the new times, that those who
had not read Goethe were old fogies and belonged
with the antediluvians. Even Henry talked this
way: when any one spoke of art he would blot a
paper with ink, then double it over and defy the
greatest artist to surpass his effect. (The least said
about art was too much for him and the Hotten-
tots!) But one easily forgave Henry: he wrote, at
least, like a Trojan. Ellery was obdurate. "I am
sorry, but it stands so written."—"But you can
alter it."—"Not one letter," replied the hardened
bard.

How Emerson loved rhyme, not tinkling rhyme but grand Pindaric strokes, firm as the tread of a horse! Rhyme that suggested not restraint but the wildest freedom. He loved it constitutionally, as he loved the Æolian harp he had placed in his study window, as he delighted in that new-found musical instrument, his ice-harp at Walden. He would stand, on a winter's day, on the edge of the frozen pond and for twenty minutes at a time throw stones across this crystal drum. What a charming sound as they fell and fell again, repeating the note with just the right modulation! That was a kind of rhyme, like the repetition of the parts in a colonnade, in the windows or the wings of a building, in gardens with symmetrical beds and walks. The return of the steps in the dance, the dance of the spheres!

It always put him in tune. His blood, at the sound of rhyme, seemed to beat with the pulse of Nature. And metre, too. As he paced along the road, twirling his stick, he loved to recite some ballad. Was it plaintive, heroic, pathetic? His mood changed with the measure: in an hour's time he passed up and down the whole gamut of human emotions. Now and again he amused himself by humming the rhythm of the common English metres, and his mind began to search for the words to fill these vacant beats. Not the poor purposeless words of the literary poets. Words like those of the old bards, indemnifying, deifying, imparadising.

For poetry had always been his secret ambition.

As a boy at school and college he had written countless verses: a short epic, *Fortus,* ballads in the manner of Campbell, a poem on astronomy, didactic odes. He even felt that poetry, could he but compass it, was the right form for his most cherished thoughts. He toiled over his verses as he toiled over nothing else. "A poem," he wrote in his journal, "should be a blade of Damascus steel, made up of a mass of knife-blades and nails, and parts every one of which has had its whole surface hammered and wrought before it is welded into the sword, to be wrought over anew." He thought of himself as "a bard least of bards," but he sent poems to his friends who were publishing magazines, Furness, for one, the editor of *The Diadem*; and in 1847 he published a volume at his own expense. Here were "The Sphinx" and "Saadi," "Uriel," "Woodnotes," sixty pieces or more, the fruit of twenty years of loving labour.

He had gradually developed a style that was all his own. A nervous, intellectual style, swift, clear and cold as a mountain stream. It was lean and spare as his own frame, quick as the steps of his feet as he swung along, lean and quick and as thrilling as the wind, the flight of the darting woodbird or the note of the locust winding off his wiry coil of song. Not sunlight but starlight, as Carlyle described it, rarefied and remote, yet expressing what felicity in the constitution of things! Were these verses dry and hard, composed of disparate elements, these verses that unveiled the soul of a

man, austere, calm and happy, for whom life was
a long revelation of occult harmonies? They
burned here and there with an inward ecstasy—
with lines too that flashed across the mind like
meteors in space.

For Saadi sat in the sun in the joy of an endless
present. And for him the front of heaven was filled
with fiery shapes.

CHAPTER XVII

CHANG TSOO and Kee Neih retired from the State to the fields because of misrule, and they showed their displeasure at Confucius who remained in the world. Confucius sighed and said, "I can not associate with birds and beasts. If I follow not man, whom shall I follow? If the world were in possession of right principles, I should not seek to change it."

How else could Emerson reply—in the privacy of his journal—when Thoreau and Ellery Channing, not to mention Alcott, took him to task for gadding about the country? He might have remarked that Pythagoras wandered, too; he might have added, with Hobbes, that in the country "one's understanding and invention contract a moss on them, like an old paling in an orchard." Instead, he spoke of his debts. "Look in my pocket, Ellery," he said on one occasion. "Three cents and a counterfeit half-dollar."

To the road, the Lyceums again! He had no alternative. So off he went, whisked away by the stormy wing of Fate and whirled like a dry leaf across the continent.

It was none too pleasant, this junketing, this wading, riding, running and suffering all manner of bumps and bruises. None too pleasant, for a decor-

ous New Englander, dragged out of house and
position for this juvenile career, carted about the
country at the tail of a discourse, to read it over
and over. (Sleeping in railroad stations and hotels
where the very air was buttered and the whole atmosphere a volatilized beefsteak.) None too pleasant, for the "Celebrated Metaphysician," as one of
the papers called him, this tumbling about in close,
dirty cars, this getting to bed at midnight in a
freezing room, getting up at five and breakfasting
off half-washed crockery, on cold fried fish and
potatoes swimming in fat.... "I'll bet you fifty dollars a day you will never leave your library and put
up with all these miseries!" ... "I'll bet I will, and
win the nine hundred dollars!"

A ridiculous vice of men, forever consulting
their dignity! They couldn't go into the quarrel,
they couldn't go into the tavern, because they were
old; or into the Abolition meeting and attempt to
make a speech—it would never do if they failed!
For himself, he looked at the wise and saw he was
very young; he looked at the stars, he thought of the
myriads of aspirant souls, and he saw he was a
stranger and a youth and had yet his spurs to
win. Absurd, these airs of age! *Ancora imparo*. He
carried his satchel still.

Like a poet, yes—no dainty, protected person,
apart and odd. A traveller on the common high-
way, a frequenter of taverns, very naturally and
heartily there. A student of botany who had learned
that a tree draws only one-twentieth of its nourishment from the ground, that it drinks in the rest

through its leaves from the outer air. A merchant of the simples and herbs of wisdom, of the laws of Plato and Buddha, who had found that if he mixed them with a little Boston water he could sell them in New York and Ohio. An economist who had discovered that the more he spent the more he had to spend, that when he communicated all the results of his thinking he was full of new thoughts. He raked the bright atoms of perception faster together by quitting his fireside and sallying out in pursuit of them. Besides, it was always an incentive to be obliged to prove his quality all over again with every stranger he met.

He learned the resources of the country. He encountered the revolutionary force in the most unlikely corners. Very young in their education were those who required distinguished men in order to see grand traits: he found them in porters and sweeps. All sorts of surprising souls turned up at his lectures: that poor Platonist Taylor, for instance, at Amesbury, and the shoemaker at Berwick, Maine, and Tufts at Lima, New York. And Thomas Truesdale, the Wall Street cotton-broker, and Rebecca Black, the seamstress, Hermann who made the toys and Edward Stubler, the druggist in Alexandria. What natural clearness of insight these people had and how they confirmed his faith in human nature! (Was that old Quaker surprised that he thought her worthy of notice? But if she had said Yea, and the world had thundered Nay, she would still have said her Yea!) It was true that man was an angel in disguise, a god playing the fool, that he wanted to be awakened, to get his soul out of bed, to be stirred from his deep habitual sleep to a sense of his own power to shake the world. He wanted to be awakened, that prosy, selfish sensualist, and who was able to do it better than Emerson himself? As a magnet separates the particles of steel in a heap of filings and rubbish, so in the minds of his listeners he separated all that was active, creative and fine from the slothful remainder. Life, at the sound of his voice, sprang out of apathy, and faith out of unbelief.

Who could resist that voice, with its wild, strange melody, with its intonations and cadences as of some Hungarian dance? Or that speaker, motionless on the platform, save for an occasional thrust of his right hand, clenched with the fingers upward? (Straight and thin as a birch-tree in winter, with his hatchet face, half Indian, half the face of an eagle, peering, peering.) His voice, one listener observed, seemed to have no connection with the physical man. It had shoulders in it which he had not, lungs far larger than his, a walk the public never saw, a fist for which his own hand never gave him the model.

He was travelling westward now, each year farther and farther. St. Louis, Springfield, Milwaukee. He was going to school to the prairies, where it rained and thawed incessantly and he stepped off the newly paved streets and was up to his shoulders in mud. Well he knew the bitter evenings, the "singers," of Illinois, when the mercury stood at 28 below zero and the landlord merrily said they had no cold weather in those regions, only Indian summer occasionally and coolish nights. He slept on the floors of canal-boats, wrapped in a buffalo-robe, in a wreath of legs, and drove in buggies across the plains fifty miles in the icy wind. And many a time he saw the waves of Lake Michigan tossing in a bleak snowstorm.

The world out there, as the settler said, was "done up in larger lots." The talk was all of sections and quarter-sections (of swamp and forest); there were placards in the hotels pleading against the fury of expectoration and saying that no gentleman could come to the public table without his coat; and he didn't need to discover that in all he called cultivation these kindly, sinewy farmers were only ten years old. How could he be surprised when the stout Illinoisan, after giving him a ten-minutes' trial, stamped out of the hall? He was more the student than the teacher in this land of wonders, where the prairie grass at La Salle was higher than the top of his carriage, higher than the head of a man riding on horseback. He had always delighted in men who could "do" things, men of the drastic class, and the Western farmers had drawn from their local necessities what stores of heroic energy! They lived on venison and quails like children of Homer.

He encountered again those men who were natural founders of cities, sensible, steady, wise and prompt in action. And towns and towns, solid and stately squares turned out as if by machinery, like cloth and hardware. And countless other marvels, inanimate marvels, unfused as yet with the electric will of man. Interminable silent forests, the raw bullion of Nature. Miles of acres at Pittsburgh, each with three or four bottoms, rich soil, bituminous coal, iron, salt (almost as many bottoms as the human soul). And the Mammoth Cave in Kentucky, where he lost the light of day, where he walked under mimic stars and sailed on Stygian streams, eighteen miles in the darkness. And relics of a fathomless past. A mass of copper, unearthed near Lake Superior (six tons? or twenty-three?), standing on end, on wedges, with a wooden bowl beside it, and axes and chisels of stone (and trees that had grown above it since it was lifted, with three hundred and ninety rings). And what strange confirmations of his reading! He happened to be glancing through Tacitus' *De Germaniis,* in Missouri and Illinois, and he noted all sorts of resemblances between the Germans of the Hercynian forest and these Hoosiers, Suckers and Badgers of the American woods.

He always enjoyed his adventures in Horace Greeley's country. (For Horace was the spiritual father of all these regions. What bales of *Tribunes* were dispersed there every day! Horace did everyone's thinking for two dollars a year.) He liked to get away from the Eastern seaboard, from Boston, Cambridge, New York, where the current of American life was so superficial. The nervous, rocky West was intruding a new and continental element into the national mind: out there the passion for Europe had yielded to the passion for

America, and he seemed to discern the dawn of a native genius. It was true that he saw little more than a certain maniacal activity—no intellectual power; true that the mass of the people had only arrived at a kind of slovenly plenty, an unbuttoned comfort, not clean, not greatly thoughtful, without dignity in its repose. Yet he couldn't but feel that all these buffalo-hunters, these rough-riders, these legislators in shirt-sleeves, were better than the Whigs at home. Wild liberty in the end bred iron conscience; and sooner or later the managing of the public lands and all the gigantic tasks that lay before them would bestow on the pioneers promptness, address and reason, authority, the majesty of manners.

For the rest, what strange people he was always meeting, each with a new horizon! That old sharper, for instance, who said his conscience was as good as ever it was: he had "never used it any." And Bassnett in Illinois who gave him his book, *Outlines of a Mechanical Theory of Storms.* (Not sound, of course, but it seemed to break a new path in science.) And Sylvester Judd, of Yale, the author of *Margaret,* who had drifted away from home and was living on "sunsets." (He said he was a minister and talked with the sick and dying. All very well, replied Emerson, if people were sick and died to any purpose; but, as far as he had observed, they were quite as frivolous as the rest, and a man peremptorily needed other companions.)

He signalized each journey by putting in his bag some Latin, French or Italian book he had al-

ways wanted to read, Martial, the *Vita Nuova,*
Beaumarchais; for classics, dull at home as they
often seemed, had a singular charm on the train.
(What genial, miraculous force he had known to
proceed from a book! When all things seemed most
sterile he would take up Plutarch or Augustine,
and read a few pages, and lo! the air swam again
with life. Homer, Plutarch, Plato, Shakespeare,
Jonson. These mighty painters of grand and heroic
behaviour were his friends and daily companions.
Was the real world about him painfully trivial,
were his actual friends so congenial to his emptiest
moods that their influence was noxious? Then he
passed in fancy into this world of words and found
himself expanding to his proper dimensions. They
were two-lived, these heroes: they lived again in
the fact that he felt their life. Books: were they
grand and tonic, did they speak of happy leisure,
of courage, vigour, cheer? Books: were they sper-
matic? In books he traversed the universe with
Vishnu, planting his foot three times—and the
whole world was collected in the dust of his foot-
step. He mounted the tripod over the cave at
Delphi. He rode on the horse of the Cid, who had
never been conquered.)

And the railroad pleased him too. Highly poetic,
this strong shuttle, shooting through forest, swamp,
river and arms of the sea, binding city to city!

CHAPTER XVIII

1850. The Fugitive Slave Law had passed both houses of Congress. Emerson awoke each morning with a painful sensation. He carried it about all day. It robbed the landscape of its beauty and took the sunshine out of every hour.

He had lived all his life in Massachusetts and had never had to submit to any check on his free speech and action. But now, at any moment he might be summoned to report and return to bondage a fugitive slave. *He* might be summoned, a citizen of Massachusetts! Then one thing was certain: everything he had, everything he could do would be given and done to defy the will of the State.

Odious news in each morning's paper. A crime to harbour a slave! Then Henry Thoreau was a criminal, and Mrs. Thoreau, and Edwin Bigelow, the blacksmith—criminals for breaking a law that no man could obey without loss of self-respect! He longed for nine lives to spend them all in breaking it himself. Boston, spoiled by prosperity, had bowed its ancient honour in the dust. The city and the suburbs were all involved in one hot haste of terror —presidents of colleges, professors, ministers, brokers: not a liberal recollection, not so much as a snatch of an old song for freedom, intruded on their

passive obedience. Webster himself had fallen—
the life and soul of the Law—and carried New
England with him.

It was time for Emerson to throw himself into
the cause, this cause of anti-slavery. He had often
awakened at night and reproached himself for not
having done so earlier. But then, he had said to
himself, he had very different slaves to free
than the negroes—imprisoned spirits, imprisoned
thoughts, far back in the brain of man, that had
no defender but himself. Had not John Randolph
said, and wasn't it true?—"We do not govern the
people of the North by our black slaves but by
their own white slaves." These white slaves, yes—
they were his proper concern: ignorance, barbar-
ity, prejudice. The one thing not to be condoned in
intellectual men was not to know their own task,
or to take their ideas from others: and how easily
their minds were destroyed by a dissipated philan-
thropy! From this want of rest in their own and
rash acceptance of other people's watchwords came
the imbecility and fatigue of their conversation.
For they could not affirm these watchwords from
any original experience, from the natural movement and strength of their own souls.

This question had often recurred in his dealings
with the reformers. As often the answer had come:
his business was to insist on central soundness, not
superficial applications. "Go love thy infant, love
thy woodchopper," he had felt like saying to the
Abolition bigots, "and never varnish your hard,
uncharitable ambition with this incredible tender-

ness for black folk a thousand miles off." But often his faith had been shaken: often he had broken his rule, on the impulse of the moment, or on some occasion of unusual provocation. There had never been any doubt where his sympathies lay. As a minister, in the old days, he had admitted a speaker against slavery into his pulpit. In a lecture in Boston he had spoken of the heroism of Lovejoy, the anti-slavery martyr of Illinois, while a "cold shudder," as one listener said, "ran through the audience at this braving of the current opinion." Then in 1837 he had spoken on slavery in Concord, to protest against the attempts to stifle freedom of speech. Every church in Boston but one, and almost every hall, was closed to the Abolitionists: and even in Concord he could not find room till the Second Church allowed him the use of its vestry. When all said, Hush! he could only say, Proclaim! He could only insist on the sacred duty of New England to maintain free discussion of every question involving the rights of man.

But slavery had never aroused him half so much as President Van Buren's removal of the Cherokees. In 1838 this whole nation of eighteen thousand souls was driven away from its lands in Georgia, put into carts and boats and dragged over mountains and rivers to a wilderness beyond the Mississippi—dragged from its fields and villages, thanks to a sham treaty signed by a handful of traitors. All but a few had protested, "This is not our act." And yet the Government had ratified the error. Emerson had always loved the Indians; he had heard of the worth and civility of the Cherokees; he knew their social arts. And the truth was out that the whites had broken faith with their allies and wards, a crime that simply confounded his understanding. Could he pass unnoticed this outrage on human nature? (Would the American Government lie? Would it steal? Would it kill?) He had written a letter to the President, for his days and nights were blackened by the news.

So far as the negroes were concerned, he had never accepted the complacent view of Boston that slavery was a part of the natural order of the world. He had never forgotten how, as a young theological student, he had visited a meeting of the Bible Society of St. Augustine while a slave auction was going on outside. The cry of "Going, gentlemen, going!" had come through the windows and mingled with the pious exhortations of the chairman: and with one breath he might have bidden for "four children without the mother" and aided in sending the Scriptures to the continent from which they had been kidnapped. He had not forgotten the manners of the Southern negroes. How much richer their nature was than that of the Yankees!—a wild cedar swamp, luxuriant with all vegetation of grass and moss and ferns, with rains and sunshine, mists and moonlight, birds and insects filling its wilderness with life and promise. Gentle and joyous themselves, they seemed to make the greatest amount of happiness out of the smallest capital. The negro's hour was coming, and the Abolitionist was logically right. But his own quarrel was not with the state of affairs. No: with the state of man.

But his feelings had gradually changed. The mind of the country was poisoned. Choate was publicly saying that "the stern old Puritans of 1620 would have spurned the rose-pink sentimentalism of resisting the Fugitive Slave Law." Seward's "Higher Law than the Constitution" had become a national joke; and a Western man in Congress spoke of the opponents of the Texan and Mexican plunder as "every light character in the House." Scholars, writers, leaders of opinion, terrified by the thought of disrupting the Union, were ready to accept any demand of the South; and New England had become the vassal of South Carolina. The refugee, whom the fame of Boston had reached in the depths of some Southern swamp, arrived there only to find that all the force of the State was employed to catch him: the famous town of Boston was his master's hound. More intolerable still, free negroes of Massachusetts were enslaved at Southern ports; and Samuel Hoar, who had gone to Charleston to protest against this infamy, had been driven out by a mob. If Massachusetts could no longer protect its own, then, Emerson said to himself, let the Governor break the broad seal of the State.

What turned the tide in his mind was the defection of Webster. Could he ever undo the mischief this leader he had so revered had wrought in the minds of his countrymen? Webster had gathered up in himself the opinions and wishes of the people. He turned this way or that, and the nation followed him; and now he had renounced, Emerson thought, all the great passages of his career. His speeches denouncing slavery, his speech against Hayne and Southern aggression, his eulogy of Adams for resisting the encroachments of the South, his speeches and writings in behalf of Hungarian liberty—what were they worth on the day when he surrendered the natural rights of every American? He had gone over in an hour to the party of force. He had made the country a jail for the slaves of the Southern planters. The fairest American fame had ended in this filthy Law.

The "solid portion of the community," in Emerson's eyes, had begun to look like sharpers and beasts of prey. He could understand at last Garrison's reply when some one urged him to keep cool, saying he was all on fire: "I have need to be all on fire, for I have mountains of ice about me to melt." He set to work to prepare for a campaign. He had a den built in his attic for any fugitive slave who happened to be passing through Concord. His mare and his covered wagon were always ready to drive a slave to South Acton to meet the train for Canada. He began to collect material for a History of Liberty. He pored over Cicero, Grotius, Coke and Blackstone to be able to quote the masters of jurisprudence as affirming that no law had any validity that was contrary to the law of Nature. Moncure Conway, a young Virginian minister, was visiting Concord at the time. He had left the South and his own inheritance of slaves and had lost pulpits in Washington and Cincinnati through his anti-slavery opinions; and he gave Emerson a number of practical arguments on the effect that emancipation would have in the South. Never before had Emerson resorted to argument, but all his mental habits were changing now. He was going to fire a gun for every one of the hundred that Boston had fired to celebrate the passing of the Law.

So Emerson "came out" in 1851. He spoke in Boston, Cambridge, at the country Lyceums. Volleys of hisses and catcalls drowned his words, but he stood quietly and waited for the noise to cease, then continued with perfect composure. He quoted Blackstone to the judges; he attacked the tameness of Boston. Of Webster he said: "He must learn that those who make fame accuse him with one voice, that he who was their pride in the woods and mountains of New England is now their mortification,—they have torn down his picture from the wall, they have thrust his speeches into the chimney. No roars of New York mobs can drown this voice in Mr. Webster's ear. It will outwhisper all the salvos of the Union Committee's cannon. . . . All the drops of his blood have eyes that look downward."

The Law itself, he said, was one that every man should break at every hazard. It was contravened by the sentiment of duty, by the sentiments of pity and charity, by the written laws themselves, for the sentiments wrote the statutes. And Massachusetts would have to take the lead. "Massachusetts is a little state: countries have been great by ideas.

Europe is little compared with Asia and Africa: yet Asia and Africa are its ox and its ass. Europe, the least of all the continents, has almost monopolized for twenty centuries the genius and power of them all. Greece was the least part of Europe, Attica a little part of that—one-tenth of the size of Massachusetts. Yet that district still rules the intellect of men. Judea was a petty country. Yet these two, Greece and Judea, furnished the mind and heart by which the rest of the world is sustained: and Massachusetts is little, but, if true to itself, can be the brain which turns about the behemoth."

During the ten years that followed, till the Civil War broke out, Emerson constantly spoke on subjects connected with slavery. His proposal was to free the slaves by purchase, the method the British had followed in the West Indies. He spoke of the assault on Sumner—"that noble head, so comely and so wise, the target for a pair of bullies to beat with clubs." Then in 1856, in a speech on "Affairs in Kansas," he prophesied the outcome of all these calamities. "The hour is coming when the strongest will not be strong enough. A harder task will the new revolution of the Nineteenth Century be, than was the revolution of the Eighteenth Century. I think the American Revolution bought its glory cheap. If the problem was new, it was simple. . . . But now vast property, gigantic interests, family connections, webs of party, cover the land with a network that immensely multiplies the dangers of war. . . . I wish we could send the sergeant-at-arms to stop every American who is about to leave the country. Send home every one who is abroad, lest they should find no country to return to. Come home and stay at home while there is a country to save. When it is lost it will be time enough then for any who are luckless enough to remain alive to gather up their clothes and depart to some land where freedom exists."

Three years later, in 1859, John Brown was hanged in Virginia. It was a sultry day in Concord, with heavy clouds and a wind blowing from the South. At noon, at the hour of the old man's death, his friends gathered at the Town Hall. Alcott was there, and Ellery Channing, who read aloud Raleigh's "The Soul's Errand." Emerson read a poem by William Allingham and made a little speech. Then the company sang a funeral hymn composed by the new schoolmaster, Frank Sanborn.

For John Brown had many lovers in Concord. He had twice visited the town as Frank Sanborn's guest: the last time, in fact, he had set out directly thence for Harper's Ferry. Twice he had spoken at the Town Hall. Standing on the platform, he had shaken the very chain worn by one of his sons who had been taken prisoner and tortured by the champions of slavery. And he slept, the last night, with a big knife by his side and a pistol under his pillow.

He spent an evening at Emerson's house and told again the story of his adventures. A Western Cid, Emerson thought him, a border hero whom Scott would have loved to paint, with his weather-beaten face, his wild eyes and the black leather stock that he wore about his neck. He said that as a boy of twelve he had conducted alone a drove of cattle one hundred miles across the plains of Ohio. He could instantly detect a strange sheep in his flock of three thousand; he could read the signals by which animals communicate with one another; he slept on his horse as readily as in his bed. He had the senses of an Indian and the faith of a Hebrew prophet; and to Emerson he seemed a figure out of some primitive epic.

Emerson knew nothing in advance of the Harper's Ferry project; but for him it was enough, when Brown was finally condemned, that no motive of spite or revenge had determined the undertaking. Brown was a lion to the last. "There is somewhat not philosophical in heroism; there is somewhat not holy in it," he had written once. "It seems not to know that other souls are of one texture with it; it has pride; it is the extreme of individual nature. Nevertheless, we must profoundly revere it. There is somewhat in great actions, which does not allow us to go behind them. Heroism feels and never reasons, and therefore is always right. . . . For the hero that thing he does is the highest deed, and it is not open to the censure of philosophers or divines." John Brown was another witness to the truth of Emerson's thought.

CHAPTER XIX

TO-DAY the carpets had to be cleaned. Yesterday came the cousins. The day before was the funeral of poor S——. And every day Emerson remembered the rope of work he had to spin. He tried to listen to the hymn of the gods and he heard this perpetual *cock-a-doodle-doo,* right under the library windows. The gods, he said to himself, should respect a life whose objects were their own. And they rolled him in the dust and jumped upon him!

Still they came, the visitors. Pale, withered people with gold-filled teeth and minds in the same dilapidated condition, drugged with books for want of wisdom. Exaggerating people who talked of "moments when their brain seemed bursting with the multitude of thoughts." (As if there were any danger!) People like those boys who watch for a sleigh-ride and mount on the first sleigh that passes, then swing to another and ride in another direction, not caring where they go so long as there is snow and company. Ladies who said that they were going to die, when all they meant was that they wanted a nap. Insane people who bit you and made you run mad also. Familiar people, with no deference, no pleasure in keeping the island of the man inviolate. And everybody, old men, young women, boys, played the doctor with Emerson and prescribed for him.

Those unfortunate days of August and September! When the two cows were due from New Hampshire and he learned that they had strayed on the way and were lost. When the annual muster approached, bringing alarms to all housekeepers and orchard-owners. When he had sprained his ankle and his hands were palsied from the crutches. When a strong southwest wind blew all day, stripping every loaded pear-tree of its fruit, just six weeks too early. (And this year he had really hoped to win the prize at the Cattle Show!) When a letter arrived saying that his publishers were about to fail. These were the happy days for Mr. Crump! The Monumentals came, in landaus and barouches, wishing his large aid in behalf of Mount Vernon, or of Ball's statue of Webster, or President Quincy in marble: and the agent-lady from the Cape who had three blind sisters (and several dumb ones) and had been advised to put them in the poorhouse. (Never!—so long as she could peddle books and demand praise and tears for her resolution.)

Visitors. Buna, for instance. It could not be said of Buna that she lived entirely for her dinner, patiently absorbed as she was in this capital event of the day. No, for she was not less dedicated to her supper, nor less to her breakfast. You had studied her character imperfectly if you thought she lived in these. No, she wished to keep her feet warm, and she liked a soft seat, and expended a skill and generalship on securing the red chair and a corner *out* of the draught and *in* the air that was worthy of a seat in heaven. In a frivolous age, Buna was earnest. She groaned, she watched at night, she waited by day for her omelette and her lamp with the smooth handle, and when she went out of the house it was a *row* for half an hour.

Visitors. Mulchinock, the poetaster. The poet sent a copy of his verses to the printer. Thenceforward he was relieved, the human race took charge of it, and it flew from land to land, from language to language. He was even forced to prove, perhaps, like Campbell, that he had written the lines, so entirely had they become the property of the race. But poor little Mulchinock, having made what he called verses, went about and read them to all who could be made to listen, begged you to befriend them and quote them and sign a certificate that they *were* verses; and, in short, devoted himself to the business of nurse or attendant to these poor rhymes, which, God knew, needed all this backing and would go to the devil in spite of it. (Alas, Emerson thought, a dim, venerable public decides upon every work. It takes its place, by no effort, friendly or hostile, but by its real importance to the constant mind of man. And this in a way that no individual can affect by praise or blame.)

Imperfect persons, these visitors, with some partial thought or local culture. Emerson could have counted on his fingers all the sane men that ever came to him. How many were degraded in their sympathies!—with native aims high enough but a relation all too tender to the gross people about them. There were women who looked at his carpet, at his cook and waitress, conventionally, to see how close they squared with the customary cut in Boston. And the heavy souls who insisted on pounding. (In vain he tried to choke them off, to avoid the slaughter-house details: straightway they began at the beginning, and thrice they slew the slain. Society *must* be distressing, and there was an end of it.) And the flatterers—as if Cathmore did not dwell in the wood to avoid the voice of praise! And the busy-minded. (Men ran away from the smallpox. Why had they no fear of the smallpox of small society, the vermin, the tapeworm of politics, of trifling city life, that was eating their vitals?) And the followers, the would-be disciples—dangerous, these. The more eagerly his school crowded about him, the more difficult it was for him to forget their love, to compromise his influence by advancing further. Was he to stop where they wanted him to stop, at the phase where they apprehended him? Was his that "hour so fair" that Faust besought to linger—linger, yes, and fester? (Flow onward, life, and leave these heights behind!) They wished him not to take another step lest they should be left in the dark. Away with this egoism, theirs and his together! A man should stand among his fellows as one coal lies in the fire it has lighted, radiating heat but lost in the general flame. For the rest, what was the value of insight that did not create independence? And the best wisdom could never be communicated; it had to be acquired by every soul for itself.

(Go back to Plymouth, my friends, to Providence, to Worcester, and mind your business too! I shall give you no categorical answers, but look beside you and speak the thought that suggests itself—"listen behind you for your wit," as Thoreau says; so perhaps I can throw your problem into a fresh perspective and start you thinking anew. In good society—say, among the angels—everything is spoken by indirection and nothing quite straight as it befalls. Who wishes to dwell in the region of two-plus-two, as if Euclid were not one's next-door neighbour?)

How different, Emerson reflected, how different one man could be in two hours! Whilst he sat alone in his study and opened not his mouth he was God manifest, in flesh. In a parlour with unfit company he talked like a fool. But at least, if those sought him whom he did not seek, he would hold them stiffly to their rightful claims. Give them cake and lemons, give them his ripest pear, if that was what they came for; give them his conversation, but admit them never into any infringement of his hours. For the rest, all praise to the farmer's scale of living: plain plenty, without luxury or show, that drew no wasteful company and escaped an army of cares. Hospitality, yes—a little fire, a little food, but enough, and quiet, quiet, quiet.

Visitors! But this was the penalty of living in Concord. *En France, tout arrive.* (Living anywhere, in fact. How rich the poorest place when sensibility arrived! How magical was poor Walden under Ellery's eyes!) It was just as Mrs. Sedgwick said of Lenox: you could go to New York or London, but sitting still, year after year, she had found that all the people she had heard of and wished to see came by, sooner or later. The cranks and bores came, but the great men came, too. And how many obscure persons who excited Emerson's wonder, speculation, delight! Poor and mean the world looked when he thought only of the great; but when he recollected the charm of certain women, the poems of many private lives he knew, when he thought of the millions he knew not, he felt how rich he was, set down in such a world, gifted with the power to communicate with such an accomplished company.

Those young Harvard philosophers, for instance, Renouf and Washburn, who walked out from Cambridge and told him such fine things of their mates in the senior class. And Eustis, with another tale of heroes. And that boy from Andover Academy, John Albee, who had so many doubts about his education, doubts about going to college —though they taught "all the branches." ("Yes, indeed," said Henry, who happened to be in the room, "the branches and none of the roots.") He was much amused when Emerson mimicked Carlyle and was glad to take the copy of Herbert's poems and keep it for a year. One could freely say, in Albee's presence, that there seemed to be a good crop of poets in this new generation.

One event never lost its romance for Emerson, the

alighting of provocative persons at his gate. Aunt
Mary, first of all, breathing fire. "The wittiest and
most vivacious person I know, the most profitable
to meet," as Henry said. "She is singular in being
really and perseveringly interested to know what
thinkers think. In spite of all her biases, she can
entertain a large thought with hospitality."

She had entertained all the thoughts of Concord.
She distrusted Alcott's theories: the superstructure, she said, was "gilded and golden," but the
foundations were "in the depths of"—she couldn't
quite say what. But Henry's "extensive mentality"
had broken down her defenses, and he always enjoyed crossing swords with her. One evening when
the sibyl had just arrived, he hastened in to read his
manuscript to her. In some passage the word "god"
was used in a purely heathenish sense, and Aunt
Mary inquired, in a tone of dignified anxiety,
"Is that god spelt with a little g?" Fortu-
nately for Henry, it was. Then Mrs. Thoreau
called on her, wearing, as usual, a cap with long
yellow ribbons and still longer bonnet-ribbons.
"Mrs. Thoreau," she presently remarked, "you
may have noticed that while we were speaking of
your admirable son I kept my eyes shut."—"Yes,
Madam, I have noticed it."—"It was because I did
not wish to look upon those ribbons of yours, so
unsuitable at your time of life, and to a person of
your serious character."

To reprove was Aunt Mary's vocation. Once
Henry James was spending the night in Concord.
(An enchanting guest, this Saul among the

prophets, who had come to Boston to live—miscast again.) Alcott and Henry were there: Alcott had the floor indeed, for one of his Conversations. He was launching out, the cloud-compeller, and all Concord kept silence before him; he was spreading his wings for a flight over the void when the irrepressible James called for a definition.—Surely, Mr. Alcott, in a conversation you won't mind a few words from your spellbound listeners? . . . But Alcott did mind. A definition? To *define* was to *confine*—so he said, and great airships are not like tugs and catboats: they must have plenty of time to get under way. . . . Another thrust from James, and the airship was on the rocks. Pythagoras said no more and Saul had the ear of the company. What a laughing rigmarole! What gusts of earnest love of humankind! Society was to blame, said James, for all the crime that was committed. Let the criminal shout from the gallows that he had never been treated kindly by a single mortal! And then he pitched into the "moral law"—by which he meant self-conscious moral judgment. Aunt Mary rose in her shroud. She did not stir from her place, but she stood upright; and, raising her hands, she clasped them above her head and anathematized this pagan.

Beaming James rocked in his seat; for when she said these things one liked oneself the better. "The finest wits," she also said, "have their sediment," and there was still hope for a sinner. "Hope lives and travels on with the speed of suns and stars."

How much women taught one! Emerson thought. You wished to please them and say something they would like to hear, and by meeting them often you gained skill in this. There was Henry, the ever-intractable, so certain that whatever pleased an audience must be bad. He loathed soapy sympathy. What daggers he looked when poor Mr. Lovejoy, the preacher, tapped his book and said, "Here's the chap who camped in the wood." Alas for Mr. Lovejoy! "Here's the chap who camps in the pulpit," said Henry. What scorn he felt for Emerson when the latter said he would like to write something like *Robinson Crusoe* that would please young and old! The fewer persons you reached, he said, the better you wrote and lectured. But who liked to please Aunt Mary more than Henry? Who liked to please the children? One evening, at supper, before one of his Lyceum lectures, Edith asked him pointedly whether his lecture would be a nice interesting story, such as she wanted to hear, or whether it was one of those old philosophical things she did not care about. Henry turned to her, taken aback: he was plainly trying to believe that he had something to say that would fit Edith and Edward.

Visitors! Delia Bacon, so shy, so proud, with her mad theory of the key to Shakespeare—a Lady Quixote not to be dismissed with any shrug of the shoulders. No mythical family pride had led her to believe that Bacon and a company of wits had written the plays. That question, with her, was subordinate, though she well said that the idea of the authorship largely controlled one's appreciation of the works themselves. ("What new worlds such an authorship would enable us to see in them!") Bacon, she thought, cringing and truckling in his life, had yet preserved a mental reservation, "perpetually set down by shining Ariels on margins that will yet give out their colours. . . . Something still sat within, in purple, crowned, unbending, that never stooped or wavered, smiling to see its 'high charms work.'" But her main concern was the clue, yet to be discovered—in Shakespeare's coffin, she thought—to the poet's inner sense, the true knowledge of all things, which the plays were written to reveal and which, through the key she had found, the world was about to learn. Sadly dubious, it all seemed to Emerson, and yet with a plausibility! And how courtly, how merely courtly she made her Shakespeare; she would not allow for the tinker element and experience that belonged to the greatest poets. But she had read much in the plays that the critics of the Athenæum would never read, much that only a noble soul could find.

She came in 1852, and Emerson placed in her hand what letters he could muster, for Miss Bacon was going to England. (Carlyle would be sympathetic.) He wished her a prosperous voyage. (With what misgivings! Could he not almost foresee the anguish that awaited her? The silent devotion, the loneliness, the poverty, that strange midnight hour in the Stratford church, with the willing vicar waiting, the terrible doubt rising by the unopened grave? And the madhouse? But even now he knew what he would say at the end, say with his Latin poet: "Had she not been mistaken she would have accomplished less.")

Then who was this at the door? Horatio Greenough, his old Florentine friend, just returned from Italy. (His professor of sculpture in Concord University.) The same Greenough shining in his study, magnanimous as ever, with his courage and cheer and depth. How old? "Forty-seven years of joy I have lived." He had made the model of the Bunker Hill Monument. ("An obelisk says but one word, *Here!* but it speaks very loud.") And he made Emerson think of the Italian heroes—Michael Angelo, Leonardo, Alfieri.

What clear light, what rare elevation of thought! The grandest of democrats, Greenough. Emerson would never have refused to fife in his regiment. What a lie, said Greenough, this theory of culture was, this drawing on helpless humanity for the sake of a single class! Wasn't everything generative and everything connected? "The rowdy eyes that glare on you from the mob say plainly that they feel you are doing them to death; you, you have got the chain somewhere round their limbs; your six-per-cent is as deadly as the old tomahawk, and war, war to the knife, is between you and us." What could any one see in the old Egyptian architecture, in the architecture of the Middle Ages, but "cost to the constituency," the toil of prostrate millions?

Emerson's notebook yawned for some of his phrases. (He would have to digest them later.)

Beauty for beauty's sake, he said, was embellishment, non-functional embellishment, and false, childless, moribund. Look at the Greeks! (How Greenough loved austerity!) The adherence of the Greeks to the osseous fabric and to all the geometric necessities enabled them, as soon as plastic ornament was to be attempted, to carry into that, also, geometric truth. No surface finish, no deviations for the sake of a luxurious variety. Had Emerson really looked at the Elgin marbles? In that procession of horsemen, though every part was fixed, yet all the attitudes of the horse were given, and one figure supplied the defects of another. Thus you observed a horse put through all his motions, so that movement was enjoyed and you almost saw the dust.

Greenough was full of sense and almost free from crotchets. He wanted to stop commerce, to insulate the Americans, and put an end to the foreign influence that denationalized them. And he spoke again of the old artists and how they taught one another, the importance of a school, of an atelier. (These lonesome New Englanders!) What abounding discourse! There were three Horatii now in Emerson's Rome: Horace Greeley, Horace Mann, Horatio Greenough. No one had so charmed and invigorated him for months.

Visitors! They were streaming to Concord from all the corners of the earth. Englishmen, Germans, Hungarians, Swedes. Representative men meet for the conduct of life! Emmanuel Scherb had been settled for a year in the town, a German exile, a grave, stately professor who had fought against the Jesuits in Switzerland. He was lecturing on Hegel in the little Orthodox vestry, and he addressed his twelve listeners and the empty benches with as much elegance and finish as if his audience had been one of lords and duchesses. Then in 1852 Louis Kossuth came, that man truly in love with the greatest future. He wanted to see the bridge where a handful of farmers had opened a Revolution; and Emerson couldn't but tell him, in his speech of welcome, that Concord reserved its honour for actions of the noblest strain. An angel of freedom, Kossuth, crossing sea and land, crossing parties, nationalities, private interests, dividing populations wherever he went and drawing to him only the good. He had got his story told in every palace and log-hut and prairie camp on the continent. He was growing popular, in fact! But Kossuth's temper had long been tried in the fire. He was not a man to forget that everything great in the world is in minorities.

Then, one winter day, Frederica Bremer arrived. (Concord in the snow, she said, was just like Sweden.) A cordial, gracious, observant little lady, delighted with the New World and its "Homes." She said that Emerson frightened her a little, that she only talked well when she could expand. (How familiar to him, that feeling!) But she argued warmly enough for her personal God, and she took him to task for his "disintegrated views," all the more deplorable in a man of such power. Lidian's brother, Dr. Jackson, happened to be staying in the house and it pleased her to see the medal his discoveries in ether had won from her own King Oscar. Emerson carried her off to call at the Manse. (There was a "home" for a traveller!) And she gave him, when she left, a *History of Sweden.*

But most of his foreign guests were Englishmen, and Emerson always liked their cheerful voices, their pride, veracity, directness. Often enough they were models of classical virtue. Thomas Cholmondeley, for instance, that tall, fair, fresh young Roman, with his full brown beard, Bishop Heber's nephew and Clough's friend at Oxford, who had spent several years ranching in New Zealand. He fell in love with Henry's nonchalant manners; they struck up a warm friendship on the spot, and Cholmondeley went off to board with Mrs. Thoreau. He asked Henry to teach him botany and take a walk to Wachusett, and Henry actually consented. A frank, happy, curious man, this Cholmondeley, delighted with New England: everything interested him, Alcott's Conversations, the preaching of Theodore Parker, the whalers at New Bedford. And what a gift he sent the following year, in return for "so much kindness"!—a gift to Henry from England. Forty-four volumes of the sacred books of India—the *Rig-Veda,* Sankara Acharya, the *Upanishads,* the *Vishnu Purana,*—in English, French, Latin, Greek and Sanskrit. A great day for Henry!—for scarcely one of these books could be bought in America. A great day for Concord. There had never been any seed-sowing to compare with it since Lane's library of the Mystics was scattered in the neighbourhood.

Clough had appeared before Cholmondeley—in 1853—the patient Clough, "secret as an oyster" (as Allingham had written to Emerson)—"opens a little at certain times of the tide, but snaps to again in a jiffy if touched, and maybe bites your finger." Patient Clough, so puzzled and yet so placid, still lost in the wilderness where Carlyle had left him, still stout, solid, reliable, discouraged with England, anxious for work, anxious to marry, anxious to find a home—perhaps in America. He had settled in Cambridge, in lodgings, and thought of opening a school there; he had gathered a few pupils and was toiling away, revising Langhorne's Plutarch. He was homesick, missed the English gardens, thought they made too many puns in Cambridge, and the wretched climate had given him a sore throat. But he felt he was "wanted" here at least, and Boston was "tolerably English," and he liked to see his book on drawing-room tables and hear himself described as "the celebrated author of *The Bothie.*" (They had bought up a whole edition, these astonishing Yankees.) Emerson gave him a dinner at the Tremont House, with Longfellow, Hawthorne, Greenough, Lowell and others; and he had him out for a Sunday once a fortnight. (He thought Walden a "prettyish pool," and altogether Concord was not so bad, a small sort of village, rather bare, with elms of a weeping kind, the woods somewhat scrubby.) Emerson would have liked to keep him longer, but he had

too good a chance to return to England. Patient
Clough, driving his furrow in the sluggish soil!
To pain and strife, he was certain, the earth would
bear golden harvests. And he said that Emerson
had reconciled him to "mere subsistence."

CHAPTER XX

EMERSON had often wished that Boston had a coffee-room, a reading-room, a club where a man might go in the afternoon and find a few congenial souls ready for a chat. The Old Corner Bookstore was a cheerful centre, when he dropped in for a moment and heard Fields's resounding laugh behind the green curtain. But a club, a club for poets and men of letters—what a pleasure that would be! Theology, law, medicine, politics, trade, all had their meetings and assembly-rooms. But literature had none. As Ellery Channing said, there were two hundred thousand souls in Boston and not a chair in the whole town for him.

With clubs in the past he had had little success. He had belonged to several, set them going, cherished them. The Transcendental Club, and the Town and Country Club, which he had started with Alcott "for the study and diffusion of the ideas and tendencies proper to the Nineteenth Century." They were protests against the muteness of Boston, but they had soon died of the disease against which they were fighting. They were pitched in too high a key—associations of voices, not of persons. The accumulated rust of solitude had creaked as it were in the joints of every member.

How insulated they had been, those seekers of wisdom in the old days, sitting on their chairs like images in some temple of Memnon—till the spirit moved their tongues! Margaret Fuller alone had been able to fuse them into some semblance of a company, and Emerson could still feel the cold sense of defeat with which they had bidden one another good-night. Often, after such an evening, he had found himself repeating Kant's remark, "Detestable is the society of mere literary men!"

But with time a warmer, softer, more genial season had awakened in the heart of Boston. That bleak intellectual spring had ripened into summer. One day, in the train, he saw across the aisle a broad-faced, unctuous man, fat as a priest, with large, gentle eyes and easy, unconscious gestures. Agassiz, of course!—the new foreign professor of whom every one was talking. There was something symbolic in this figure. The influence of Agassiz, the laughing, talking, exciting, commanding professor, so eager, so expansive, so responsive, had begun to work like yeast in the University. Wherever he moved and spoke, a warm breeze, laden as it were with rain, stirred people's minds, and the old provincial reticences and rigidities, the ice and the cobwebs, melted under his voice. Agassiz was a symbol; for a tolerant, skeptical, secular, sympathetic atmosphere, a certain spontaneity and enthusiasm had spread through Boston. Poets and historians had appeared, scientists, essayists, travellers. The renaissance, faintly prefigured in the days of Channing and Everett, was at last in full tide.

Just so; then why not use the power of the tide? Emerson was hungry for so many facts, natural and human facts, discoveries, hypotheses, inventions, and he wanted to hear ideas that differed from his own. How fast the right company kindled one another's interest in their own studies! One had no thoughts at home; then easily and at once—with a few genial companions—the old motion began again in one's brain. The cloud lifted, the horizon broadened, fancy and humour flowed, and life seemed once more of an infinite opulence. Any skill, for Emerson, success, mastery, conquest in any form over men or matter, was a spur, a delight, an incentive. And Boston was full of these conquerors now, waiting for a chance to meet.

A young man named Woodman, Horatio Woodman, a lawyer and lover of lions, was the impresario. He had often dined with Emerson at the Albion, and in 1856 he proposed a monthly dining club that would bring together the best minds in Boston. Longfellow and Lowell were ready to join, and Oliver Wendell Holmes, and Agassiz and R. H. Dana. So the Saturday Club was born. There were soon a score of members: beaming Henry James, Tom Appleton, "prince of rattlers," with a steamer-ticket for Europe always in his pocket, giant Felton, the Harvard Porson, E. P. Whipple, the essayist, Samuel Gridley Howe, the teacher of the blind, Whittier, Sumner, Prescott, John Lothrop Motley, who had just returned from Holland, with his high animal spirits and the face of another Byron; and Dwight (editor now of *The Journal of Music*) and Frederic Hedge, who had settled down as professor of German at Harvard, survivors of the old Transcendental circle. They chose the Parker House as the best place for their meetings, the large front room on the second floor overlooking the statue of Franklin in the grounds of the City Hall.

Emerson had little luck in persuading the Concord authors to come to the club as his guests. Alcott complained of the want of simplicity in Longfellow, Lowell and Holmes and would not be drawn away from his rural affairs. Ellery appeared once, wretched and full of contempt for these genial worldlings. Henry Thoreau looked in, after one of the meetings, and said it was all cigar-smoke —"no salt, Attic or other"; but then, as Henry remarked, the only room in Boston where he ever felt at home was the waiting-room at the station. But Hawthorne became a member, a silent member, who kept his eyes steadily fixed on his plate ("sprawling Concord owl," as Henry James described him, "brought blindfold into the brilliant daylight and expected to wink and be lively like any little dapper Tommy Titmouse or Jenny Wren") ; and Rockwood Hoar, the judge, Elizabeth's brother. Judge Hoar valued the Book of Common Prayer for the special distinction it gave his native town: "O God who art the author of peace and lover of Concord"; and many were the happy talks that he and Emerson had on the subject of Scott. (That poet who played ever a manly part.) When the Concord members found it difficult to get home again in the evening, he had his big, black horse and carryall driven over to Waltham to meet the last train. Then they all drove home the ten miles on the starlit country road, and Hawthorne, once in the darkness, would begin to talk.

Longfellow and Agassiz, at either end of the table, were the two poles of the club, Longfellow with his soft voice, his glints of humour and his flavour of books and travel, and the irrepressible Agassiz, lounging in his chair, laughing and crying at once, eagerly turning to right and left, unconscious as an infant, with a lighted cigar in each hand, smiling and forcing the attention of all about him. One could easily understand how Agassiz, in Brazil, had upset the customs of the country. He had asked the Emperor to allow ladies to be present at his lectures, against all the laws of etiquette, and had opened the study of science to the women of South America. In just the same way he had secularized Puritan Harvard. He came to Concord often, examined turtles with Henry, lectured at the Lyceum and always stayed with Emerson. He attracted the whole village when he spoke there, and for weeks every head bubbled with Natural History.

Emerson himself talked little at the club, but he listened, as Holmes remembered, "with a look never to be forgotten, his head stretched forward, his shoulders raised like the wings of an eagle, and his eye watching the flight of the thought which had attracted his attention, as if it were his prey, to be seized in mid-air and carried up to his eyry." But Holmes and the lusty Lowell, with his brown and bushy beard, whimsical, boyish, were in their

element. What wit, what amusing topics! Some
question of Yankee phrases, perhaps, always a
happy theme for the author of the *Biglow Papers*.
Or a story of the prize-ring, the deeds of Yankee
Sullivan, Heenan and Sayers. Holmes, busy as a
wren (with a queer little smiling face which he
said he considered a convenience rather than an
ornament),was a great lover of sport. He knew all
the points and styles of the winning horses. He
liked to chat with the giants at the circus. He joked
with the prize-fighters, measured and studied their
muscles, like a good professor of anatomy who was
also a poet; for he loved a symmetrical growth in
horse, man or tree. "My nature," he said, "is to
snatch at all the fruits of knowledge and take a
good bite out of the sunny side. After that, let in
the pigs." Emerson delighted in Holmes's wit, so
sprightly, sparkling, finished, and he made a little
speech on the Doctor's fiftieth birthday. *The Atlantic Monthly* had just been launched, with Lowell
as its first editor, and several of the members contributed to every number. (They told a story of a
meeting when the copies of the new issue were
brought in, and each one seized a copy and sat
down to read his own article.) Emerson wished to
pay his tribute to the Autocrat, who flung his wit
about like sea-sand and gave each month such a
staggering blow to the Dunce-power of the world.
He spoke of the Doctor's correction of popular
errors in taste, behaviour, science. A man of healthy
perception whose thoughts left only cheerful and
perfumed memories.

In the twenty years that followed, Emerson seldom missed a dinner of the club. In this large, discursive talk, truths, he found, detached themselves as thoughts, like spars flaking off from the eternal wall. He heard the news of the universe from his fellow-members—news of astronomy, botany, art, politics, of a dozen different realms— each from the lips of a master. And his theories and observations were put to the severest test in this atmosphere of sharp, critical discussion. His style was growing more and more concrete. The practical wisdom of the man who had dealt with men had gradually taken the place of the cloudy dreams of old. The Franklin in Emerson's nature had come to the front, and the Saturday Club certainly had something to do with it. His face had changed, too. The brooding smile remained, but an air of sagacity and authority had settled on his features. A steely force had passed into his chin. He looked like an eagle now, with those eyes and that beaklike nose and the deep lines that swept across his cheeks.

In the summer of 1858, he and several of the members joined in forming the Adirondack Club— the "Philosophers' Camp," as people called it later. Never before had he entered the primitive wilderness; never had he seen at close range the guides and trappers of the northern forest. Lowell and Agassiz and Rockwood Hoar and Professor Jeffries Wyman, the zoölogist, were among the party; Holmes had no taste for the woods, and Longfellow refused to go when he heard that Emerson was taking a gun. "Somebody will be shot," he said. They camped on Follanbee Lake, in a shelter of bark, and slept on hemlock boughs, while the wolves prowled about and they heard the cry of the loon. Agassiz was busy as ever, with inexhaustible spirits, studying the plants and animals. He found a fresh-water sponge that had never been classified, and every day, while the others gathered around him, he lectured on the elements of Nature and dissected a fish or a deer. The dinner-hour was a frolic, with Lowell's humour playing over all, puns and wit and learning and tags of poetry, and John Holmes and Judge Hoar and Agassiz to fill the forest with the echoes of their laughter. They dined on venison and trout and foaming mugs of ale, while the owls gathered to listen.

To Emerson it was very strange at first; but he soon grew into the camp-life. He had refused to hunt or fish; then, as the days went by, the primitive man awoke in him and he, too, wanted to shoot his deer. (He could see only a "square mist" when the time came.) The ways of the guides absorbed him. They put on their coats to sleep and took them off in the morning; they paddled on the lake bareheaded and wore their hats in camp. They reversed all the habits of civilization. A new species of men, these doctors of the wilderness, self-sufficient, serving and served by no one. They built their own shelters, killed and caught their food, cooked for themselves and could even make their clothes. Their lives were complete and rounded, independent, the perfect circle of means and ends of which

Emerson had always dreamed as the life of Nature.
The Civil War put an end to these holidays in
the woods. On the subject of war Emerson had
often reflected. War had this great value, he
couldn't but feel: it shook society until every atom
fell into the place its specific gravity assigned to it.
Good sense and foresight came to the top, and
Ulysses at once took rank next to Achilles. In a
lecture given in 1838, he had suggested two means
of establishing peace that were going to be heard
of later. First, a Congress of Nations. And sec-
ondly he said, "The manhood that has been in war
must be transferred to the cause of peace before
war can lose its charm and peace be venerable to
men." (The germ of a famous essay by Henry
James's son a generation later.) But war as a situ-
ation was a new experience to Emerson. He almost
welcomed it in 1861 as restoring the nation to
reality. "We have been very homeless for some
years past," he said, "but now we have a country
again. We have forced the conspiracy out of doors
. . . It was war then and it is war now; but declared
war is vastly safer than undeclared war."

He had entered the political arena with his anti-
slavery speeches. No use attempting to keep out of
politics now! He had followed as long as he could
the advice of Pythagoras, eschewed the political
bean, confined his thoughts wholly to the "state of
man"; but the "state of affairs" had grown too all-
engrossing. In January, 1862, he made a speech in
Washington and proposed the policy of "Emancipation as a platform," with compensation to the

owners who remained loyal. Sumner carried him
off to see the President, and Lincoln's first remark
was: "Oh, Mr. Emerson, I once heard you say in a
lecture that a Kentuckian seems to say by his air
and manners, 'Here I am; if you don't like me,
the worse for you.'" A native, aboriginal man, this
Lincoln, Emerson thought, as an acorn from an
oak, with a face and manners that disarmed suspicion, with a fund of fables and proverbs, too,
which in an earlier age would have earned him the
fame of an Æsop.

One of Emerson's Concord neighbours, Cyrus
Stow the butcher, had come to Washington a few
years before to realize an old desire. He had retired from his business in comfort, and he wished
to see the great men of the country making the
laws. He returned a few days later, disillusioned.
He had entered the Capitol with awe and reverence, and in those marble halls, he said, with a
lowered voice, were members of Congress "drinking and swearing *right before me.*" Emerson
himself had never had any illusions in regard to
politicians, but the war had straightened their
backs. The members of Lincoln's cabinet whom he
met impressed him with their sincerity—Chase and
Seward and Stanton. He spent four days in Washington on this occasion. He called upon Seward in
his dingy State Department, and Seward took him
to church the following morning (Emerson mar-
velling much at the Egyptian stationariness of the
Episcopalians). Then he went to see Lincoln again
and found his two little boys, seven and eight years

old, having their hair "whiskeyed" by the barber. He talked with Welles, the Secretary of the Navy, and with Senators Sherman and Colfax, and the Senate Chamber delighted him with its noble proportions. He had seldom had such a bath in the world of public affairs. He had never believed very heartily in government. "That nation is best," he had said, "which is governed least." But the war had altered his feeling, at least in a measure. "The country is cheerful and jocund," he wrote in his journal, "in the belief that it has a government at last." Government to win the war, government to establish freedom: in this Emerson believed with all his soul.

And then the President made him a member of the Board of Visitors at West Point. Here was a new opportunity to examine at close range a new species of men, and Emerson set out at once on his visit of inspection. John Burroughs, who saw him there, took him for an "eager, alert, inquisitive farmer," for he had a "kind of rustic curiosity and simplicity. . . . When the rest of the board looked dull or fatigued or perfunctory, he was all eagerness and attention." And indeed he was greatly drawn by the Spartan ways of these young military monks, their exercises in riding, drawing, shooting, in geology and engineering. Like the guides in the Adirondacks, they, too, were masters of the art of self-reliance!

CHAPTER XXI

AFTER the storm came perfect days, a warm October. What colour in these heaps of apples, more lively and varied than the orange, with its greenest leaves—balls of scarlet fire! And what gaiety and depth they gave to russet Massachusetts! The social fruit in which Nature deposited every possible flavour: whole zones and climates concentrated in apples.

What a harvest in wartime! Pears, perfect for once, and in what profusion! Passe Colmars, Seckels, enough to fill three barrels, and four barrels of Gloutmorceaux. Had Emerson ever doubted his law of compensation—he who had written to William the other day that the first of the year found him in as poor a plight as the rest of the Americans? Not a penny from his books since last June, no dividends from the banks, no lecture-engagements. But a hundred barrels of apples for the Quincy market!

What splendour in this humble town!—a step from his door: the Lincoln hills dressed in their coloured forest. And what reserves and resources! Had he ever had cause to doubt them in the long, mottled years? He thought of some of his neighbours: Cyrus Stow ("a spoonful of wit," as Ellery said, "and ten thousand feet of sandstone"), and that solid village worthy who, reading his paper in the grocery, always read a passage through three times before venting his opinion, and the loyal Concord carpenter, with his comment on the price of lots in rising Chicago: "Can't hardly believe that any lands can be worth so much money, so far away." Had he ever done justice to the common farmer and labourer? A hundred times he had felt their superiority, and yet he continued the parrot echoes of the names of literary notabilities who, if he had brought them into the presence of these Norsemen, would have shrivelled into shadows. He saw the young farmers in their Sunday clothes. What power, what utilities they had, and how meekly worn! The cold, gloomy day, the rough, rocky pastures were opportunities for them. And yet there was no arrogance in their bearing. A perfect gentleness, rather.

The war was already won, he couldn't but feel. The success of the North was sure, rooted in the poverty of New England, its schools, its thrifty industry, in the snow, the east wind, the life of the farm and the sea. A nursery of obstinate vigour, and how gracious, too, in this royal revel of October! He remembered Henry Thoreau's oaken strength, that unhesitating hand of the labourer accosting his task, whenever he walked or worked. And Henry had loved apples, too, loved them as Plutarch loved them, and praised them as well.

He could scarcely believe that Henry was dead. Six months ago, and "enjoying existence as much as ever" at the last. It was only the other day he had made his snow-house, crept in with his lamp and shouted to Henry to join him. (Playing his favourite game, proving that every kind of life could be lived in Concord. Was he not an Eskimo for an hour?) It was only the other day he had gone with Henry to call on Perez Blood. Perez was sitting alone in the dark, in his woodshed, in his astronomical chair. They looked through the famous telescope, saw Saturn's rings and the sunlight on the mountains of the moon. (Who but a Concord farmer would have spent his inheritance on globes and books of astronomy?) Then Perez died, and they drove in a wagon to the auction, and Henry pointed out the English hawthorn abloom on the neighbouring hill—and the sweetgale blossoming, and the swamp-pinks by the river—to the *pee-pee-pee* of the kingbirds. The woods and the fields, said Alcott, were sorrowing for Henry. "There has been none such since Pliny," as Alcott said again, "and it will be long before there comes his like. The most sagacious and wonderful worthy of his time, and a marvel to coming times."

A marvel, as it seemed, only to coming times. Concord had scarcely known him, far less Boston. Longfellow and Lowell had misprized him, and Rockwood Hoar had confirmed them in their skepticism. No matter, he had thriven, as he said, on solitude and poverty. He had found all his human hopes confirmed in the smell of the water-lily, and the future would understand him. One had only to print his journals, Emerson thought, as he turned those copious leaves, to create a plentiful crop of little Henrys. Young men of sensibility would fall an easy prey to the charming of Pan's pipe.

The Concord oaks were falling. Aunt Mary, Henry's Cassandra, was the next to go—in far-off Williamsburg, eighty-eight years old, and still a boarder, with a face unwrinkled still, pink as of old, and the blue flash in her eye, and the yellow hair cut close under the mobcap! She had loved death all her days, and often her friends had wished her "joy of the worm"; and when they laid her away in Sleepy Hollow the event had such a comic tinge in their eyes that they feared to look at one another across the grave.

The ancestral oaks were falling; oaks never to be replaced, Emerson felt again, re-reading Aunt Mary's letters. What force between these lines! "After all, some of the old Christians were more delivered from external things than the modern speculatives, who are anxious for society, books, ideas, and become sensitive to all that affects the organs of thought. A few single grand ideas, which become objects, pursuits, and all in all!"

But the new growth was forming under the old. Alcott, the phœnix, had re-risen from his ashes and plumed himself afresh; and Concord was a picnic now with all the children. Indomitable Alcott, despised and rejected! He was aqueous, vaporous, yes —another Indra, destined to seven incarnations. He had taught; they stopped his mouth. He dug in the earth and emerged again, a philosopher. Again they scorned him, and Alcott emerged as a poet. He had carried his wares to the West, at fifty-five (a peddler once more, with a carpetbag and a new assortment of "notions")—come home, knocked on the door again at midnight, half-frozen, hungry, still smiling and serene. He had a queerish look in his face and a dollar in his pocket. His overcoat had been stolen; he had had to buy a shawl. But at least he had "opened the way," and next year things would be better.

They had made him Superintendent of the Public Schools in Concord. No great vindication now. He had grown a little too vapourish perhaps, and these matters of organization could scarcely interest him. But how much he might have accomplished, once, with a chance like this! The salary was not to be mentioned; but "Hope and keep busy" was Mrs. Alcott's motto, and Louisa had made a "battering-ram" of her head and was driving a way for them all through the rough-and-tumble world. She had earned four dollars first for a pile of sewing, then five for a story, taught school in the barn, bought paper for her father (so that he might keep on with his diaries though the heavens fell) ; and the publishers thought she could write a book for children that would carry the world by storm. Did Emerson know that years before he had been Louisa's Goethe? She had found in his library one day the *Correspondence with a Child* and had instantly thought of herself as another Bettina. She had written letters to her father's friend, letters she had never sent, left wild flowers on his doorstep and sung Mignon's song under his window.

The young people in Concord were very gay, with dances, festivities, plays, and the Alcott girls to lead them. It was always a lark for Emerson when he piled them into the haycart, bedecked with flowers, and carried them off for a swim and a picnic at Walden. (For he was the master of revels, now that Henry was gone.) The school was going well, with the new young master, Frank Sanborn, a senior at Harvard when Emerson met him first at one of his lectures and offered him the position. He had made his mark already—had defied the bailiffs who had come to Concord to seize him, at midnight, on suspicion, as a friend of John Brown. He had not appeared when they summoned him, for some part he had never taken in the Harper's Ferry raid. (Did they think they could simply kidnap a citizen of Concord? The whole town assembled and drove the bailiffs away.) The school was flourishing now, with Sanborn's Prussian assistant, Reinhold Solger, who lectured on history and geography so well that Emerson was going to school again himself. And what boys and girls they had!—if parents counted for anything: Emerson's and Rockwood Hoar's, two sons of Henry James (Robertson and Wilky), three sons of Horace Mann, three daughters of John Brown, and Julian Hawthorne.

The Emersons gave tea-parties every year so that all the boys and girls might come to the house, and Mrs. Emerson took them into the garden and gave them bouquets of flowers. "Did you speak to her?" Emerson asked his son, when he heard of some new pupil. "I hadn't anything to say." "Speak, speak, if you haven't anything to say. Ask her, 'Don't you admire my shoe-strings?'" On Sunday afternoons he came to the front entry at four o'clock and whistled for the children, and they all went out for a walk to Walden, the Cliffs, or Peter's Field—some spot he had found perhaps during the week. He liked to make it a mystery.

The Hawthornes had returned to Concord after their years of exile, and Hawthorne, who had always wanted a tower to write in, had built one at Wayside, like Hilda's tower in Rome. He was doing his best to work; he locked himself in, pulled down the blinds, scarcely stirred from the house. But something had happened; what was it? Had Europe broken the spell of his old New England? Had the war unsettled him? He had no opinions, but who had more vehement "views"? He rejoiced in the shattering of the Union. He had felt in the Consulate at Liverpool that the Southerners were not his compatriots. They were better apart, he said, and "I hope we shall give them a terrible thrashing and kick them out." He was changed; he had lost that radiant spring and vigour; he had wasted away; he tottered as he walked.

Was it really Hawthorne, that phantom on the road, so white and still? He would turn away and hide in the woods to avoid you. Passing his house, you saw him painfully dragging down the hill the logs he had cut on the ridge. Such embarrassed motions! And his hollow eyes besought you not to approach. He had put himself into a dungeon, he said, and could not find the key to let himself out. You passed again, and there he was aloft, moving slowly along the top of the ridge, on the path his feet had beaten as he composed his stories; pacing back and forth, his dark frame cut clear against the sky, in the spaces of the mingled branches. Once Emerson met him there, face to face on the ridge—brooding, brooding, trying to think out his tragedy, *Septimius Felton*. He couldn't seem to get it, and he said, as Emerson paced along beside him: "This path is the only remembrance of me that will remain." Then the news came from New Hampshire: he had wandered away and died in a village inn.

They buried him in Sleepy Hollow, in the splendour of May. Longfellow and Lowell were there, and Holmes and Agassiz and Alcott, and the meadowlarks and the bluebirds. How noble he looked at the last, with that calm and powerful head! These mute green banks, Emerson thought, were already full of history; heroes and poets were leaving their names and virtues on the trees. They would sleep well in this quiet valley where the beautiful night and the beautiful day came in turn to sit upon the grass.

Emerson had besieged Hawthorne; he had never lost hope of surmounting his caprice and one day conquering a friendship. He had bathed in Hawthorne's moonlight, and not long before, in New York, he had found another sun. Walt Whitman, a journeyman printer, had sent him a strange book called *Leaves of Grass,* a shaft from the void of

Brooklyn. He had felt a sudden thrill as he turned the pages, that unmistakable thrill he had felt when he found Carlyle, and Coleridge and Landor. There was nothing sterile or stingy here, no sign of excessive handiwork, none of the lymph in temperament that was making American wits fat and mean. It was free and brave, this book, with the courage of treatment that delighted him, and the large perception. He wanted to see his benefactor, and he felt like striking his tasks and running to Brooklyn. And he wrote, with fullest heart, to the unknown author, "I greet you at the beginning of a great career."

Emerson found him at last, in his wilderness of Brooklyn. They walked together to the ferry, three miles from Portland Avenue, where Walt lived with his mother, and dined that first evening at the Astor House. Emerson was strangely drawn to this great ruddy animal, with his buffalo strength and his rich emotional nature, calm like his own but so different in other ways. He felt over-trained at times, too intellectual, and Walt refreshed him, gave him something he needed, put something into his tissue that he never found in Concord. And Walt glowed with pleasure in his company. They shared the same belief in the Inner Light; as Walt said, they were like two Quakers together. Walt had absorbed Emerson in his carpentering days, and that message of "Man Thinking," of an individual correlative with the cosmos, had expressed, in a form that excited him, the idea that was taking shape in his own poems. Emerson, for him (he had said in an open letter), had discovered a new continent, the continent of "interior America." And for Emerson, Walt was in many ways the new man he had prophesied—a Taliessin, a true American bard, with the largeness and optimism he loved in the primitive epics.

They met a dozen times or so, usually in New York, and once or twice in Boston, when Walt came up to direct the printing of a new edition of his poems. Walt was a curious monster. He liked to dine at the hotel without his coat, and once he refused to drink out of his glass and called for a tin cup. Emerson was a little repelled by this too much "fellowship"; he liked a statelier manner, a manner that seemed to say, "I am I and you are you." And some of the poems in the second edition of *Leaves of Grass* offended him. He could not see the significance of *Children of Adam;* and for three hours, one clear February day, he walked up and down with Walt under the elms of the Common, begging him to suppress it—to give the book a chance to be read, give the people themselves a chance to read it. (For this, Walt said later, was the sole burden of Emerson's argument.) Walt had had doubts himself, but as Emerson pushed the point he became finally convinced of his own rightness. He never wavered again. Emerson, in spite of his own words, had given Walt his lesson in self-reliance.

Was Emerson annoyed when the new edition appeared, with his phrase and his name blazoned on the back of the cover? (It seemed that he alone of

the critics of America had really fathomed the
book.) A storm broke over his head. Once more
letters appeared in the papers saying he had lost
his mind; and the "trippers and askers" came, demanding to know how *he* could possibly defend a
passage like this, or this. Emerson held his peace.
To the end he was grateful to Walt for the Ap-
palachian largeness of his outline and treatment.

He wanted to introduce Walt to the Boston men
of letters. He suggested inviting him to the Saturday Club, but Longfellow and Holmes said, No.
(A "rowdy," Lowell called him, "a New York
tough, a frequenter of low places.") Concord and
Boston were at variance again, for Alcott and
Henry had liked him as much as Emerson, and together they had proposed to invite him to visit the
town. But Mrs. Alcott said, No; Sophia Thoreau
said, No; Mrs. Emerson said, No. Walt and New
England were plainly incompatible. He would certainly not have been happy in such a hostile atmosphere, and Emerson did not insist. Besides, Walt
positively refused to come. He loved Emerson; he
had liked Henry; he thought well of Alcott. But
one literary man at a time was enough for him. So
Emerson continued to see him in New York.

CHAPTER XXII

ONE day in 1866, when Emerson was lecturing in New York, he met his son by chance at the Hotel Saint Denis. They spent the evening together, and Emerson read aloud some poems he had been writing. One of them was called "Terminus." "It is time to be old," the poem said:

> "The god of bounds,
> Who sets to seas a shore,
> Came to me in his fatal rounds
> And said: "No more!
> No farther shoot
> Thy broad, ambitious branches and thy root."

He smiled as he read the lines; and indeed why had he written them? He was just setting out on his usual Western tour, vigorous as ever in appearance, fresh and young at heart. It was only a premonition. He had sixteen years of life before him and six years of work. But he felt within him a legacy of ebbing veins.

His curiosity, his enterprise were as keen as ever. His Western lectures took him to Chicago, Milwaukee, St. Paul—across the Mississippi in a skiff in the dead of winter. Minneapolis strongly attracted him, as a place for a young man, and "Fond du Lac," he noted, "is a wonderful growth, and shines like a dream, seen this morning from the

top of Amory Hall." At home he liked to talk with
drivers and stable-men, and he went with delight
to Magner's horse-training lectures in the stable of
the Middlescx Hotel. At Rarey's exhibition of
horses in Boston he was also an eager spectator, and
he said that Rarey, the trainer, should have been
made a doctor of laws for his personal influence.
(What control this man had over his horses!)
Feats of any kind had never lost their charm for
the lover of heroes. Then once an unknown mechanic named George Tufts, who was crippled by
some disease, sent him two or three letters, one containing the line, "Life is a flame whose splendour
hides its base." Emerson was stirred by these letters, which criticized his own point of view, and
while staying at Saratoga he set off on a journey
of several days in a fruitless effort to find the man,
who had moved away from the village from which
he had written.

His curiosity, in fact, seemed to grow with the
years. He dreamed of all the worlds he would have
liked to conquer. What a pleasure it would have
been to go with Agassiz to Canada, with Asa Gray
to study the trans-Mississippi flora, with Jeffrics
Wyman to share in his excavations! Three thousand years of life would never have sufficed to sat-
isfy all his interests. Egyptian history, for instance,
and Sanscrit literature, and the riddle of the Chaldæan Oracles. And algebra, astronomy, chemistry.
He could have his days with Agassiz, at least, examining the marine life on the rocks at Nahant.
And he took his turn at the telescope at Williams-

town, observed the four double stars in Lyra, the two hundred stars of the Pleiades. There, for a moment, he left the world behind him and lost himself in the sense of the sublime.

For visiting he had never greatly cared. "The strength of the Egyptians," he said, when some visit was proposed, "is to sit still." But at John Murray Forbes's island of Naushon he always felt at home. He had met Forbes first about 1848, on the steamboat from Detroit, and the latter had persuaded him to stop over and see Niagara Falls. Forbes was building his railroad to Chicago: a shrewd, humorous, open-hearted man, a Highland chief in the guise of a Boston magnate, with a great love of poetry, Scottish ballads, and a large impersonal interest in the welfare of the country. He had broken with the Cotton Whigs, helped the Free State men in Kansas, and entertained at his house, on two successive nights, John Brown and the proslavery Governor of Missouri. In the Civil War he had gone to England on a largely successful mission to enlist support for the North and had acted as counsellor to the Secretaries of the Treasury and the Navy. On his island in Buzzard's Bay, with its rolling sheep-downs, he kept open house, with his yacht and his horses; and Grant, Sherman and Stanton mingled there with poets, painters and writers. Forbes was the life of the company, in his unassuming way, the Highland chief at home, now toiling away at his papers, drawing up bills for Congress, now calling for a song, "Bonny Dundee," for instance, or "MacGregor's Gathering."

Emerson loved this Naushon. Its dells, ponds and groves always refreshed him. The pebbles, too, on the beach, the jostled rainbow of pebbles that stirred him to add some lines to his poem "Seashore." And the hawks and the herons that hovered over the waters, and the gliding ships beyond. There was always the best of conversation in the house of this Yankee nobleman, who shot and rode and sailed so well and controlled with such practical wisdom such a multitude of facts. And great was Emerson's joy when his daughter Edith became engaged to the eldest son of his friend, a young man who had been taken prisoner in the war and escaped and rejoined his regiment and had finally been present at Lee's surrender. The marriage took place in the following autumn, and presently Colonel Forbes came to the rescue of Emerson's business affairs. For Emerson, who had figured and fought like a merchant to make money for Carlyle, had a very vague idea of his own accounts. The contracts for his books were unjustly unremunerative; he had never received from them more than six hundred a year, and an agent who had given him every quarter a masterly statement (he thought) of his other investments was found to have defrauded him. He was on the point of defaulting when Colonel Forbes intervened. The returns from the publisher's sales were soon doubled.

In the summer he often took an excursion to some corner of New England. He camped on Monadnoc in 1866, with his son Edward and his daughter Ellen and a party of their friends, and surveyed from this Olympus the vast champaign, forty ponds and a hundred farms and farmhouses and the circle of distant mountains, with the clear songs of the thrushes rising from the green belts below. Two years later he climbed Mount Mansfield and found George Bradford there in the Mountain House. They scrambled up together to the "Chin" and saw Lake Champlain lying below them, like a piece of yellow sky. They peeped into some caves where bears and panthers had been seen that summer and rose the following morning in time for the dawn.

At Marston Watson's, too, Emerson occasionally visited—that beautiful park "Hillside" on the slope above Plymouth which Henry Thoreau had surveyed in 1856. Alcott and Watson himself had carried the surveyor's chain, and Ellery and Alcott had both written poems describing this friendly villa where the Transcendentalists of old had gathered. And he still enjoyed his visits to the country colleges, Amherst, Williams, Dartmouth, where, after making a speech, he would sometimes stay for several days talking with the students. At Dartmouth the President disapproved of emulation and forbade the literary societies to elect members by merit. Even the parts at Commencement were assigned by lot: it "removed disagreeable excitement from the societies." It would remove still more, said Emerson, were there no college at all. He advised them to take morphine at the college commons.

At Dartmouth in 1863 he had given his address

on the "Man of Letters." His old subject, but inexhaustibly precious; and he wished to say that if the army was badly led, as the country complained in those dark days of the war, it was because the population was badly led, because the scholars, the seers had been false to their trust. They had not stood by their order but had deferred to the men of this world. He wished to say again that scholars are bound to stand for all the liberties, against slavery, arbitrary government, monopoly, oppression—to express his hope that some of these listening students would become men of letters, critics, philosophers. The material prosperity of America had beaten down the hope of youth, the piety of learning; and was it not true that all vigorous nations had balanced their labour by the power of the imagination? The scholar was the carrier of ideas that were to fashion the mind and the history of this breathing world, the imparter of pulses of light and shocks of electricity.

Did Emerson know what excitement filled the souls of his hearers, what possibilities seemed to rise before them, what visions of past and future? He had so plainly never doubted the truth of what he said; he took it so for granted that every one must see it! All the mythology of Arabia spoke in his voice, the tree of Paradise, the adventures of the Indian gods, of the gods of the North, Thor, Odin, Balder. A whole Valhalla of happy inspirations, upon which he himself had fed, with which he had lived, breathed in the words that floated through the chapel. A current of exaltation ran from soul to soul, for this was the note of the bugle calling every man to the battle of thought.

He was making many speeches now, aside from his regular lectures. He had spoken in 1860 at the Music Hall in Boston in memory of Theodore Parker, who had just died in Florence, his old friend of the Transcendental circle whose history could never be omitted from the annals of Boston, a speaker of bitter truth, strong, eager, inquisitive of knowledge, with a flaming heart, valour and independence, whose place, Emerson said, could never be supplied. He spoke, too, on the centenary of Robert Burns, of Humboldt and his favourite Walter Scott. The delight of generous boys, he called the latter—could he ever forget his own joy in *Marmion* and *The Lord of the Isles?*—a wise, great-hearted man. In Burns he found a joyful common-sense, aggressive, irresistible, musical arrows of satire that yet sing through the air and the secret of taking from fairs and gypsies the speech of the market and the street and clothing it with melody. And there was the wonderful Humboldt, with his solid centre and expanded wings, marching like an army. "As we know," he said, "a man's natural powers are often a sort of committee that slowly, one at a time, give their attention and action; but Humboldt's were all united, one electric chain, so that a university, a whole French Academy, travelled in his shoes."

He spoke, too, at a banquet in Boston in honour of the Chinese Embassy. He had always admired

China. Its etiquette, he had said, was as great in its way as the prophecy of the Hebrews; and the wisdom of the Chinese sages was part of his book of life. Then Froude arrived from England, and he welcomed him at a public dinner in Boston. And he tried to speak again on the three hundredth anniversary of Shakespeare. He had prepared elaborate notes—(all criticism, he had written, is only a making of rules out of Shakespeare's beauties)—and then he had left them at home. He had never been able to speak extemporaneously. Once at an anti-slavery meeting at Worcester he had risen at the request of the chairman and stammered and halted through a five minutes' speech, so that all the people were astonished at his awkwardness. And on this occasion he rose, calmly looked about him for a moment and then sat down serenely; he could not think of a word to say on the poet of all poets he had loved from his earliest youth.

He gave readings in Chickering Hall to a class that his publisher Fields had organized for him. He went through his favourite authors and selected poems and passages of prose: examples of courage, examples of the "dire," lay sermons, bits of history, from Gibbon, Plato, Wordsworth, *The Cid,* Carlyle; and he had the pleasure of hearing, after one of these afternoons, that Herbert's *Poems* had been sold out in Boston. On Mondays at three o'clock he lectured at Mechanics' Hall, with a red curtain behind him and, for audience, the grey-haired faithful who had heard his earliest lectures and whose grandchildren sat beside them now. Then in 1870, with a class of thirty students, he began a course at Harvard. His subject was the "Natural History of Intellect," and what he hoped to do was to make a supreme effort and methodize his thoughts. But method was not for him. The beautiful phrases rolled out with as little connection as ever, and in the end he confessed that he had failed.

"I write," he said, "anecdotes of the intellect, a sort of Farmer's Almanac of mental moods." He had written nothing else, he had spoken nothing else for half a century. And who cared now, as his hands fumbled with the manuscript, as he turned over a dozen pages, turned back another dozen, skipped, let the pages fall upon the floor—who cared for order and system in these thoughts? If you blew your nose, one listener said, you lost the drift of the lecture and were never able to pick it up again. But the lectures had no drift that was not the drift of the speaker; they were simply truth seen through Emerson's temperament. "His deferential entrance upon the scene," as the elder James recalled it, "his look of enquiry at the desk, and the chair, his resolute rummaging among his embarrassed papers, the air of sudden recollection with which he would plunge into his pockets for what he must have known had never been put there, his uncertainty and irresolution as he rose to speak, his deep, relieved inspiration as he got well from under the burning-glass of his auditors' eyes and addressed himself at length to their docile ears instead: no maiden ever appealed more potently to your enamoured and admiring sympathy." And what he said was always the same thing, that spiritual is greater than any material force, that thoughts rule the world. He had written much of the scholar. "We paid you," he had conceived men saying, "that you might not be a merchant. We bought and sold that you might not buy and sell, but reveal the reason of trade. We did not want apes of us, but guides and commanders." And he was the incarnation of his own idea. He had reinstated, alone in the nineteenth century, the ancient figure of the sage, the giver of laws. He had lived always in the mountain, seeing all the details in their place and tendency. He had had a new census and calendar; for a long September day between sun and sun had held centuries for him in its rosy and yellow deeps, and his calendar had been thoughts and his action *as thou ought*. He had been greeted by omens that were prosperity and filled him with light. He had been an opener of doors for those who were to come after him. And every man had been to him for all men, the universe in a mask. Wherever snow fell or water flowed, wherever day and night met in twilight, wherever the blue heaven was hung with clouds, wherever were outlets into celestial space, wherever was danger and awe and love and truth, there Beauty, plenteous as rain, had been shed for him.

> And well could honouring Persia learn
>   What Saadi wished to say:
> For Saadi's nightly stars did burn
>   Brighter than Jami's day.

CHAPTER XXIII

TWO long journeys marked these later years, one to the Far West, the seat of the youngest of civilizations, and one to the seat of the oldest, Egypt and the Nile. Long flights for the old eagle who preferred now to sit at home in his eyry. But there was a touch of Fate in these last two pilgrimages. Emerson had always combined in his nature the Western pioneer and the Eastern sage. He was setting out to survey the extremities of his empire.

In the spring of 1871, he was much fatigued after his lectures at Harvard. So Forbes, the master of railroads, suggested a trip to California in a private car. Edith and Colonel Forbes and Wilkinson James and one or two other young people formed the party. Emerson was going to see the Golden Gate!

At Chicago, the great Pullman himself, a grey little bearded man, saw them off. The car and the outfit, he said, were the best that he could do; if they took the trouble to order it, they could have as good a dinner on the train as they could ever get at Parker's. Emerson was in high spirits; it seemed to one of the party that he had "a certain great amplitude of time and leisure." George Bancroft had sent him a gift of Goethe's *Sprüche in Prosa,* and he worked away at his German. He worked a little, too, on the manuscript sheets of *Parnassus,* the anthology he was editing of his favourite poems. He told one of the ladies a story about a friend of his son's in the West. This young man had a vineyard, but he fell off a bridge into the water and was eaten by a crocodile. "This may not be exact," he added, "but nowadays one must finish a story well."

At Salt Lake City, with the other men of the party, he hastened to the theatre. *Marriage by Moonlight* was the play, or *The Wildcat's Revenge.* (Emerson had travelled very far from Concord.) Then he called on Brigham Young. A stout, red-faced customer, dressed in a long cloak, ready for his drive, who remarked that "the one-man-power really meant all-men's power." Young seemed not to know who his principal visitor was, but his secretary asked: "Is this the justly celebrated Ralph Waldo Emerson?" Quietly self-sufficient, Emerson thought this emperor of the Mormons, with plenty of homespun sense, more of a man than he had ever supposed.

The alkali deserts of Nevada reminded Emerson of Asia and the Bible. Then in San Francisco he went to a miners' theatre, he visited the opium dens, he gave two or three lectures. "All left the church," the newspaper said, "feeling that an elegant tribute had been paid to the Creative Genius of the First Cause." He was sorry to miss the "skatorial queen," a Concord girl, famous as a skater, who was giving a public performance. She sent him a ticket, saying that if he came late she would gladly repeat her act. But one of his lectures occurred on the same evening.

Then came the great adventure, the visit to the Yosemite. The pine-trees there, the sequoias, the curves of the Royal Arches, the foam of the Vernal Fall, soft as carded wool, filled him with astonishment; and climbing the trails, he let the reins drop on the neck of his mustang and gave himself up to the wonder of the wilderness. And the joys of another friendship! A young Scotchman, John Muir, was tending a sawmill in the valley. Emerson had heard of this botanist who had explored the whole country to the Gulf of Mexico, who had slept now and then in a wrinkle of the bark of a redwood, who loved the mountains and lived in absolute solitude, sometimes watching sheep; and he rode over to see him. Muir was entranced at this unexpected encounter, for he had read Emerson's *Essays* with passionate enthusiasm and was only too happy to show him the sketches he had made, the collection of dried plants which he kept in the loft of the mill. He quoted, in a voice trembling with excitement, lines from Emerson's poems; he said Emerson was the first visitor to the valley who had ever admired the pine-trees warmly enough. He was learning to write himself and remarked that he preferred Alice Cary to Byron. ("A great mistake," said Emerson. "There is a certain scenic and general luck about Byron.") Then he tried to persuade his poet to run away for "an immeasurable camping trip back in the heart of the moun-

tains." He was disgusted with these indoor Boston
people, with their notions of propriety, who had
somehow got hold of this great man and refused
to let him sleep out in the woods. "You are yourself
a sequoia," he said at last. Emerson had planted a
tree at Mariposa, to commemorate his visit; but in
Muir he had planted thoughts of an even hardier
life. Through this tall, raw Scotchman, this
Thoreau of the Sierras, he had taken possession of
the West.

At home again, in the summer of the following
year, he awoke one morning early, at half-past five,
and saw a light in his closet. The house was on fire!
The children were all away, so Emerson ran to the
gate and called for help. The neighbours quickly
assembled and moved the books and furniture out
on the grass. In three hours the fire was out; the
walls were standing but the roof was gone, and the
whole interior of the house was wet and charred.

For a week Emerson seemed to have suffered no
harm. He went with his wife to the Manse, and a
room in the courthouse was fitted up as a study for
him. An English publishing house had threatened
to print a volume of his scattered writings which
he did not wish to preserve, and had only agreed
to desist on the understanding that he would give
them soon a volume of essays. He tried to work;
then two weeks after the fire he fell into a fever;
and, although he rallied soon, his memory began
to fail. His friends, meanwhile, had collected contributions of more than sixteen thousand dollars to
rebuild his house and send him on a vacation, and

late in October, 1872, with his eldest daughter
Ellen, he sailed again for England.

Six months in London and Paris, Italy, Egypt. A
hail and farewell to Carlyle: the bitterness of Carlyle's dissent in the Civil War was forgotten now,
and the old men parted with all their first affection.
Breakfasts with Gladstone and Browning. A visit
to Oxford, where Emerson heard Ruskin lecture.
He thought the lecture a model; but later, in Ruskin's rooms, the latter continued his lamentations
on the state of modern society until Emerson could
bear it no longer—he rebuked this bird of night.
And in London he found Charles Newcomb, his
old Brook Farmer friend of thirty years before,
writing novels, of all things in the world, but not
for the public to see, oh, no, not for the public to
see. In Paris, Lowell was awaiting him, and he
had a few words with Renan, Turgenev and Taine,
who sent him the next day his *English Literature*.
Then in Florence he met Hermann Grimm, with
whom he had corresponded for many years.
Grimm had sent him a letter which Alexander
Thayer, who was writing the life of Beethoven,
had brought to Concord. He had said that Joseph
Joachim and himself were Emerson's first readers
among the Germans, adding, "I have endeavoured
to write my book about Michael Angelo so that it
would stand the test if I read it aloud to you." Emerson had been touched by this friendship: it almost connected him with Goethe, for Frau Grimm
was the daughter of Bettina von Arnim, and he had
sent this German lover all his first editions. "I have

the same craving," he wrote, "and the same worship for a new thought as when my first intellectual friendships gave wings to my head and feet, and new heavens and earth." He had recommended to Grimm young William James, who had gone to Berlin as a student of medicine. And here they were at last, thrown together in Florence, where Grimm was now at work on his *Life of Raphael*.

From California to Florence, he had spun his web of relations. And now, before going home, he wished to see the tomb of "him that sleeps at Philæ." George Bancroft received him at Cairo, and they breakfasted with the Khedive; then, with a company of friends, he sailed up the Nile. Unbroken sunshine and the green ribbon of the river, and, sitting on the deck, he read again Goethe's "Conversations with Eckermann" and watched the peasants on the shore, erect as ancient philosophers of the School of Athens. Never had he seen such grace of forms and motion. Egypt for him was the land of eternal composure, the opposite of America, and he quoted again the proverb, "The strength of the Egyptians is to sit still."

In Concord, on his return, the whole town had gathered to meet him at the station. The church bells tolled, and a cheer went up from the crowd as the train drew in and stopped and Emerson appeared on the platform. A band of music preceded his carriage through the streets and the school-children escorted him. An arch of triumph, covered with leaves and flowers, had been erected at his house; and the house had been restored. All the books, the pictures, the loved familiar objects stood again in their places. Emerson was overwhelmed. He crossed the threshold, looked about in astonishment, then returned again to the gate and made a little speech to his fellow-villagers.

The journey had revived him. His thick black hair was gone forever. He had been almost bald indeed when he went to Egypt, but those forty days of rest in the sun had covered his head with a new crop, downy and snowy white. He stood more erect than ever, and the sternness, the occasional scowl, that had marked his face had given place to a look of ineffable calm. You met him on the road, so tall and slender, wrapped in his black cloak, with his peering, questioning glance and that smile, as some one described it, "slowly, very slowly growing until it lit up his whole countenance with a refulgent beam (the whole performance dominated by a deliberation as great and brilliant as the dawn.)" You met him on the road, you saw him coming, you wondered if you would ever survive the onset. Then up your spirits went, soaring aloft, in the light of that quiet glory.

Within he felt no change: no wrinkles, no used heart, but unspent youth. He had drawn, he felt, the white lot in life. And age could never alter his own happy temper: had he not been born cheerful and well-adapted to the tone of the human race? The forest awoke in him still the feeling he had had as a boy. He could always find something there he had never seen before, and he thought that, to Nero, longing for new pleasures, a walk in the woods ought to have been suggested. His eyes, so old and wary, still gathered their hourly harvest. Yes, life for him was still absurdly sweet.

He carried a compass in his pocket. "I like to hold the god in my hands," he said. The needle of life, for him, had always pointed north. But he knew that his working days were almost over. One lived and learned and acquired skill in writing, as an old carpenter acquires skill in wood. What a pity that now one's organs should betray one, that one's eyes, health, fire and zeal of work grew weaker every day! He found himself nervously vigilant, until writing became a terror and only at rare moments could be attain the intellectual *élan* that once was a daily gift. "The strong hours conquer us," he had written to Carlyle, "and I am the victim of miscellany—miscellany of designs, vast debility and procrastination." The weeks ran by as a web out of a loom, a bright stripe for day, a dark stripe for night, and these ran together into an endless grey. He thought of proposing an indignation meeting.

Honours were raining upon him, degrees from universities, the nomination as Lord Rector of the University of Glasgow (Disraeli won the election), his appointment as Overseer at Harvard by President Eliot. His mind was quiescent now and his radical feelings had vanished. He had become once more the child of seven generations of ministers, and his vote alone prevented the abolition of compulsory chapel at Harvard. Books came by every post, with flattering dedications, and visitors

poured into Concord: Lord Morley, Leslie
Stephen, James Bryce, Lord Camperdown, Gold-
win Smith, Bret Harte—the flower of two generations of Europe and America. He sat for his
portrait, again and again, protesting. He was "not a
subject for art." Meanwhile, "Emerson days" were
celebrated in the schools throughout the country.
He had said in a speech at Concord that the town
had no seaport, no water-power, no cotton, oil or
marble; the granite was better in Fitchburg and
even the Concord ice had bubbles in it. The town,
then, was reduced to manufacturing school-teachers for the Southern and Western market. Let it
stick to that staple, he said, and make it the best in
the world; let it turn out the best possible article.
Concord had followed his advice, and his fame
had spread West and South in the wake of the
teachers. As Oliver Wendell Holmes remarked,
"They are doing us up in spices like so many dead
Pharaohs." Emerson had become a classic.

He took little pleasure in this incense of adula-
tion. He had often mocked at Goethe for spending
so many hours counting his medals. That velvet
life had seemed to him incongruous with genius;
poverty and reproach and danger were its true
adornments. There were greater pleasures in old
age than this. Thinking, for instance, of the stories
about his contemporaries that he wished he might
have told. Counting over and over the tale of his
friends: Carlyle, Thoreau, Agassiz, Rockwood
Hoar, Alcott and Greenough and Muir, Newcomb
and Margaret Fuller and Father Taylor. Carlyle,

in memory of their friendship, had bequeathed to Harvard College the books he had used in writing his *Cromwell* and *Frederick*. They had ceased to write to each other since their last meeting in England, but the tie that had weathered forty years could never be broken now. Why should Emerson read those works, he had often said to himself, when he had the man himself, one who could sit under the trees of Paradise and tell him a hundred histories deeper, truer? Those pages that looked to others so rich and alluring to him had a marrowless air: it was the warm hand and heart he had an estate in, and the living eye he would never cease to discern across the sparkling sea.

Many were the pleasures of age. Watching his dreams, for one, those quasi-optical shows that suggested in one's structure what magazines of talent and invention! What dialogues they carried on, those different personalities one harboured in one's soul! What a rush, when the mind awoke, came from some hidden quarter to break the drama into a chaos of parts, then particles, then ether, like smoke dissolving in a wind, as if the gods were jealous! A pleasure to think of the dangers he had escaped, a pleasure to realize, too, that any failures in future signified nothing. He had found expression, he had set his house in order. He had noticed years before that when summer opened he feared it would be short, but that after the heats of August he was reconciled, like one who has had his swing, to the cool of autumn. So it would be, he felt, with the coming of death.

For some time now his memory had been hiding itself. He forgot names, he forgot the commonest words. "After a while," he said on one occasion, "the—the—the—how do you call what stores up water till it is suddenly—suddenly—what shall I say?—not squeezed out?" "A sponge?" "No, no." "The clouds, perhaps?" "Yes, the clouds began to roll up and threaten rain." He wanted an umbrella, and he said, "I can't tell its name, but I can tell its history. Strangers take it away." His perception, his humour, his vivid interest remained, but in lecturing he confused the sheets of his manuscript, reread sheets he had read a moment before and then stopped bewildered.

But he still persisted in working—writing, travelling, lecturing. Lecturing, for instance, at the University of Virginia, where the war was not forgotten and they wished to insult this Yankee, and the students laughed and talked, and Emerson was obliged to stop at the end of half an hour. ("They are very brave down there," was his only comment. "They say just what they think.") A prodigious force, he said to himself, that native bias of character whose impulsion reached through all the years and kept the old man constant to the same pursuits as in youth. For twenty years he had worked at his *Parnassus*. He kept the poems in his "Black Anthology," so called from its leather covers. He read them over with his daughter and included his newest favourites along with the loves of his childhood. The book contained, among recent American poems, several by Bret Harte that Emer-

son found in the newspapers, and one by Forceythe
Willson of Wisconsin, whose whereabouts Lowell
had tried to discover until at last he found him living in the house next to his own on Mount Auburn
Street in Cambridge. He had written not long before an essay on Plutarch to be used as an introduc-
tion for a new edition of the *Morals* by Professor
Goodwin, and he had compared the old version
with the Greek original. But composition was beyond him now. The English publishers were press-
ing him for the new volume of *Letters and Social
Aims,* and he could scarcely put two sentences together. His family appealed to Elliot Cabot of Boston, an old friend, half-monk, half-dilettante, a
lecturer on Kant at Harvard. Cabot was only too
happy to help the old man with his scattered
papers. He came out to Concord and went over the
journals and selected and prepared the essays as
Emerson himself had prepared them in the past.

In Concord, meanwhile, a generation had appeared in whom the soil made fertile by Emerson's
presence had burst into happy bloom. The Hawthornes had vanished; of the family of Henry
Thoreau one aunt alone was left to bear the name
in America. But the Alcotts had stood their
ground, and the world had swung their way. Louisa
was famous now, and May was beginning to make
her name as a painter. The station-master's son was
a musical genius, Judge French's son was a sculptor. Goodwin, who had studied with Clough, was
already a famous scholar. And in Frank Sanborn
the village had its Boswell. It was curious, too, that

in several notable cases the voice, the manners, the very smile of Emerson could be recognized moving about in persons to whom he bore no blood-relationship.

Ellery Channing still made rhymes, still aired his crotchets, and Alcott walked the woods, looking for odd coils of roots and branches and building rustic temples to the geometry of beauty. The gay and tireless Alcott, with his long silvery locks and his courtly manners, winding along the wood-paths in his wide straw hat, his arms filled with the treasures of the brush. He was still lecturing in the West, still faithfully keeping his diary (a whole library now of bound manuscripts, fifty volumes or more) and writing sonnets in honour of his friends; and at last, in 1878, his old dream and Emerson's of a Concord University was partially realized. The School of Philosophy was opened for summer sessions. The Hegelians from Saint Louis invaded the town. Under the huge elms on Alcott's lawn they built their tabernacle, with walls of pine shakes and Gothic windows, and a strange new jargon began to be heard in the woods and fields of Concord. They were very Prussian, these strangers, with their "categories" and "totalities." A new generation assembled in this twilight of the old Concord gods. Eager young men and women from every corner of the country came to drink at the spring of the poetry of Nature. There were garden parties and boating parties on the river, and the wood-paths rustled with muslin dresses, and Walden Pond rang with the voices of youth. It might have been forty years before, in the days when the Brook Farmers came to consult the oracle, and some of the old circle assembled, too. Elizabeth Peabody, the "grandmother of Boston," as people called her now, the champion of lost causes for half a century, drowsed in her chair on the platform. Alcott often spoke, and Emerson read a lecture on aristocracy. And then one summer day Walt Whitman came to Concord. He, too, was a patriarch now, serenely wise, stamped by those long years in the Civil War; and the old scores were forgotten. He came to visit Sanborn, and he drove out to Walden and placed his stone on the cairn that marked the spot by the pond where Henry's cabin had stood. Then he dined and spent an evening at Emerson's house. Emerson said very little but sat in his chair, smiling, and under the play of the lamplight Walt watched with all his old love the face of the Mystic Trumpeter of his youth. (A just man, poised on himself, he thought, all-loving, all-enclosing, and sane and clear as the sun.)

Seventy-eight! with a heart as light as ever—and a twelvemonth still to live. Emerson was not too old to enjoy his swim at Walden, where he still scorned a towel—(spring still made spring in his mind, and he was never old!)—not too old to receive a party of Methodist ministers who came to pay their respects. He seemed a little doubtful at first, as though he thought they might put him through his catechism, but, once reassured, became affable and charming. He had forgotten what he had written: he glanced through *Representative Men* and said

it seemed as if something had been omitted, "here
—and here—and here" (touching the table as he
spoke). And once he took his writings from the
shelf, and, glancing through them, smiled, as he
said to his daughter, "Why, these things are really
very good." Did he know that the Emperor of
Brazil had read him from end to end, that he had
his disciples in India, for whom he shone serene as
the evening star? That the Prime Minister of Russia kept the *Essays* at his bedside, that a student in
Siberia had been imprisoned for having in his possession a copy of *Self-Reliance?* His fame had
spread through the world, in spite of the *Saturday
Review,* which ridiculed his "occasional jets of
nonsense." ("His works," this friendly journal still
maintained, "are nothing, mean nothing, say nothing.") But what was fame? he had said to himself.
He had thought of the fossil snails and leaves
and ferns that had come down safe from antiquity, surviving all the shocks, upheavals, deluges,
wherein everything noble in art and humanity had
perished. They had come down, staring and perfect, into our daylight. What was fame, he had
said to himself—immortal life before the eyes of
mortals, if every snail and fern and dead leaf
shared it?

He had written once of a certain country where,
when threescore years had passed, a mist or dim-
ness, a sort of autumnal haze, settled on the figure,
veiling all decays. It was Emerson's country now.
He was living in a dream when he went to Longfellow's funeral in Cambridge, when he wandered

up to the coffin and gazed at the face of the dead. "I cannot remember his name," he said, "but he was a good man." When he looked up at the portrait of Carlyle that hung on his study wall and said, "That is my man!" When his wife sat beside him, and he contrived to express with a smile how long and happily they had lived together. When he spent that last evening in his study, and his son read aloud to him "Paul Revere's Ride"; and he took apart as usual the brands in the fireplace and swept the hearth for the night. When Alcott came to say good-bye to his friend, and Emerson held his hand and said, with smiling affection, "You are very well—keep so, keep so." And when Alcott turned to go and he called him back once more and grasped his hand again: "Good-bye, my friend!"

Gradually, year by year, the outline had grown indistinct and the halo gayer and brighter, till at last there was left only a sense of presence. And the strong gods pined for his abode; for the universe had become his house in which to live.

THE END